Three Minutes of Magic

of

by

Geoff Docherty

ISBN: 978-0-9566648-0-8

Three Minutes of Magic

by

Geoff Docherty

Previous Publication by the Author
No 1 Best Seller
"A Promoter's Tale"
(Omnibus Press)
Foreword by John Peel
Preface by Dave Stewart

Geoff Docherty, My Manager.

"Didn'Promise Anything – Delivered Everything."

Brand New Mercedes Van (Complete with bunk beds)
Top class PA System (Genesis)
Major Record Company Deal (Warners)
Major Publishing Deal (Island Records)
Major Tours/ Gigs/ supported by WEA (Faces/ Slade/ Free/ Capt Beefheart/ Ten Years After/ Wizard/ Marquee Club/ Reading Festival/ BBC Radio (John Peel) Old Grey Whistle Test.

"All with unselfish ingenuity, tenacity, enthusiasm and dedication. Thanks a million".

Terry Wilson Slesser (Beckett), Vocalist

Grateful thanks to:
Gillian Baxter
Peter Watchman
Terry Wilson Slessor
Syd Simpkins
Geoff Hope
Dhasuni Rodrigo

and special thanks to
Karen Dawson
for her tireless help in bringing this book to fruition.

Preface

This is the story of one man's attempt to manage and take a series of unknown groups from the obscure wilderness of the unknown to the dizzy heights of world wide fame. Having already reached the top as a successful promoter of a whole plethora of major bands such as **Led Zeppelin, The Who, Pink Floyd, David Bowie, Rod Stewart & The Faces, Van Morrison, Country Joe & The Fish, Captain Beefheart, Roxy Music, Free, Jethro Tull, Deep Purple, Supertramp, Black Sabbath, The Jam, Ten Years After** and promoting **John Peel's** all time favourite gig, it gives a unique and highly interesting insight into the pitfalls and heartache which he encountered. Thoroughly absorbing as well as pacy, it is a must read not only for music lovers but also for discerning observers of the frailties and weaknesses of human nature. To miss it would be a reprehensible failure to explore a true and fascinating adventure story. To read it will give immense satisfaction to those who pride themselves on exploring new avenues of untold human emotions.

3 Minutes of Magic

Chapter 1

It was a bright Saturday morning in spring 1973 as I walked into a town centre coffee bar, known as the Bis Bar with the £10,000 cheque from Warner Bros Records nestling safely in my pocket. Having just secured a major record contract with the group I was managing, it all seemed like a faraway dream. The question now was what would it lead to and how long would it take to reach the stardom we all hoped to achieve? It was a prospect which was ultimately to prove both fascinating and challenging. Having already been a successful promoter with major bands such as **Pink Floyd, Led Zeppelin, The Who, David Bowie, Eric Clapton, Rod Stewart, Santana**, and dozens of others, it was my earnest intention to try to emulate them. However, was it just a fanciful dream or could it one day become a reality? I certainly hoped so as I pulled up a chair and sat down in order to allow me to take everything in while quietly absorbing its relaxing and stimulating atmosphere. The group I now found myself managing were young, talented and highly enthusiastic as well as eager to make their mark in a rapidly unfolding musical revolution. While sitting there that morning in deep contemplation, I was positively enthralled at such an exciting prospect as I thought back to how it had all started. At the time, I was working at the Bay Hotel both as a doorman and promoter while in the year 1968, the emerging psychedelic scene was rapidly gaining a stronghold throughout the whole of the UK. Gripped in this stimulating and exhilarating time, I realised that groups such as **Pink Floyd** and **Jefferson Airplane** had already infused young and impressionable minds into a new and more thought-provoking phase. Having previously spent six and a half years in The Fleet Air Arm during which I had served over two years on the aircraft carrier Ark Royal, I had already experienced a multitude of new and fascinating horizons in various parts of the world and unknown to me, this was to be no exception. Here, it must be said that each person in their own inimitable way unceasingly look for new and hopefully exciting challenges throughout their life. Fortunately, I was no different as I began exploring ways of opening up a future that would encapsulate a stimulating and worthwhile foray into the heady and exciting world of music. I could sense the Bay Hotel, having already experienced a personal appearance by **Pink Floyd** was beginning to capture and inspire people's imagination while drawing them closer together despite being aware that everyone who attended hoped to develop their own distinctive path in life. Fortunately, music was to become the one unifying factor which had successfully culminated in bringing many disparate factions under one collective roof, especially at the Bay Hotel. By now, Mr Dixon, the recently installed hotel manager had become more liberated in his outlook and was soon beginning to give me a free hand. Whether it was by accident or design matters little. What does is that it became an important factor in everything which followed and for this I am extremely grateful.

One night while standing in the Bay Hotel foyer I was approached by a music loving regular. "Are you Geoff Docherty?" he questioned. "Yes, why do you ask?" I replied. "Well, we're in a band called **This Years Girl** and I was hoping you would give us a gig." "Have you much of a following?" I inquired. "I'd say we have," answered the diminutive guitarist who possessed straw coloured hair together with a cheeky effervescent smile. His name turned out to be Jackie Ingram and on first sight he failed to conjure up visions of Hollywood stardom or masses of teenage girls swooning at the stage door. Fortunately however, experience had taught me that looks, while helpful, are secondary to talent no matter what direction that person may have chosen to follow. It was now time for a quick appraisal knowing that an unknown group playing in front of seven or eight hundred discerning people can be quite a daunting or exasperating experience. This is especially so if their musical aspirations fail to be allied to some semblance of genuine talent, no matter how embryonic it may be. "Let me think about it," I replied. Within days his insatiable and incessant propensity to be the classic hustler was beginning to have an effect, especially as he had a number of qualities I greatly admired, namely enthusiasm, determination, and friendliness. "Where are you playing at next?"

I inquired. "At the Three Tuns in Durham on Wednesday," he answered with an assured confidence which was proving to be highly infectious. "All right, I'll come and see you," I replied with as much conviction as I could muster. On hearing these words his face lit up and though it appeared to be no big deal, to him it was to prove an important step in finally gaining a local and loyal following.

Once there, I found they played a mixture of blues together with covers from American West Coast bands including **Jefferson Airplane, The Byrds** and from England, **The Pretty Things.** For such a young group they appeared to be well ahead of their time while the crowd who were mostly from nearby Durham University seemed to enjoy them. It was certainly an eye opener and I was immediately captivated. A few weeks later at the first available opportunity, I booked them to headline at the Bay. With a surprisingly large crowd in attendance they soon proved to be more than excellent as an appreciative and enthusiastic audience shouted for more. Later, the diminutive Jackie Ingram came into the office to be paid with a flush of excitement clearly apparent on his face accompanied by a huge and incomparable smile. It was to prove a highly satisfying moment for both of us as little did I know that fate had predestined our paths to become inextricably linked. A few weeks later, the drummer, whose name was Syd Simpkins approached me in a local hostelry known as The Rosedene and asked me to manage them. Having already seen them live and being impressed by what I had heard, I immediately agreed. So began my first excursion into managing bands, although I never realised what it would entail, or the difficulties which lay ahead. A few weeks later with my unrestrained enthusiasm having wantonly cast aside any lingering or uncertain doubts I may have held, I arranged for them to play at the famous Marquee Club in Wardour Street, London. At the time, I had become friendly with influential Radio One D.J **John Peel** who I had earlier brought to the Bay and found to be very friendly as well as approachable. Before their appearance, I contacted him and asked if he would go along to see them. "Of course" he replied and after doing so, wrote a small complimentary piece in a popular music magazine known as The Disc and Music Echo. Each day the group and I usually met in The Bis Bar in order to meet and discuss music or any relevant news. In doing so I soon came to realise they were young and inexperienced about life and appeared to look to me for some semblance of spiritual or physical guidance. Unfortunately, whether I could provide them with this was certainly a matter for conjecture as well as proving to be an unnerving experience both in terms of responsibility and lack of management know how. Nevertheless, our collective enthusiasm remained undiminished as we pressed ahead in a determined effort to reach the starry heights of world wide fame and fortune. In a situation of this nature, naivety can be a wonderful and innocent thing. While sitting on those high stools in the Bis Bar, unknown to us, we were all unwittingly steeped in an immense surfeit of it. Under these circumstances, a cool and dispassionate appraisal of the way ahead seemed far from important. What really mattered to the band were the pretty girls they had met the night before and **Pink Floyd** or **The Pretty Things** latest releases. This youthful camaraderie and exchange of musical ideas was proving to be a natural way of emphasising that their way of life had now entered a more objective and meaningful purpose. Fortunately, it was also filling a cavernous and meaningless void which gave them hope that one day they too would be playing at Middle Earth in London and possibly surpassing even **Pink Floyd's** achievements. However, was it fantasy or just an idle or passing dream? Who knows, but it certainly breathed new and invigorating life into their hopes of emerging into a world where their music would attain the status which they felt it fully deserved.

Outside, I parked my recently acquired 3.4 litre silver Jaguar which perhaps was my way of making a statement that I had already achieved some measure of success. Its cream leather seats and wood panelled facia created this kind of ambience and as I drove along the seafront I began imagining myself managing a top band. Whether it was a form of escapism or wishful thinking, I was unsure. But **This Years Girl** were different and I felt there was always the possibility that they could "make it." If they did, it was immensely exciting to think that I would also be an integral part of it. In fantasising at such a possibility a warm and satisfying feeling immediately began racing through my thoughts. Fortunately, as I was already promoting major world wide groups and had been privileged to feel a lot closer to them than the average person, nothing could be discounted. A few days later I pulled up at The Bay to find **Country Joe & The Fish's** roadies setting up their equipment. Inwardly, it was a very satisfying feeling to realise that they had come all the way from the West Coast of America to play at our little and seemingly insignificant hotel on the seafront. Unknown to me at the time an added bonus was that it was to undoubtedly become one of my all time favourite gigs. Once on stage, we were soon to find that there was a fighting and aggressive edge to their lyrics which were encapsulated in their famous anti Vietnam song "I Feeling Like I'm Fixing To Die Rag. What Are We Fighting For?" It was a song which was to become a rallying call for change, especially for the young after countless thousands of young Americans had sacrificed their lives in a futile and seemingly endless war. A few hours later, **Country Joe** had majestically succeeded in converting another eight hundred or so committed people to his cause. It was the deep conviction and heartfelt passion in his voice which positively shone through while making a great impression upon everyone present including me. All the while the audience were spellbound as I quickly realised that any group with this quality and talent couldn't be ignored.

By now, The Bay wasn't just a venue where you came to see bands. It was also a school of learning, friendship and hope, as well as bringing together many disparate factions who were able to freely discuss the merits of any interesting music or current topic. There was a whole new world of music out there and I could sense **"This Years Girl"** wanted to be a part of it. By attending The Bay, **Pink Floyd, Country Joe**, and **John Peel** (who had all appeared there) were to become the canvasses which had been indelibly imprinted in their youthful minds. Now, they wanted to create a lasting and impressionable one of their own. To be aware of this was incredibly exciting, as well as challenging, and in some ways, mind blowing. Meanwhile, the burgeoning and impatient surge of their youth was about to propel them into the dark and mysterious depths of the rock & roll arena. What lay ahead and how would they fare? No one really knew, and in some ways, no one really cared. However, only time would tell.

Sitting in the relaxing confines of The Bis-Bar, the big plate glass windows allowed the band a panoramic view of everything that was taking place outside. If a pretty girl passed by their youthful heads would unerringly swivel, just like Elvis's hips. Being a member of a group gave them a collective strength of purpose and unity which I recognised could quickly becomes infectious while hopefully emerging on stage. My experience as a promoter had already taught me that if this essential ingredient comes across to an audience, they usually pick up on it. Fortunately, if and when it does, it invariably instils a lasting appreciation of their music. There was of course one other important facet to be considered. In those first heady days the talk was of innovative and creative music and not of money or gross percentages. Divested of such corporate trappings, the way forward seemed positively uplifting while peace and love reigned supreme throughout the rapidly emerging psychedelic scene.

Within days, two consecutive gigs in Dundee and Elgin were arranged by a local agent named Jimmy Llewelyn, later to become a nightclub owner. Hours later, the band set off for the long journey to Scotland in the group's van. Watching their young hopeful faces packed into the back together with their on stage equipment immediately brought pangs of guilt to my conscience. To bundle four human beings into such cramped conditions, especially as I wasn't travelling with them seemed tantamount to cruelty. However, at 7am the following morning I was awoken by a frantic knocking at my front door. On opening it I was confronted by a dishevelled and tired looking group. "When we got there, they knew nothing about the gig and had never even heard of us," protested Syd Simpkins the drummer. "We've been travelling all night and have had nothing to eat," he continued with a voice clearly steeped both in anger and bitter frustration. As I stood listening, on realising the mood he was in, it seemed he wouldn't hesitate to employ an act of severe physical retribution should anyone else dare incur his wrath, no matter how minor the offence Knowing this, I immediately dressed and drove to the agent's house before awakening him. As I began airing a series of protestations at his lack of organisational abilities he remained cool and seemingly unperturbed. He smiled as if to placate me and I realised my words were failing to convey the gravity of the injustice that had been so cruelly perpetrated against the band. This was to be my first setback in managing and set me thinking. Could people be trusted and did they care, or was this merely a bitter and uncomfortable foretaste of what to expect in the future?

A few weeks later, while on a visit to London, I visited the Ellis Wright Agency in Regent St who were to become the forerunners of Chrysalis Records. On entering, for some strange reason I sensed I was about to be involved in a futile exercise. Whether it was intuition, or a faltering belief which questioned whether the group were ready or good enough yet, counted for little. What mattered was that we had driven nearly 300 miles in order to make the effort as I knocked nervously on their door. "Come in," shouted an authoritative and welcoming voice. After gingerly opening it, I was confronted from behind an imposing wooden desk by Terry Ellis, who subsequently went on to co start Chrysalis Records with Chris Wright while simultaneously managing **Jethro Tull** to world wide success.

Once inside his office, I couldn't help noticing it looked austere and lacked carpets, or for that matter something to make it feel more welcoming. Nevertheless, it was London and gave us a small glimmer of undiminished hope. "I'm the manager of a band called **This Years Girl**. I'm hoping you will take them on and help to get them some worthwhile bookings," I requested with a mixture of awe and trepidation. "Have they got a record contract?" he inquired. "No, not yet, but I'm hoping that we'll get one soon," I replied with as much assurance as I could possibly muster. "Write to me with their details but I can't promise you anything," he replied rather indifferently while looking down at his desk. I swallowed hard before turning to leave. It was hardly the sort of reception I had hoped for, and yet in reality, I had offered him very little. Suddenly, I looked down. Why I'll never know but it seemed to ease the pain of a seemingly futile response. "That was the brush-off, lets go back to Sunderland," prompted Syd the drummer with a disillusioned look painfully written across his unlined and youthful face. His despairing and frustrated voice seemed at odds with all his hopes as I felt a certain pity towards him. Rejection is of course always a bitter pill to swallow and for it to be thrust so readily on the group's young shoulders was clearly an unsettling and unwelcome experience. Later, at the junction of Wardour St and Oxford St we stopped and bought ice creams. As we slowly began to consume them, in some strange way it appeared as if we were licking our newly opened wounds before setting off on the long journey home. After three days of sleeping in the van, our first uneventful and hopeful trip to London was finally over.

Back in Sunderland, I still had a lot to look forward to but it seemed that no one at national level was remotely interested in the group. A few days later, they played at a packed Quay Club in Newcastle, a great little venue that had a friendly and most endearing atmosphere together with some excellent music. Once the group hit the stage, I was pleasantly surprised at how magical an evening could be when discerning and friendly people are able to merge into one joyous and appreciative crowd. As they danced, it was as if they had been transported into another world in which the uplifting and mesmerising music reverberating around the room was all that mattered. Looking back, it was undeniably exciting and liberating all at the same time. Suddenly, in the tight confines of the club an attractive girl eased past and smiled. It was both warm and welcoming while unfortunately not one which necessarily promised anything more than polite pleasantries at the end of the night. Nevertheless, its warmth settled nicely into the vibes already being created and I felt at home as I looked around and continued to soak up the friendly atmosphere. It soon became apparent that the music from the West Coast of America had found a new home and **John Peel's** efforts to alert everyone to its potential was already bearing fruit. Despite being packed, it was attended by a wonderful mix of people. No one intruded into other people's space, seeming to glide by as if floating on a cushion of warm and invigorating air. As there appeared to be no unnecessary rules or petty restrictions, it reminded me of The Bay in Sunderland. In doing so, I realised how important it was that this kind of friendly ambience was steadfastly maintained within its confines. As the group played on, their indomitable spirit and enthusiasm were an absolute joy to witness. Later, after having watched the group play, I emerged in the streets of Newcastle firmly convinced they had opened up a whole new dimension in my own and other peoples thinking. Could they expand the evening's success into something on a much grander and awe inspiring scale? Once again, only time would tell.

When managing a young and inexperienced group, they invariably possess a certain innocence and naivety which can be positively endearing. At this stage, constructive criticism, however well intentioned can appear to be hurtful or damning, and may even open up wounds which may take a long time to heal. However, praise, if expressed too warmly or enthusiastically can lead to a group developing wild and unrealistic delusions of grandeur long before they have achieved or deserved such a stature. Conversely, sitting on the fence while cloaked under a welcoming sign of diplomacy can be construed as a form of cowardice. With a group, human emotions can be extremely sensitive, especially if stardom fails to appear on the horizon as readily as they had anticipated. For any band or their manager, patience and forbearance becomes a prime requisite which weighs heavily under the realisation that impending failure is more than a possibility. During one radio programme, **John Peel** while reflecting on the meaning of life had once posed the question, "what does it all mean?" With a young group whose music is failing to hit the heights, you could ask the same question. Eighteen months later, with their hopes and ambitions crushed by an overwhelming lack of response from people who failed to appreciate what they were trying to achieve, they decided to split. Fortunately, there was time for one last gig which was to be a farewell showcase at The Bay Hotel with myself promoting them. Unbelievably, for a local group it was virtually a sell out and I was immeasurably pleased that they had outdrawn many major names who I had recently been promoting there. Later that night, they left the stage to rapturous applause and despite the overwhelming camaraderie and warmth which was enveloping them in a sea of endless backslapping; it was finally and irrevocably over. In witnessing such a sad spectacle, I recognised the full flush of their eager and youthful enthusiasm had imploded into a thousand fragments of disillusioned hopes and broken dreams. Later, after everyone had finally departed, I walked the length of the stately and seemingly cavernous ballroom deep in a myriad of thoughts. The jukebox remained noticeably silent while there was an eerie and ghostly feeling about the place. As I continued to look around, a broken glass lay in the corner amidst a pool of its previous contents and inwardly I felt an immense loneliness and sadness. Music can undoubtedly be tremendously uplifting as well as fulfilling.

However, there are times when even this fails to lift flagging spirits that have been shredded into an abundance of highly disappointed emotions. Just then Mr Dixon the manager who resided on the premises walked in before informing me he wished to lock up as I quickly acknowledged his presence. For him, it had been a highly successful night, but as an elder statesman, he failed to appreciate the poignancy of the occasion. Fortunately however, in the light of the morning, I would have time to contemplate and reflect on what might have been. Inquests of this nature invariably have a distinctive ring of abject and disillusioned failure while strangely, others appear to relish the very fact that it has taken place. Inside, pride coupled with determination cannot remove the disappointment of being ignored at national level. Hurt feelings are however, a part and parcel of life and can conjure up untold apathy as well as self pity. Ironically, unknown to me at the time, it is all part of the healing process which ultimately allowed me to gather renewed strength in an attempt to find new and exciting challenges.

Managing my first band had certainly been an invaluable experience despite being one which had failed to fulfil both mine and the group's expectations. Fortunately, it did bring with it a measure of invaluable experience together with myriads of unanswered questions. Next time,-oh! how often did I say those two fateful words while mindful that for anyone to admit defeat so readily could be construed as a lack of moral fibre or even cowardice. While pride is undeniably an admirable trait, in managing a band, a surfeit of it can prove to be both costly and fateful as well as soul destroying. Add a touch of madness and the portents for a roller coaster of emotions are far greater and more nerve wracking than any fairground ride. Then why do it you may well ask? Lock statisticians, mathematicians and psychologists in a room for endless hours and I can assure you they will find immense difficulty in arriving at a plausible answer. I can only describe it as a gut feeling which hypnotises you into believing that next time it will be different. But will it? If only we could foretell the future. Fortunately, as a promoter, through the personal recommendations of a friend living in London (Micky Grabham), I would soon discover an unknown group called Free who would bring the ballroom back to life. Whether it was fate or a fortuitous piece of luck matters little. What does is that they restored a sense of equilibrium to my musical judgement and for that I will always be grateful. What was so special about them? Unquestionably, there is only one word, talent. Unfortunately, being so close to them, they had unwittingly made success look far too easy. Paul Rodgers just seemed to step up on stage and sing. Paul Kossoff merely plugged his guitar in and proceeded to play some wonderful searing notes while the rhythm section Andy Fraser and Simon Kirke were tightly locked together. However, there was one major difference in that they were young, unknown and relatively inexperienced compared to other major bands. Sitting in the dressing room and observing them, they seemed so normal and down to earth. As their stature began to grow, it lit a vibrant spark in me having made success look so effortless. To be involved in managing someone as successful as they were seemed such an exciting prospect as well as creating a wonderful aura of opportunity. Dad had always said "you have to pay for your learning son." Unknown to me, his words were to be truly prophetic.

Chapter 2

One night, having climbed the stairs of a local nightclub after a fairly uneventful but enjoyable night, I ordered a refreshing drink. Soon, a group took to the stage and started to play which immediately aroused my interest. "What's the name of the band?" I inquired of Tommy Clinton, the manager of Annabel's in Sunderland where this unknown group were playing. **"Beckett,"** he replied. "They're pretty good, where are they from?" I inquired. "South Shields," he informed me. By now, a few years had elapsed since my previous attempt at managing and I had continued to be a successful promoter in my own right with bands of international repute. Before long I had moved to Sunderland Locarno a Mecca ballroom that held 3,000 people which I had named "The Fillmore North" on the night I promoted there. Doing so had allowed me to acquire a vast multitude of contacts in the record business which I was confident would prove to be more than useful. **Beckett's** excellent blend of vocals coupled with an electrifying stage presence were certainly spellbinding as well as compulsive listening. On stage they appeared totally relaxed which made it appear as though it was their birthright or second home. At the conclusion of their set I casually approached the lead singer and after some initial small talk, asked if I could manage them. "Oh I don't know" he replied in a nonchalant and carefree manner. "There are lots of people who want to manage us. Anyway, who are you?" he questioned. "I'm Geoff Docherty from The Fillmore," I replied. "Well I'm Terry Slesser and I'm not sure we want anyone to manage us at the moment," he informed me curtly before turning away and heading towards a pretty girl. He's a bit cocky and fancies himself I thought. Nevertheless, his stage presence was excellent and I couldn't help wondering if I was confusing confidence with cockiness. Left standing there, and considering his lack of interest, I quickly dismissed the idea and thought no more of it.

Later that night, in a surprising development, he suddenly approached me. "Excuse me," he began in a much friendlier tone. "I've been talking to Kenny Mountain our rhythm guitarist and he says you know a lot of people in the business. Maybe we should have a meeting and talk about it," he suggested. His words sounded more sincere, while seeming to have acquired an impassioned urgency which gave the impression he regretted not taking me more seriously the first time we had met. I smiled inwardly knowing that I'd already met most of the major groups and had an underlying conviction that I could draw on that experience to help him and the group. "Alright," I replied with an enthusiasm which had immediately been rekindled. Shortly afterwards I began having serious doubts and realised I needed time to think about embarking on such a high risk venture. Here, it must be pointed out that managing an unknown band is not to be taken lightly and at the same time can be extremely costly if things go wrong. However, despite these reservations there was something about this group which captured my imagination. Unknown to me, when setting out at the start of my second venture into the problematic path of band management, there were to be many untold triumphs and heartaches. The next unanswered question was could I succeed in taking them to the dizzy heights of an enduring and successful musical conquest? Right then, I certainly hoped so.

A few weeks later, after signing them to a management contract, I had officially become their manager. Within days I realised that Kenny Mountain, the rhythm guitarist who was older and more experienced than the others appeared to be their guiding mentor. Having been the lead singer in his previous group **Yellow**, he also possessed an excellent voice as well as an unflustered attitude to life. But could he steer the group on to the glorious path of success, or for that matter, could I? Terry the lead singer was tall, athletic and extremely charismatic. Once on stage there was an exciting magnetism about him which held the audience spellbound while exuding an aura of total self confidence Arthur Ramm the lead guitarist was blond, good looking and very unassuming. He also appeared to take everything seriously and possessed an uncanny knack of remaining amazingly calm under duress, no matter how extreme the circumstances. The rhythm section consisted of the diminutive Billy Campbell on bass and Alan Craig on drums. Alan Craig-what memories. He was so carefree and amusing that within five minutes of meeting him, if you weren't laughing there was something seriously wrong. Mood swings? He didn't know the meaning of such a thing as his outlook on life remained constantly upbeat. With these five individuals already formed into a promising and cohesive unit I began the long and tortuous journey that was to lead to a kaleidoscope of adventure with an amazing array of highs and lows. In the hard world of rock management, unknown to me, it was to be an unforgettable and invaluable experience. A few weeks later Arthur, who had already played in Hamburg with a previous group arranged for **Beckett** to play 15 consecutive nights at The Top Ten Club in Hamburg where **The Beatles** had previously played after the Star Club was burnt down. Our accommodation turned out to be a rather seedy hotel known as The Pacific not far from the Repherbahn where as fate would have it, the legendary **Beatles** had also stayed. Before leaving, Arthur had warned us to stockpile tins of food as The Pacific was self catering with only one communal gas cooker to serve its many residents. In his quiet and undemonstrative manner, Arthur delighted in regaling us with tales of his previous experiences at the Top Ten where many other British groups had cut their teeth including **Ten Years After** and **Rory Gallagher**.

When you finally stand on the stage where **The Beatles** once played as complete unknowns, it's an awe inspiring experience. The fact that it is now the band you are managing who are playing there is equally so. In Hamburg, visiting tourists seemed compelled to visit it as though accepting it was a poignant shrine to British music together with the memory of its most famous protégés, **The Beatles**. Once inside, a sense of pride wells up inside you on realising that four seemingly insignificant human beings from Liverpool had taken on the world and won. But there was so much more to it than that as I began to think that if they could do it, why not **Beckett**? Fanciful or fleeting dreams are an inescapable fact of life. In reality they are invariably harmless and can be a constant source of inspiration or even fun. However, in my eyes the youthful **Beckett** had real and unquestionable talent. I also knew it was my job to utilise it to their best advantage while attempting to secure that all important record deal.

A few hours after arriving, the group were up on stage and undergoing a rigorous and compulsory sound check. Within minutes their music was reverberating around the history steeped interior of the empty club. "Too loud," shouted the aggressive and uncompromising voice of Ricky. On hearing it the group looked apprehensive and I understood why. He was the chap who had once booked **The Beatles** which had elevated him to a status far higher than his tiny frame could ever hope to achieve. Having been suitably admonished, the group then kicked in with another song while looking uneasily at each other for some semblance of reassurance. By now, a nerve wracking tension had crept into the proceedings and I couldn't help feeling extremely sorry for them. "You are still too loud," he cried out in a voice laced with a mixture of critical and uncompromising derision. "I've turned you down on the house PA but your stage settings are still too high," he warned in a voice which continued to be abrasive as well as highly unsettling. Knowing he had previously sent one group home without ever playing for allegedly failing to comply with his strict and implicit instructions, added to the tension which now hung ominously in the air. After a few more hesitant starts, having turned down, **Beckett** began to play exceedingly well as their confidence was noticeably growing. Meanwhile, the ever busy waitress stopped to listen and smiled, as if giving them her own distinct seal of approval. I smiled back as her eyes immediately wandered back towards Terry on stage. It soon became apparent that he was already capturing her heart as he began to energetically move his slim, athletic and sensual figure to the beat which appeared to be for her sole benefit.

Okay, that's fine" said Ricky after hearing a few more numbers. I heaved a huge sigh of relief knowing the band would now be playing that night and were about to be thrown in at the deep end. As the clock ticked ominously away, I couldn't help wondering what sort of audience it would be, and more importantly, would they like or appreciate the band? A few hours later, at eight pm, they duly climbed up on stage to a half empty club, having to face the punishing prospect of playing eight half hour spots. These were interspersed with eight half hour breaks until finally finishing at four in the morning. This was to be their baptism of fire into Hamburg and they were faced with having to play this gruelling routine for fifteen consecutive nights. It was a long and arduous prospect but I needn't have worried. With two excellent vocalists in Terry and Kenny, they sailed effortlessly through the first night. Later, the club began to fill up as people began dancing rhythmically and joyously to their music. Fortunately, Ricky looked happy and by the end of the night the group and I had soon cemented a worthwhile and lasting friendship with him. While performing each night, it soon became noticeably apparent that the group were becoming considerably tighter and more relaxed. There was an indefinable magic about this small dark and seedy club which was hard to quantify. As it rocked to the energetic and pounding beat of five youth's intent on making their mark, I began to relax. Each night the club would fill up and the portents were extremely encouraging as I danced, smiled, listened, and then smiled again. They were undoubtedly happy and carefree days while managing the band seemed to be a wonderful way of striving to reach the very top. But could their best endeavours possibly take them there? It was the sixty four thousand dollar question and only time would tell if there would be a million dollar answer.

Meanwhile, many people who regularly attended the club all claimed to have personally met **The Beatles**. Whether they had or not seemed immaterial, although I'm sure many of them did. What really mattered was that **Beckett** had become the new usurpers and the burning question was could they attain even a fraction of what their famous predecessors had? Realism tempered with dreams can be a heady and overpowering mixture. An appreciative crowd enthusiastically and endlessly shouting for more soon raises expectations. In doing so, the dreams become ever more fanciful as the reality of fulfilling them becomes a distinct possibility. Fifteen days later, it was time to go home. Hamburg and the Top Ten Club had proved to be an uplifting and stimulating experience which I look back on with extremely fond memories. On arriving at the Port of Harwich, a customs officer immediately ordered us to unload every piece of equipment from the tightly packed van onto the dockside. On being informed of this I was furious as it had been more than a Herculean task to fit it all in. Realising they were searching for drugs, I was adamant that they were wasting their time. "You're joking,"

I protested. "We have just disembarked from the ship after a 19 hour trip and we're very tired. Surely you are not going to make us take it all out? Why don't you just let us go?" I pleaded. Despite my impassioned words the stern faced customs officer remained unmoved. On complying with his order, and after a surprisingly quick check, we repacked the van before finally being allowed to continue the long journey home. Once outside the dockyard, the group suddenly began to snigger. I looked at them in a questioning and bemused manner, failing to see any apparent reason for such a display of uninhibited mirth. "What are you all smirking at?" I inquired, having had my curiosity aroused. "Nothing," they replied in a dismissive and disdainful manner as if to indicate the question was far too preposterous to warrant an answer. However, as the journey continued, the sniggering became unmistakeably louder and more pronounced. "Look, there must be something the matter. What is it?" I asked for the umpteenth time. "You didn't have any dope in the van did you?" I urgently inquired. At this point one of the group spoke up amidst a bout of further riotous laughter. "Well, we did have some cannabis hidden in the bass drum but I was confident they wouldn't undo all the nuts to remove the skin," he chuckled triumphantly. "Are you crazy?" I shrieked in disbelief. "Don't you realise what a serious offence this is? If they'd have discovered it I would have been held responsible because I was the one who signed the carnet," (a customs declaration document). On hearing my protestations, a sheepish look crossed their faces having realised the seriousness of my concern. "Don't ever do that again," I warned. The group remained silent as the van continued on its long and laborious homeward journey. "Look Geoff, if we had been caught we would have admitted it," volunteered one of them a few minutes later. I looked at him with a disbelieving frown on my face but said nothing. This was to be my first baptism into the world of musicians who were intent on making it on their own terms while alerting me to the real and possible dangers which lay ahead.

A few days later, my home telephone rang. "Geoff, Lionel Conway here." (He had previously worked for Dick James of **Beatles** fame and once managed **Elton John**) "You know that group you keep telling me are excellent? Can they play at The Marquee tonight?"

he inquired. "Warner Brothers Records are holding a special promotion there and the group they have booked are unable to play," he informed me. I glanced at my watch which indicated it was 10am and we were three hundred miles from London as well as having no idea where the group were. I had to think fast knowing these opportunities certainly didn't crop up every day and instantly recognised it was a heaven sent chance to play in front of a major record company. "Yes, we'll be there," I confidently assured him. "Good," I'll see you tonight," he answered before ringing off. After a series of frantic phone calls, hours later we were on the train from Newcastle Central Station while our roadie Brian Berks set off on his own to drive the equipment in the battered old Ford Transit to London. For him, it was a race against time as by now it was fully loaded and extremely slow. I also realised that if he pushed too hard there was the very real danger of it breaking down and yet there appeared to be no alternative. Nevertheless, it was too good an opportunity to miss as I impressed upon him the importance of not stopping, excepting for fuel. Fortunately, experience had also taught me that it was important for the group themselves to arrive on stage fresh as well as relaxed. I'd first noticed this at Newcastle Mayfair Ballroom when I'd booked **Rod Stewart & The Faces**. Rather than face the tedious and wearisome journey by road, they had flown up and as Rod bounded energetically onto the stage like a finely honed athlete, there was an unmistakeable and supreme confidence about him. Despite the hall being oppressively hot and sweaty, his energy levels never dropped and the group proved to be a revelation. Conversely, at other promotions, some groups would turn up looking weary and dishevelled from their long arduous drive. This, together with a lack of sleep, once on stage, it soon became apparent they lacked sparkle as well as enthusiasm. With **Beckett**, I was determined not to fall into such a soul destroying trap, especially for such an important gig. Soon, the rest of us had boarded the train at Newcastle Central Station, before settling comfortably into the allocated seats. Unknown to them, during the journey I carefully scrutinised their behaviour. Fortunately, they seemed relaxed and unconcerned, seemingly unperturbed at the importance and magnitude of the task that lay ahead. As the journey continued, I casually checked their young faces in order to comfort and reassure myself that they were ready. I thought of The Marquee and all the famous groups who had played there. Suddenly, heady dreams of major stardom began racing through my thoughts as I desperately tried to remain outwardly cool. This, together with their noticeably calm and unruffled demeanour became instrumental in instilling within me an inner confidence that they might just be able to pull it off. After fifteen consecutive nights in Hamburg they were so well rehearsed, I felt they could have gone on blindfolded and still performed amazingly well.

Nevertheless, as a manager, there remained a multitude of worries racing through my mind. What if something went wrong? Would Warner Brothers be impressed enough to sign them? Then again, would the equipment arrive in time or would one of the guitar strings snap and throw the group into disarray? Normally, I knew they could take these things in their stride, but this was no ordinary gig. A major record contract was in the offing as I kept repeatedly mulling a myriad of things over in my head. Never in my wildest dreams had I expected things to be happening so quickly. Hamburg, and now headlining at the famous Marquee Club in London in front of Warner Brother executives all seemed like an apparition. Was this to be the final payoff for all the years of steadfastly promoting local and major bands? I certainly hoped so. York, Doncaster, Peterboro, Welwyn Garden City. As the names flashed up I realised we were nearing London and the pressure was beginning to build. Remarkably, the group seemed relaxed and it appeared to be just another gig to them although I knew different. While serving on The Ark Royal aircraft carrier I'd been fortunate enough to travel all over the world and experienced some mountainous seas before entering calmer waters. The ship was big and strong and no matter what buffeting it suffered, it always came through unscathed. Sitting there on the train it seemed a strange but apt analogy. **Beckett** had also experienced some rough and difficult gigs but always seemed to possess the same capacity to weather whatever fate threw at them.

A major record contract. It's easy to say but in reality to acquire one is no easy task. I was fully aware of this and sitting next to five young hopefuls who were desperate for success, failure was unthinkable. However, it was a possibility that had to be faced. The thought of it continued to haunt me. There was no escape from realising that in order to create the initial buzz in London; I had unreservedly built the group up to be something special. Suddenly, a series of doubts began to flood through my mind once again. What if they were summarily dismissed as just another bunch of uninspiring hopefuls? A cold and frightening shiver ran down my spine as the train finally pulled into Kings Cross. The group began purposefully walking up the long and seemingly never ending platform. In my mind it was a platform of hope, of dreams come true, and a stepping stone to greater things. Meanwhile other passengers hurried past, oblivious to the importance of our visit. Ironically, I knew that they too would have their own incalculable dreams, but what were they, and did everything hinge on what happened in the next few hours? There was no time to waste as we took the luxury of hailing a taxi in our haste to let Jack Barrie, the legendary manager of the Marquee, know that we had finally arrived.

By now, it was 8-15 pm and when we arrived, he quickly informed me that unless the equipment arrived by 8-45pm it would be too late to go on. I immediately thought of "Berksey" huddled over the steering wheel, all alone and struggling to make it. He can only be described as a deeply determined character that would unfailingly pull out all the stops. However, I also knew that fate, together with an old van, could conspire against even the best of intentions, no matter how honourable they might be. The fact was, everything now depended upon him and for the first time I felt exceedingly vulnerable. I glanced around the dark interior of the club which was packed with record company executives together with an assortment of their secretaries and friends. I wandered into the bar where everyone seemed to be drinking on expenses and it clearly showed. Glasses were being unashamedly clinked while people warmly greeted each other in what appeared to be a happy and carefree mood. I glanced at my watch for the umpteenth time, knowing it was nearly 8-45pm and there was still no sign of "Berksey." Back in the dressing room, I noticed the group looked uncharacteristically nervous. I tried to smile but was unsure if it was having the desired effect. I momentarily glanced at Terry who never was a worrier. He immediately smiled and how I envied him. Just then Jack Barrie approached me with a deep worried frown written across his weather beaten face. Having already sensed why and before he could speak, I began pleading for more time. "He'll be here in a moment. You've got to give us a little longer," I pleaded in a heartfelt and seemingly distressed manner. He stared at my impassioned face in the full knowledge his decision could affect us for the rest of our lives. He glanced at his watch and suddenly, it all seemed so unfair. To travel all that way only to be thwarted for the sake of a few minutes was undeniably a highly disturbing and nerve wracking experience. Meanwhile, people continued to drink at the bar, unaware of the intensity of the drama being played out. Where was "Berksey?" My mind was in a turmoil as time raced on. I fully realised he could be stranded on the motorway but somehow my faith in him remained undiminished. If there was one person who would move heaven and earth to get there, I knew it was him.

It was now 9pm. Jack Barrie approached me again, ominously shaking his head, accompanied by a disgruntled look of anguish on his face. By now, it seemed all was lost. In a last desperate effort to placate him, I pleaded, cajoled, and pleaded some more. In frustration, I threw my arms up in the air, but it was all to no avail. "Sorry, it's too late now," he instructed with words which were both deeply cutting and cruel. Suddenly, the damning and heartbreaking realisation hit me knowing the chance of stardom had inextricably slipped away. I was distraught knowing that we had tried so hard and this was to be the humiliating and fruitless culmination of all our efforts. "Listen Jack. If "Berksey" had broken down he would have rung here to tell me, but he hasn't. Please give us just a few more minutes," I begged in a last despairing attempt to salvage something from our seemingly despairing hopes. Before he could answer, as if by a miracle, the back door suddenly swung open and in ran a breathless "Berksey." "Sorry I'm late," he exclaimed. I looked at his sweat drained and unshaven face while his broad smile clearly illustrated how relieved he was. Jack looked at me for what appeared to be an eternity before he spoke. "Okay, get them on as fast as possible," he instructed. His words hit me like a sledgehammer as I breathed a huge sigh of relief. "Thanks Jack," I replied before hurriedly informing the group they were playing. Within a few hectic minutes the group and I had frantically manhandled the equipment on to the stage where **The Stones, Jimi Hendrix, Led Zeppelin, The Who, David Bowie** and hundreds of others had all cemented their reputations. "Hurry up Geoff, get the group on," urged Jack impatiently. I nodded in acknowledgement knowing there was no time for a sound check. It was to be a defining moment knowing the group were about to be thrust into the most important gig of their lives and only fate could decree what would happen. "Ladies and Gentlemen, from the North East of England, a highly recommended group, **Beckett**," announced the DJ in a cultured and reassuring manner. At this, four of the band immediately stepped on stage, before quickly plugging in. I looked towards the vocal mike and immediately noticed Terry was absent. I dashed backstage to find him nonchalantly brushing his hair while looking in the mirror. "Terry," I screamed. "Quick, get on stage, you're holding everyone up." He turned and looked at me with a twinkle in his eye and a confidence which somehow calmed my innermost fears. With a self assured and relaxed flourish, he dashed through the dressing room door, immediately joining the group on stage.

Within minutes, the bar had emptied and a packed Marquee was about to see if this unadvertised and unknown band could fulfil the record company's hope of unearthing new and genuine talent. It was a nerve wracking moment as I swallowed hard. Everything now hinged on their performance as they kicked in with a precision and tightness that quickly eased any worries I may have held. During the second number, Terry began to energetically work the stage, his long black hair swirling behind him as his slim athletic body began responding to the beat. Meanwhile, "Berksey" was peering over the bass amp, his sweat stained face worriedly checking the equipment in the full knowledge that he'd had no time to tape the leads down. Just then, Arthur, the young blonde haired lead guitarist who was always so quiet and methodical in his approach, unleashed a searing solo. Terry immediately held his vocal mike near the frets to accentuate it as it hung in the air. It was showmanship at its very best and the crowd immediately applauded. This was manna from heaven for Terry. It was what he thrived on and there was no stopping him. Later in the set, Kenny Mountain stepped forward to showcase a Chuck Berry medley in his wonderful attacking style, while his distinctive voice whipped up the crowd's enthusiasm to even greater heights. It was his piece de resistance and never failed to send an audience into raptures of appreciation and delight. During all this, Ian Ralfini, the managing director of Warner's and Martin Wyatt, his trusted assistant, were watching intently. Everything now hinged on their decision as I glanced over to find they were huddled in deep conversation. What were they saying? Or more importantly, what were they thinking? I wondered. I was already aware that they had recently signed a group called **America,** whose single, "Horse with No Name," had charted in both Britain and America, while their album of the same name had reached No 1 in the American Billboard Chart and stayed there for five weeks. Not only that, they had achieved this success within a remarkably short time of signing. What about if they decided to sign **Beckett** and the same thing happened to them? It was a heady thought as an overpowering and invigorating feeling of euphoria began to surge through me when suddenly, reality kicked in. Warner Bros were an international record company with exacting standards, but just how exacting were they, I wondered? Meanwhile, the group were up there, heroically and majestically fighting for their very lives, underpinned by a fierce determination to impress. As I watched, I felt helpless; knowing the weighty and heavily laden baton of responsibility I sometimes held had been passed and it was all up to them. As the minutes ticked away, I became concerned. Was it the pressure? Or were doubts' beginning to eat into the very fabric of my thoughts knowing America was beckoning with just five signatures and a decision away? As a young boy I'd always dreamt of going there and with a successful band I knew it would be even more of an exhilarating adventure. In the past, the major groups I'd promoted had often woven mystical tales about how exciting it was when they had made it and toured its major cities. Dreams, we all have them and without life's challenges they would appear to be meaningless, or less worthy. That is if we are ever fortunate enough to achieve them. However, right then, this was no dream. It was reality and could actually happen.

After a faultless set and four rapturous encores, the group were finally back in the dressing room. Minutes later, Martin Wyatt entered and approached me. "How long are you in London for," he inquired? "We go back tomorrow," I replied. Can you call into my office to see me before you go?" he requested. I noticed his face possessed a warmth, together with words which sounded sincere and very encouraging which immediately lifted my spirits. However, there was still no decision and to be left in such a void was proving to be most disconcerting. The band looked at me expectantly not having heard what he said. "You were excellent," I proudly informed them. However, in reality, I knew it wasn't necessary as I realised the audience had already shown its appreciation in a far more positive manner than I could possibly have expressed in words. Suddenly, Terry turned and left, before walking into the bar to be greeted by hordes of well wishers keen to tell him how invigorating the group had been. Among them were a number of attractive girls who could visualise a star in the making and it seemed he wanted to capitalise on his good fortune and who could blame him. Nevertheless, despite the euphoria, there were a myriad of other worries. I knew that in the rock business any form of success can be transient or short lived, no matter what the circumstances. Next morning in Oxford St my head was awash with excitement as I gingerly walked up the steps leading to Warners and announced my arrival to Bernie the attractive receptionist. It was a significant moment as she casually threw me a warm and welcoming smile. Somehow, it felt as if this was my true spiritual home and immediately put me in a more relaxed frame of mind. "I have an appointment with Martin Wyatt," I quietly informed her. "Have a seat," she beckoned. As I settled into the comfortable leather cushions, I began to hope it would be the first of many such visits. Minutes later, Bernie stood up to check some files and I couldn't help noticing how shapely she was. For a brief moment it was a pleasant distraction until I realised this was not the time for admiring glances. Soon, I was ushered into Martin Wyatt's office whereupon he gave me a huge smile. By now I was experienced enough not to get carried away. "Everybody liked the group," he began. I smiled inwardly knowing he wouldn't have invited me in to see him if this wasn't the case. Nevertheless, it was a positive start as I became impatient to hear what he might have to say. "Have you got the group under contract?" he questioned. "Yes," I replied confidently. "How long for?" he inquired. "Eight years," I answered with the confident assurance of someone who was excitedly hoping for some groundbreaking or startling news. He paused for a moment before speaking in a somewhat calm and relaxed manner as his voice broke what appeared to be an unending silence. "We'd like to offer you a recording contract for an album and a single with an option for another four albums. We'll also give you an advance of £10,000 on signing, (now worth around £100,000). What do you think about that?" he asked. Outwardly, I continued to remain calm but inside my heart was racing with excitement. **Frank Sinatra, Rod Stewart, The Eagles**, **Aretha Franklin** and a whole host of other major artistes were on the label and here we were being offered the chance to join them. Suddenly, he became silent, as if unsure of what he was about to say. "Let me tell you about a new label we are starting," he began. "It's to be called Raft Records which is an amalgam of our two surnames, Ralfini and Wyatt. **Family** and **Linda Lewis** have already signed and we want your group to join them. It will still be a part of Warner Bros but it will be more specialised so that we can give it our personal attention without any interference from the American side," he pointed out. On hearing this I had very little time to think but it seemed we were being invited to join the start of a new and revolutionary label. Hardly had he taken breath when he kicked in again with a series of encouraging words making me realise just how enthusiastic he was to sign the group. Only a few weeks earlier, Chris Wright, co-founder of Chrysalis Records and manager of **Ten Years After,** had travelled up to the NE to see the group play at a working men's club in South Shields. Unfortunately, on picking him up from the station in an old Triumph Herald, it began raining heavily whereupon I quickly discovered that my windscreen wipers were malfunctioning. This caused him to spend the entire journey crouching under the dashboard in order to hold two loose wires together to ensure I could see through the torrent of water rapidly filling the windscreen. Later, and to this day, we both laugh at the absurdity of it as here was the head of a multi million pound record company desperate to keep the wires in contact with each other in the hope of staying alive. Fortunately, he succeeded and after seeing the group, immediately offered me a major deal with his record company to which I'd been giving serious consideration. Now I had a rival offer and had to think fast as experience had taught me that in life, and especially in the record business, enthusiasm is the one thing you must capitalise on. Delay, or prevaricate, and I was fully aware that the chance might slip away. With this in mind I decided to go for the Warner Bros offer, knowing it was too tempting to refuse. "Sounds very exciting to me and providing the percentages are agreeable, we'll be happy to sign," I cheerily informed him. He immediately stood up before shaking my hand. "I'll get the contract drawn up and I'm sure you will find it very fair," he assured me. On the way out I glanced at the platinum and gold albums hanging on the wall in reception. As I did so the delightful Bernie smiled. Suddenly, I felt ten feet tall as if I had just entered the gates of heaven with my head swirling in the clouds.

Once outside in Oxford St. people were hurrying past as if the world was about to end. I walked slowly and calmly in an effort to take in everything that had just taken place. Ironically, **Led Zeppelin's** office was just a short distance away in the same street and I remembered the euphoric feeling when I had finally succeeded in booking them for three gigs in the same year. In many ways it was the pinnacle of my promoting career and I'd never dreamt anything resembling how I felt that day could ever be repeated. However, it seemed it had and I was more than grateful. That first night at The Bay Hotel in Sunderland when I was paid £2 for my evenings work on the door, seemed a long time ago, but still remained fresh in my mind. On the bus home after that first night I'd thought of the attractive girl guitarist who had been playing there who was just a distant memory. Now, Bernie the receptionist had replaced her and I considered it a fair swap. There was a whole abundance of other memories too and hopefully, fresh ones were about replace them. I'd also succeeded in bringing five NE lads to London and given them a real chance of achieving their dreams. Could they succeed? It was an exciting and all encompassing thought.

Despite having clinched a major record contract, I was under no illusions. I recognised that there was still a lot of hard work ahead, although I was sure it was a challenge the group would relish. Hadn't they just come back from Hamburg where the **Beatles** had played and went on to make it? Inevitably, comparisons and dreams of untold success began to creep into my thinking. Having left Warner Brothers offices after hearing the excellent news, just a few hundred yards away was The Marquee where the **Rolling Stones** had played before making an international name for themselves. I'd also been fortunate to see them live at Newcastle City Hall where tickets were like gold and mounted police had to be used in order to force the crowds of people away from the stage door. Soon fantasy and dreams began merging into one as I picked up the pace. Euphoria is merely a word but it encapsulates so much when it is endlessly spinning around in your head. Achieving a major record contract can have this effect as an unending series of heady dreams continually began surfacing. Just then I bumped into someone and quickly apologised on realising I had momentarily allowed myself to become detached from the reality of a congested thoroughfare. Meanwhile, I continued to dream. First, there was flying to America before going on to conquer it and entering the charts at No 1. Following this would be a series of headlining gigs, while being paid huge sums as well as receiving a succession of platinum albums from a grateful record company. Thoughts of a big house with a swimming pool and a multitude of beautiful bikini clad girls sitting around its edges also began to come into this heady and illusory equation. Soon it became hard to separate fact from fiction. Hollywood and stardom conjured up dreams of meeting famous stars such as the beautiful **Elizabeth Taylor, Richard Burton, Frank Sinatra, Mick Jagger, The Beatles** and a whole cavalcade of others. To us mere mortals, they were celluloid or rock idols who were beyond reach. On the other hand, I had never dreamt I would meet **Robert Plant, Jimmy Page, Eric Clapton, The Who, David Bowie, Van Morrison** or **Captain Beefheart**, and yet in reality, I had. Meanwhile, the thought that I was about to meet the group and give them the good news, or should I say startling news was certainly an intoxicating one. In theory, I'd just earned a thousand pounds for my mornings work but the money was the last thing on my mind. It was the challenge and excitement that lay ahead which actually stirred my innermost emotions. Later, I had the gratifying task of informing the group of the wonderful and exciting news. An almost telepathic grin crossed their faces as if they already knew, but surely that was impossible. "Martin Wyatt came up to us after the gig and congratulated the group on an excellent performance," said Terry. "He wouldn't have done that if he didn't like us, would he?" His logic was certainly true and I felt ecstatically happy for all of them knowing that in Hamburg they had worked their socks off and now it had all paid off. Inside, there was an overwhelming feeling of elation coursing through my blood. The group were now about to embark on a journey which could ultimately lead to superstardom and I was convinced they had the talent to achieve it.

Chapter 3

Two weeks later, after the official signing and photographs had been taken, we were driven in a record company limousine to a Greek restaurant for a private reception where we were treated like superstars. Over in the corner, the black curly headed "Berksey" sat quietly with a contented look on his face. In many ways he was undoubtedly the real superstar. I recalled how, without his Herculean and unstinting effort, none of what was taking place might have happened. Outside, the limousine driver sat patiently awaiting our departure. Inside, I felt a quiet unease that he should have to do this and asked if I could be allowed to invite him in to join us. "It's his job," pointed out a record company employee in a somewhat uncaring and derisive manner. Just then I thought back to my short stint as a railway porter when it had been my job to carry other people's luggage and I immediately recognised how he would be feeling. A few minutes later, I asked again. "Oh don't worry about him, he'll be all right, it's his job to wait" came the reply. Soon, the group and I were to learn his name was Dennis Goodman and were subsequently to become firm friends. I later learnt that he often drove **Dianna Ross, The Eagles, Aretha Franklin** and dozens of other top recording stars whenever they were in the UK. By an amazing coincidence he had once worked in Sunderland as a tea salesman and had also served in the last war. Gifted with a wonderful and engaging personality, his private and personal asides on the stars he drove always made fascinating listening. In a rather bold and characteristic fashion, he was to slip a demo of **Beckett** into the tape deck while driving Ahmet Ertegun from London Airport. "Who is this band?" he inquired as Dennis smiled inwardly before replying. "It's a group we have just signed to the WEA label," he replied. (Warner, Electra & Atlantic had just amalgamated). An intrigued Ahmet, the owner and co founder of Atlantic Records then asked him to leave it on so that he could listen to it. Dennis chuckled heartily when he later related the story to me. It was to prove an invaluable introduction because at a later date, he went on to offer the group a major record deal on his label. "He's only a chauffeur," someone once suggested from the lofty heights of their gilded cage. How short sighted such an utterance would prove to be, as he was far from that. Besides being one of the nicest and most personable people you could ever wish to meet, he was also the confidante of virtually every major star and executive who recorded or worked for the company. I often used to play him at table tennis in the basement, and believe it or not, and unknown to everyone else, I always felt he was the real star of Warner Brothers Records in London. Sadly, he has now passed away but is far from forgotten.

Once back in Sunderland, I walked into The Bis-Bar with the cheque nestling safely in my pocket. It was a strange sensation as it was only a piece of paper, but it was what it represented that mattered most. The Chase Manhattan Bank will pay you £10,000 it said in large letters. It was to prove a very comforting feeling knowing that someone had such overwhelming and compelling faith in the band. Words certainly couldn't describe how I felt at the time, not my words anyway. In fact, a literary genius would find extreme difficulty in expressing how wonderful and joyous I felt at that very moment. For a completely unknown and unadvertised group to go to London and, against all the odds secure a major record company contract in such a short space of time, I can assure you was a truly invigorating feeling. History is undoubtedly littered with conquering heroes but in their own small and undemonstrative manner, in my eyes, this is what the group had now become. A whole new avenue of dreams and endless possibilities had opened up. While still in a state of shock, I kept asking myself why it had happened. Had fate decided to bestow its many favours on us having caught it in one of its rare benevolent moods? Or was it because the group had wholeheartedly deserved it? Being of a suspicious nature, an element of caution quietly and stealthily began creeping into my thoughts. While doing so, I began exploring any potential pitfalls which may hamper or forestall their future progress. Fortunately, despite my natural reticence, there didn't appear to be any and I felt that this time, surely nothing could stop us.

Outside, the hustle and bustle of Park Lane in Sunderland seemed a world away, with the Bis-Bar's big glass windows enclosing those inside in a warm and welcoming cocoon of complete relaxation. As usual, Debbie and her friends were in attendance, while the local boys, with their latest military jackets emblazoned with gold or colourful badges discreetly kept an eye on proceedings. To say it was a hotbed of free love may well be an exaggeration. Nevertheless, it was certainly the forerunner of many sexual liaisons, which gave it an added feeling of camaraderie and lasting friendships. Music was of course, high on the agenda, as was a daily visit in order to fulfil the unbridled fantasies of their youth. Suddenly, **Beckett** were news. It may have been understated but it was undeniably a talking point. Shy by nature, there was an inner pride that I found hard to subdue. People smiled, girls wandered over, there were handshakes, and yet, deep down I was aware the group hadn't sold a record yet. Optimism coupled with caution is a confusing and gut wrenching feeling. What if it all goes wrong? On the other hand, what if it all goes right? These two thoughts gnawed into my subconscious in a search for the answer. Unfortunately, there wasn't one, not yet anyway. With the cheque still nestling safely in my pocket, I looked around and realised that in many ways the Bis-Bar had become my second home. Each evening, they obligingly cooked me an evening meal of my own choice with fresh vegetables which I had earlier purchased. Where else could you have possibly obtained this sort of service at minimal cost? Most days, Debbie seemed to be present. Her sexuality was the passport that opened doors and meant she never paid to see her favourite bands. Hers was a licence to thrill. Her refined voice added a touch of class for those fortunate enough to experience her physical attributes. Captivating, sensual, and single minded, what other attributes could a girl want? In Debbie's case, it was rock stars all the way. Backstage at one gig she openly bared her breasts in front of interested onlookers of which I was one. Was she an attention seeker or someone just looking for thrills, or perhaps both? With her, excitement was the name of the game and how she enjoyed life's temptations in her quest to exact its rich and seemingly ever present rewards. "Hi Geoff, heard about the group and the advance they got from Warner's," she began as I smiled knowingly. A cheque of this nature had quickly elevated the group to new heights and I sensed they had now become possible targets. "Are they going to tour America?" she inquired. I liked that about Debbie. She thought big and wasn't afraid to ask pertinent questions if it meant another conquest. "I hope so," was my calm and hopeful reply. On hearing this, she immediately leaned back in her chair which was a ploy she often used to gain time and attract attention. Her long sensual legs were now clearly visible and in the daylight, very unsettling. I looked around as she patiently and temptingly awaited my reaction. I already knew there was no denying she was skilled in the art of seduction as I'd personally witnessed it on many previous occasions at The Bay Hotel. However, for some unknown reason, it never seemed to cheapen her. "Where are the group playing at next?" she shamelessly inquired. "At a college in London," I replied whereupon her face became pensive as if disappointed at not being able to be there. Seconds later, she turned to survey the array of trendy cars parked outside in an effort to identify the owners who periodically entered or alighted from them. Her calculating mind soon spotted a Marcos sports car which looked sleek and streamlined. Unfortunately however, there was no sign of its owner. Nevertheless, it mattered little as Debbie was young and had time on her hands. Soon, she stood up to leave and as her expensive perfume wafted into my nostrils I realised it was her way of leaving her calling card. Having reached out and opened the glass door, I watched in quiet admiration as her curvaceous figure and long sensual legs quickly began disappearing into the distance.

Rock & Roll encompasses music, sex, and unfortunately, possible self destruction. Whether it is drugs with their often pernicious habit of destroying its partaker, it unfailingly provides an excitement and successive highs. Sex, which is even more readily available for those who "make it," also provides an abundance of unlimited pleasure. Put the two together and looking at it rationally, they are an irresistible combination. Those groups who consistently succumbed to the temptations of drugs often reminded me of alcoholics who constantly crave another drink. Their limited willpower is matched only by their insatiable desire to escape reality in order to enter into a fantasy world of utopian dreams. In doing so, they hope it will alleviate or obliterate their seemingly insoluble and endless problems. Unfortunately, they fail to realise its cruel and ultimately devastating affects on the well being of their bodies. Witnessing such a sad spectacle as I personally had with Paul Kossoff of **Free,** really brings the futility and stark reality of it home. His willpower had become non existent while his body constantly craved more. As I watched others treading the same path it became something which I found quite sad. However, music was the path they had chosen and I soon found drugs were too well entrenched for my despairing words to have the slightest affect. Apathy, once established is a cruel and stubborn trait to overcome or exorcise. Anyone who harbours lingering doubts has only to consult the list of deceased rock stars that not only got old before their time, but also succumbed to its humiliating and degrading repercussions.

Soon, the word about **Beckett's** successful and jubilant foray into London had reached a much wider audience. "I hear they have signed a major record deal. When is the album coming out?" people would ask. In Sunderland, it was undoubtedly an achievement which meant in the musical world they were now on the ascendancy and had quickly been elevated to local celebrities. How did I feel you may well ask? Quite naturally, I was extremely happy while reminding myself of the many bands I had promoted that had acquired a major record contract and subsequently faded into the heartbreaking vacuum of everlasting nonentity. It was to be a sobering and in many ways a cheerless thought as I conveniently pushed it to the back of my mind. Nevertheless, I remained as excited as everyone else. A working class lad walking out of Warner Bros with a major record contract and a £10,000 cheque seemed like a fairytale and fantasy all rolled into one. In the rarefied atmosphere I now found myself working in, caution, or a reasoned clarity of thought was becoming impossible. Suddenly, long held dreams appeared to be rapidly turning into reality and to speak about anything other than success seemed highly inappropriate as well as foolhardy. A few days later, I drove through to guitarist Arthur Ramm's house at South Shields. As usual, his house was immaculately clean and orderly which in many ways reminded me of his guitar and equipment. "Arthur, we need to start a joint bank account for the band" I quietly informed him. "To make sure everyone knows what is happening to the money, we'll register it so that three signatures are required for any withdrawals. This will include any two of the band as well as my own." Arthur listened attentively before nodding in agreement knowing we both implicitly trusted each other. A few hours later the deed was successfully concluded after I had safely deposited the cheque at Lloyds Bank in Fawcett St, Sunderland.

Managing a band with a major record contract together with money in the bank, certainly smacks of unqualified success. Self confidence soars as people begin to look at you in a different light. This soon manifests itself into what appears to be a reverential attitude while your words have attained a far higher value or interest than you ever intended. Meanwhile, a television appearance on the much respected "Old Grey Whistle Test" together with a radio slot on **John Peel's** "Top Gear" helped to consolidate their recently elevated position in the eyes of the local community. Suddenly, they had become "hot," while the roaring flames of expectation began to reach untold heights of unparalleled optimism and dreams. "Don't ever get big headed son." Having recalled dad's cautionary words they seemed at odds with what was actually happening. My two plus two Jaguar E Type parked outside his colliery house only a few yards from Castletown Working Men's Club provided its own telling story. One day dad proudly climbed in before we made our way to the nearby cemetery in order to place flowers on my beloved twelve year old brother Donald's grave. Once there we both prayed and dad liked that as it gave him a form of solace and helped relieve the burden of sadness we both felt. However, from such sadness comes hope as his knurled hands carefully placed the flowers on the grave. We both realised rock music, success, and possible stardom faded into insignificance when compared with the feeling we both felt at that moment. To be so close to someone you once loved is in its own way, very comforting. While standing there, an inner strength began to surge through me, willing me to succeed. "I'll do it for him and dad," was my quiet but determined thought at the time. Dad liked the E-Type, especially as he'd never expected one to be parked outside his house, let alone being driven in one. He also had a great sense of humour. He laughed a lot and always seemed to giggle at his own jokes which made them seem even funnier. He was inherently cautious, a trait he studiously passed on to me and my brother Leo. "Don't waste your money son. Always keep some in the bank for a rainy day. You never know when you might need it," was another piece of advice he often proffered. Being of an older generation, he'd never heard of **Led Zeppelin** or **Country Joe**. However he had heard of **John Peel** and liked him after meeting him. Seems a contradiction really but that's the way he was. People used to ask him for tickets to see the bands but he called my promotions dances. "It's a rock concert Dad, I would point out." At this, he would giggle and make light of it. How could anyone possibly take offence at such simplistic naivety?

Unfortunately, within a year, all the money from the advance had been spent. A new Mercedes van, new equipment, wages, petrol, bed & breakfasts and lack of decent paying gigs all took their toll. With the advance now spent, the band was unable to keep their head above water without being heavily subsidised and was costing me serious money. A hit single was desperately needed but unfortunately, there didn't appear to be one on the horizon. A series of gigs including supporting **Rod Stewart & The Faces**. **Free**, and **Ten Years After** all failed to stem the financial losses. Ironically, critical acclaim and respect seemed to increase in direct proportion to their financial plight. Praise and respect comes in many forms and **Beckett** continued to receive it by the bucketful. Unfortunately, this helped engender a feeling that it was only a question of time before the big breakthrough came. Knowing or feeling this, together with the constant praise they were receiving instilled within me a determination not to give up hope. It's a truism to state that nothing ever comes easy and being fully aware of this was proving to be a rallying call whenever serious doubts or difficulties arose.

Out front, Terry and Kenny continued to be superb as were the rest of the group, but it was readily apparent that something vital was missing. But what was it? This was a perplexing question which had to be resolved and it seemed it would come to a head sooner, rather than later. To ignore it and hope it would right itself was no longer an option as I continued to experience mounting losses. Eventually, this caused me to make one of the most difficult and heartrending decisions of my career. A friend of Kenny Mountain had constantly been regaling us about an incredible guitarist who lived in Newcastle and whose name was Bob Barton. One night, I decided to go along to see him and sure enough, he proved to be excellent while also possessing a great voice. If he was in the band instead of Arthur, it might just clinch it, I thought. Here, it must be said that desperation is never a good bedfellow to make far reaching decisions of this nature. However, I was also aware that procrastination or indecisiveness can often be accompanied by their own damaging limitations. The addition of another excellent singer, making three top class vocalists now in the band, would surely create a lot more interest, was my considered thought at the time.

It must also be pointed out that just prior to making my decision I'd seen **The Doobie Bros** live at Reading Festival and was amazed at how fantastic they were. With three excellent vocalists they proved to be a revelation while my trusted and knowledgeable friend Chas McIver thought exactly the same. As each vocalist sang, backed by superb harmonies, they had the whole festival really rocking. I was amazed and the sell out crowd fell in love with them and refused to let them off stage. The other serious consideration which weighed heavily on my mind was the fact that the record company were crying out for a hit single and the band had been unable to write one. Very conveniently, Bob Barton had written what I regarded as a potential single and this proved to be a major factor. Whatever you may think, making a decision of this nature is far from easy. A tortuous mixture of human emotions and friendship, together with a guilty conscience, all conspire to give you sleepless nights. The long arduous eight thirty minute spots for fifteen consecutive nights at The Top Ten Club came to mind. There was also the gig at The Marquee that had clinched the deal which was also uppermost in my troubled thoughts. Conversely, the group had had a year to capitalise on their good fortune and were no longer capable of sustaining themselves without further injections of my hard earned and rapidly depleting cash reserves. Bearing all this in mind, I talked the group into replacing Arthur with Bob Barton. Unfortunately, three years later, I was to wholeheartedly regret this decision especially as Arthur is one of the nicest people you could ever wish to meet. On hearing the news, he was devastated. To this day he is the only musician I cannot face without feeling both sorry and guilty. It seemed I had ruthlessly and selfishly taken the chance of stardom away from him in my quest to increase the band's chances of making it. Having honestly thought it was the correct decision at the time, I will explain later why it proved to be a serious and doom laden error of judgement.

A few months later, with Bob in the band, **Beckett** released their first single (which Bob had personally written) entitled "Little Girl." Despite receiving considerable airplay including **John Peel's** immensely influential "Top Gear" radio programme, it failed to enter the charts. When a single which experienced and highly discerning people are tipping for major chart success fails to achieve their initial and enthusiastic predictions, an inevitable air of despondency begins to creep in. It is also a very unsettling time, especially for the band as the realisation of failure begins to seep into their very lifeblood, draining them of hope and inspiration. Sights which have been optimistically aimed have to be lowered in a depressing reality check. The group quickly develop an air of hurt pride, while a feeling of aimlessness and lassitude begins to creep in. Sensing this, the record company soon becomes embroiled in an unavoidable malaise of its own. Inevitably, the familiar treadmill of inferior or sub standard bookings have to be undertaken with minimal fees. Also, continual and repetitive support slots can be morale sapping or demeaning. Long distances have to be travelled and once on stage, people invariably disappear to the bar to await the appearance of the better known and equipped headliners. Depression, together with a group continually playing to sparsely attended gigs does not inspire them to reach great heights. Ironically, or should I say fortunately, while labouring under such constraints, camaraderie seemed to increase in direct proportion to each setback. Meanwhile, as a promoter, I was in the providential position of being able to secure the group invaluable exposure by giving them a slot as support to **Free** when 3,000 people were present. Also, I put them on to support **Rod Stewart & The Faces,** which I am very proud to say turned out to be **John Peel's** all time favourite gig. Watching all this from the sidelines, I sensed, or should I say hoped, it would be only a matter of time before the dying embers of our faltering dreams turned into a hotbed of roaring flames.

Here, it must be pointed out that managing a band in the blind belief that they will almost certainly "make it," is in my opinion a highly dangerous and foolhardy preconception. Unfortunately, there are no set rules or instruction manuals to guide you, and in many it is like walking a tightrope which has been strung across a dark and dangerous precipice. Falter, or momentarily stop to take breath, and you are liable to fall into a steep and bottomless abyss from which there appears to be no escape. Knowing this, and being prepared for any eventualities which may lie ahead, your belief in the music must remain strong and unyielding. Optimism and tenacity together with an undying faith in the band remains a strong motivator. It is also comforting to know that if the band can come up with just "three minutes of magic" culminating in a hit single, it will dramatically change things overnight. However, quietly hidden in the murky depths of a troubled mind, you can't help wondering if it is merely wishful thinking together with an unrealistic assessment of their song writing potential. As time inexorably passes by, it becomes an outright obsession as well as a desperate necessity. Meanwhile, you are fully aware that to pressurise or constantly instil fear into the band in order to achieve such an aim could be classed as inhumane, or a form of unwarranted megalomania. Nevertheless, unpalatable as it may be, circumstances will eventually dictate that it has to be done, despite risking the unpleasantness and contempt which it may well bring. When the much sought after success continues to elude a band who have been led to believe they had every chance of "making it," apathy, disenchantment and internal strife soon become everyday hazards. Unfortunately, their disillusioned hopes quickly spread an inherent desire for the band to rid themselves of their seemingly incompetent manager. Amidst such strife, someone has to shoulder the blame as your own vulnerability, together with its wounding criticism, soon becomes apparent. This is the point where you begin to waiver as your own strength of character is tested to breaking point. To appear unmoved is to be accused of being stubborn, insensitive, or ineffectual, which is their way of applying pressure. "Familiarity breeds contempt" is a well known proverb as vitriolic remarks cloaked with unhelpful suggestions are readily aired and begin to wear you down. Amidst all this, dad's timely words of warning came to mind. "Unfortunately son, some people can see everybody else's faults but their own," he would say in a situation such as this. Of course everyone must be allowed their own viewpoint, but when you are personally subsidising each and every mistake, it hurts just that little bit more. Here, it must be pointed out that for some strange reason, most band members I have managed never seemed to read a daily paper. In failing to do so, I'm convinced that this leads them to a distorted view that the world has been specially created just for them and their music. A further corollary of this is that they become too full of their own importance and quickly dispense with their supposed altruistic intentions once possible stardom beckons. You may well ask if this is sour grapes or merely an honest observation. As I said earlier, everyone is entitled to their opinion. However, I can assure you, I have personally experienced it.

As ever, time is a great healer. The sun shines, someone smiles, and suddenly all past disagreements are forgotten in the indecent haste to try again. With it comes a renewed surge of energy which is highly infectious as it grips everyone in its thrall. Through all this, there remains that one remaining hope. Can they conjure up the necessary "three minutes of magic" which ironically is all that is required? The group know it, you know it, and the record company know it. It's a tempting and haunting question which becomes fixed in the brain, urging even greater effort. With the odds lengthening as time passes, respite becomes impossible. The merest hint that things may soon change keeps the utopian dream alive. Soon, in a moment of self doubt, you begin to question your own values. Are you being foolish and reckless, or is there a realistic chance that they have the ability to finally come up with the goods? As the pressure builds, all three possibilities come into the equation, but only time will tell. Suddenly, and without realising it, the ticking of the clock, the days of the month, and the passing of the years all rush by with indecent haste. Its cruel, it's tortuous, and it's exasperating, but it's the price fate exacts upon you when you are seeking that tempting and elusive success. Before long, a demo tape is thrust into your hands and it makes uninspiring listening. I hold back the tears knowing that to criticise at such an early juncture would be pointless, especially as there's always the distinct possibility that you are woefully wrong.

Ironically, the latest hit single by **Free** entitled "All Right Now" comes on the radio and it seems it is for them, especially as the royalties keep pouring in. In a moment of inspiration, a brainwave hits me. I'll give Andy Fraser the bass player who co wrote it a ring and ask if he'll write the group a possible hit single. Among other things he wrote "Be Good To Yourself," which was a big hit for **Frankie Miller** and everybody really liked it. "Sounds like clutching at straws to me," advises a friend who possessed a natural and overwhelming propensity to be sceptical. "Sorry Geoff, it's better if the group write a hit song themselves. That way it improves the feel because the singer can put his own emotions and self belief into it," Andy informs me. Of course he was right on both counts, but it failed to soften the blow.

So you want to manage a band? Enduring and undying faith must be the first prerequisites in your make-up before you all head off to London full of hope and great expectations. If the group succeed, and it's a big if, they deserve total respect for having had the courage to pursue their long held dreams. If, however, they fail, as I said earlier, be prepared to receive a barrage of brickbats and non stop criticism for your pains. Still, its fun trying, especially in the initial stages when sheer enthusiasm and determination carry everything before them. Along the way, I can assure you an assortment of sceptics or critics will appear with indecent regularity. This is where your strength of character and enthusiasm proves to be an invaluable asset. Possess it, and you will find you are almost half way there. However, finding the other half presents a much greater problem. So what advice can I proffer? I'm sorry, but I'm afraid I can't as there are far too many imponderables to consider. A few days later, re-energised and fully rested, I breezed into Warner's reception to find the highly delectable Bernie sitting there. As usual, she beckoned me to sit down as I quietly decided it had been worth the long 300 mile drive just to see her. Her pleasant personality, together with a few free albums certainly helped soothe frayed nerves as well as engendering a feel good factor. She gave me a warm sensual smile, but then again, she smiled at everyone who came in. Later, she smiled again but it was no use. **Rod Stewart** who was signed to the label had probably asked her out already and even though I think I'm just as good a footballer, I don't think this will impress her. While in Warners, some shock news reaches me. Ian Ralfini and Martin Wyatt have had a major disagreement with their American bosses and have decided to leave the company forthwith. It's a bitter blow, and suddenly, the two people who were so enthusiastic about signing the group have gone. I immediately stand up and walk casually into Raft's empty office which is now directionless and lacking any experienced person to take the helm. Within days I realised that all the promises and excitement on signing had dissipated into thin air, while our long held dreams had quickly turned into abject disillusionment. However, despite being emotionally disappointed, I knew it was time to show resilience, fortitude and determination as well as the indomitable will to win. With these four attributes, I knew anything was possible despite the ever mounting crisis which had not only overtaken us, but had thrust a seemingly poisoned dagger deep into our hearts.

When in London, the group more often than not stayed at The Maddison Hotel in Sussex Gardens. Here, I must confess the word "Hotel" does seem a rather grandiose title for staying in one spartan room consisting of eight single beds packed closely together in a dark dingy basement. It had nothing but a dim light bulb to illuminate it while the air conditioning proved to be a broken window which didn't appear to have been cleaned since the coronation of Queen Victoria. However, the room did have one undeniable advantage. It was relatively cheap by London standards and there was no infestation of mice as they had elected to move next door in order to look for the merest scraps of food knowing there was little or no chance of finding any there. Meanwhile, the never ending search for that elusive world-wide success went on. A few days later, I met the ex boss of Warner's, Ian Ralfini, in Dingwalls where he apologised wholeheartedly for what had happened to the group and his much lauded Raft Records. Despite the predicament we now found ourselves in, I really liked him and felt he had been genuinely sincere when he had first made those promises. Unfortunately, and to my immense disappointment, fate had chosen an irrevocable and different path for both of us. However, I held not the slightest grudge, while retaining a deep respect for him. Nevertheless, it was time to take stock. We were still signed to a directionless label which no one seemed to know what to do with and it was as if it was an embarrassment to Warners. Nevertheless, I remained resolute in my determination to keep my own and the group's morale intact. Later, I sauntered into the Speakeasy and was delighted to find the legendary **Chuck Berry** playing on its tiny stage with **Marc Bolan** grooving away near the front. To finally see a living legend performing just a few feet in front of me in such an intimate atmosphere was indisputably a brilliant and exciting privilege. "Roll Over Beethoven," "Johnny Be Good" and "Sweet Little Sixteen," all brought back wonderful memories. I recalled listening to Terry and Kenny Mountain winding up the set at the end of each night in Hamburg with a medley of his songs which in itself was truly mesmerising. However, to see the real thing was something really special and another unforgettable experience. At the conclusion of his set, John Entwistle of **The Who** was in the restaurant said "hello," before inviting me to join him. While sitting there, I thought of the wonderful night I'd promoted them at The Bay Hotel and at Newcastle Mayfair when they were unable to play due to Roger Daltry's fog bound non appearance, but subsequently appeared 17 days later to a tumultuous reception. John, who always spoke quietly, seemed to shun the limelight and this, together with his natural modesty, made him a truly endearing character to meet. "I hear you are now managing a group," he began. I threw my head back and laughed. Whether it was an indication that a certain intake of alcohol was having its effect, or my immense delight that he had heard of them, I was unsure. "Yes, although I don't think they are as big as your band, not yet anyway," I replied. He chuckled before eyeing the girl sitting beside him as thoughts of Sunderland's own Debbie came to mind. Was the girl sitting with him because he was a major rock star, or was she truly in love with him? Perhaps it was a combination of both. Later, I moved back to the bar while noticing the girl serving there was really stunning, before reluctantly deciding that with both **Chuck Berry** and **Marc Bolan** in attendance, it would be a futile exercise to attempt anything other than the pleasantries of ordering a drink.

Meanwhile, constantly promoting and mixing with rock stars has the false and disarming effect of making you believe it's your rightful home. There's a tendency to take it for granted and in some ways assume it will go on for ever. In reality, it's perfectly obvious that you shouldn't. However, reality has its own Machiavellian manner of springing its devious surprises on the unwary. In rock management, without a hit single, it must be pointed out that you are invariably working for very little, or indeed nothing. Also, in managing an unknown group, you have entered into one of the most precarious and unappreciated occupations in terms of a future or rewarding career. Having done so, you are gambling on a group's talent, not to mention their future attitude should even the merest morsel of recognition ever come their way. Nevertheless, it remains an intriguing challenge together with the chance to prove your optimism and judgement are not only well founded, but will eventually be rewarded. Then of course your own ego has to enter into the equation. To admit you have one may in itself be distasteful, but recognising that you have acquired such a dangerous affliction is a step in the right direction. Conversely, modesty comes in many guises and is an attribute which most people admire. However, in the record business, and for that matter in any walk of life, you meet both sets of people. Give the wrong person power together with a huge salary and invariably their insufferable ego quickly begins to rear its ugly head. It's frustrating, it's bedevilling, and it's irritating. Ironically, such a person seems to revel in repeating that famous and tiresome quote. "The harder I work the luckier I get." On hearing it, I would inwardly smile at my own version. "The harder I work the greedier I get." Or should I say "the more pompous and unforgiving I become." Fortunately, there are some wonderful people in the record industry and these are the ones who invariably become successful as well as enduring. **John Peel** being a great example, sorely and greatly missed as he is.

Walking up the steps to Warner Brothers offices in London after you have been signed is a huge and satisfying thrill. It not only brings you into contact with major stars, you also begin to feel part of a very friendly environment. On occasions, Roger Chapman of **Family** would walk in. Unknown to him, it was a bigger buzz than he will ever realise as it was his group which first kick started my promoting career at The Bay Hotel. Polite as ever, he always smiled and said hello. No histrionics, no big deal, just a refreshing civility which was most encouraging. One day, up on the third floor, I decided to make myself a cup of tea. As the sink was inconveniently situated at the other end of the building, I discreetly emptied the teapot out of a small window above an insignificant looking side street. Moments later, an irate woman who appeared to be spitting fire charged into the building covered in tea leaves. She immediately demanded to meet the perpetrator of such a heinous and despicable act. Nick Lloyd, the managing director's assistant immediately entered and inquired if it was me. At first, I was speechless with guilt and fearing the repercussions of her ever increasing wrath, decided to deny all knowledge of it. The woman immediately looked out of the window where I was standing and quickly spotted the residue directly beneath it. Dad had always said that "a white lie doesn't hurt son," as I guiltily maintained my innocence. Still seething, she eventually departed while threatening all manner of repercussions amidst a torrent of unstoppable and abusive words. Nick looked at me and laughed. "Was it you?" he asked. "Yes it was," I confessed amidst more hearty laughter. "Let's go and have a cup of tea in the café around the corner," he suggested. This one incident is indicative of how friendly everyone at Warners was and how informal the atmosphere. Whenever **Beckett** were playing a gig in London, Nick would take me into their storeroom which was full of spirits and an untold selection of bottled lagers before stocking up a big cardboard box with a lavish assortment of both. There were also dozens of other kindnesses constantly being shown towards the group which made being there all the more enjoyable. Ironically, despite Raft Records folding, we were still signed to Warners who had now merged with Electra and Atlantic to form WEA Records. I can categorically state on behalf of myself and the group that we all loved being there and still have warm-hearted and wonderful memories of every visit.

Once back in the hustle and bustle of Oxford Street, the harsh reality of trying to make it quickly grips you in its thrall. Mixing with stars is all very encouraging, but I can assure you it's not the same as being one. "Bubbling under," as the expression goes is an unenviable position to be in. The initial excitement of being signed is soon dampened by the lack of sales together with the loss of its potential earning capacity. It cannot be denied that platinum or gold albums give a group status as well as respect. Having achieved such a stature, their name is on everyone's lips causing them to exude total confidence. Soon, a reverential retinue of followers appear to smooth their every whim which allows them the luxury of being able to concentrate solely on their career. For a lesser group watching from the sidelines it proves to be a wonderful incentive. Limousines, platinum albums, beautiful girls and a respectful bank manager all become an unstoppable driving force for any unknown group. I always think of Wilf Wright's words, who is a highly experienced manager, and a close friend of Jimmy Page. "In order to make it, you have to have an engaging and pleasant personality," he advised. Has he ever said a truer word. Fortunately, most of the stars I met were far from being unfriendly or egotistical. **Rod Stewart & The Faces, The Who, Eric Clapton, Deep Purple, Santana, Free, Led Zeppelin** and every other group I worked with apart from **Roxy Music** (excluding Eno)**, Ginger Baker**, and **Barclay James Harvest's** drummer all proved to be the epitome of inner modesty and natural friendliness.

One night while inside the Marquee, I met Mick Hinton, the production manager for **Led Zeppelin** who I had become friendly with. "Fancy going to the Playboy Club in Park Lane?" he asked. "I know some of the bunny girls there and I'll introduce you to them," he informed me enthusiastically. I smiled at such a tempting invitation, knowing that meeting a string of glamorous and sexually alluring bunny girls was certainly not to be sniffed at. However, and to my consternation, just then a fight started in the passageway leading to the bar whereupon I quickly noticed a muscular looking chap knocking the living daylights out of a smaller youth. For a split second I hesitated, knowing it was none of my business, but suddenly, instinct kicked in. I recalled how a courageous bus driver had once fearlessly rescued me from a savage beating by four unruly youths in the Bay Hotel car park. Now it appeared the shoe was on the other foot. No one needs to remind me that managing a group and fighting are worlds apart. However, I have always inherently believed in justice. Anyone who continues to inflict further serious injury on a person who is palpably incapable of defending himself is bordering on barbarism, insanity, or is just a plain and ruthless bully. In a situation of this nature to procrastinate is to greatly increase the chances of the victim being seriously hurt or hospitalised. However, to act hastily seriously increases your own chances of accompanying him. Being aware of this, I instinctively rushed him from behind before placing him in a headlock and immediately charging him down the narrow passage towards the entrance door, which had glass panels. Surprise was total, but unfortunately the door was locked and the momentum was such that his head went straight through one of its large glass panels. Once outside, to my great relief, there wasn't one cut or scratch on him as he continued to mouth off about what he was about to do. Shortly afterwards, a big fearless roadie who had become sick of his tiresome and threatening rants went outside and gave him the hiding of his life. Unfortunately, while this melee was taking place, Mick Hinton had quietly left and I never did get to meet any of those bunny girls or Hugh Hefner. If I remember correctly, **The Q Tips** fronted by **Paul Young** were playing that night and I thought they were excellent.

A few days later I met up with Pete Erskine of The New Musical Express. "Now that Raft Records has folded who are you going to sign for?" he inquired. It proved to be a pertinent question, but little did he realise how desperate the situation was. After levelling with him, he kindly arranged to interview the group. Within days a full page featuring them appeared and this was to prove invaluable publicity as I read it over and over again. A morale booster such as this is an unbelievable tonic as it restores your belief in human nature while giving a struggling band a new and encouraging sense of purpose. The following day I rang him and thanked him wholeheartedly. They say the pen is mightier than the sword and it was never more so on this occasion. Quiet and undemonstrative by nature, he laughed and we all laughed with him. Ever the gentleman, he thanked me and he'll never know how good he made us all feel. Unfortunately, he is now deceased, but I can assure his family, he is far from forgotten.

Back in Sunderland, it was time to pay another visit to the small cafeteria situated upstairs in the public museum and library as it was so quiet and relaxing. On the floor below, I could see students poring over expensive leather bound reference books which, because of their rarity, everyone was forbidden from removing. As I observed their studious and unlined faces, which in some cases appeared bemused, I began wondering if any of them would ever end up playing in a band and realise how hard or soul destroying it could be. Before long, I finished my tea and decided to wander around in order to view the exhibits. I tried to imagine how it must have been during all the different eras which the exhibits represented. Ironically, in many ways music is like a visit to the museum. On hearing a song or track, each person's imagination quickly decides if it is enjoyable. The lyrics may paint a picture of intense pain or unparalleled joy while portraying a writer's future hopes, past disappointments, or observations on his or other people's lives. Each listener then interprets them in a manner that appeals to their own emotions, which hopefully become a lasting and pleasurable experience. In the case of a group however, it can be strikingly different. If they lack the necessary vision it becomes difficult for them to perceive that other people may have a markedly different viewpoint from their own. This can then translate itself into a one dimensional perception about a song they have written. Conviction or self belief is of course an admirable trait. However, if it proves to be misguided through a reluctance to accept the mediocrity of their offering, then I can assure you trouble almost certainly looms.

Please allow me to give you an insight into what can happen when, as a manager, you enter into an A & R meeting in order to play your bands demo tape or CD in the hope of capturing that elusive record contract. With the day of reckoning having finally arrived, you nervously enter the record company's hallowed portals. On hearing the first song, you can't help noticing the head of A& R together with his colleagues quickly develops a pained, almost sickly expression on their faces. Inwardly, you begin to cringe as you soon realise they are far from enamoured with what they are listening to. "It needs a bit more bass," you meekly suggest in a last despairing effort to salvage something from the meeting. "It's only a demo. If you put them in a proper studio it will sound much better," you cry out in anguish. The pained expression on their faces then turns to one of incredulity. On seeing this you desperately force a smile while hoping that one of them possesses the merest morsel of humanity which will indicate some semblance of sympathy or understanding. Three songs later the tape finishes as two of them hurriedly dash out with a palpable look of relief on their faces. You squirm uncomfortably as it appears that that they have just been subjected to some unearthly cacophony of noise which could quickly prove to be both debilitating and life threatening. "It's not what we're looking for at the moment" stammers the head of A & R as he quickly hands you back the tape. You glance at his face which appears to indicate that he's genuinely sorry that it had to come to this. Unfortunately, it immediately hardens in the clear and unmistakeable hope that you have got the message and will leave the premises without further delay. In a clear sign of indifference to your feelings, he begins to look away, which is his way of signifying he has a very busy schedule and isn't interested in discussing the merits of any particular track. Suddenly, an awkward silence descends over the room. "Thanks for taking the time to listen," you respectfully inform him in an effort to indicate that despite his outright rejection, it hasn't blunted your manners. Finally, you turn to leave having realised that all is lost. Once again he smiles, which is far from convincing as his expression turns to one of relief on realising you are finally departing. Once outside, the immense disappointment immediately surfaces, especially having travelled three hundred miles in a futile effort to attend the meeting. Your own instinct is to cry, but the tears won't come. Not only is it unmanly, it reminds you that it was sheer folly to have even contemplated entering the building in the first place with such an unrealistic offering. "Why did I listen to the group," you mutter under your breath as reality kicks in. Unfortunately, there are still bills to be paid and a group struggling to make it. Right then, the possibility of it ever happening seem not only extremely remote but also forlorn and born out of sheer desperation and folly. Suddenly, life seems aimless and without any real rationale. However, this time it's not self-pity which crushes your hopes but the realisation that in the final analysis, what had just occurred was inevitable, quickly hits home. Your enthusiasm plummets to an all time low and it seems there is no way forward on realising months of hard work have been ignominiously consigned to the reject bin. Unfortunately, the much hoped for "Three Minutes of Magic," which the group have assured you could be a hit, have proved to be three minutes of tortuous embarrassment. Days later, it's time to take stock and re-evaluate or find a sensible reason for continuing. Depression, lethargy, and possible bankruptcy have become an everyday part of life as you continue to wrestle with your ever increasing doubts. For everyone else, music seems to be fun and an enjoyable form of relaxation. However, far from being enjoyable, it has become a wearisome burden and an all consuming way of life. How it ever happened you have no idea, but it has. To stop would be a retrogressive step, while to continue will set a dangerous precedent. It's confusing as well as disquieting, but there appears to be no way out. Suddenly, the telephone rings and you are in no hurry to answer it as it might be a gig in London for £75 which will inevitably lose more money as well as swallowing up two days of needless and unappreciated effort. Then again, it could be the producer from **John Peel's** "Top Gear" radio show who wants the band to record another session. On answering it, it proves to be the local equipment shop informing you that the group's amp and speaker are ready and you owe them £25 for repairs. Five blue ones and more heartache. It's only rock and roll but I like it.

Chapter 4

The air of despondency now hanging over the group had a distinctly terminal feel about it. It seemed that luck had all but deserted them and jokes were no longer funny. Fortunately however, not once did the group complain, especially as it was me who had chosen to sign for Raft Records. Inwardly, I began wallowing in a cloud of uncertainty as to what to do next and which direction to take. However, when circumstances may appear grim, talent and determination have a wonderful propensity to muster new found energy in the face of extreme adversity. Fortunately, within days Richard Robinson was appointed as the new company head of WEA Records. Disabled from a crippling disease and unable to walk, he operated from a wheelchair and quickly appointed Shaun Murphy as the head of Raft Records. Unfortunately, Shaun's dislike for the group and its music soon became readily apparent. It appeared that his own personal taste was light years away from where the group were at and this quickly manifested itself in his obvious lack of enthusiasm. Perhaps this was coloured by the fact that he also managed **Soft Machine,** who, at the time, were the darlings of the emerging progressive scene and far removed from what we were attempting. In many ways they were to be applauded for having the courage to pursue and present their own ideals, no matter what the reaction of a rock audience may have been. However, it remained paramount his own personal prejudices on becoming head of the record company were tempered with a mixture of reality, objectivity, and impartiality. The next and most important question was could the group win him over? If so, it had to be done promptly as time and finances were beginning to reach a critical stage and I knew he had yet to see the group live. When he did, there remained every possibility that his viewpoint might suddenly change. Was it wishful thinking? I fervently hoped not. During those early days, it must be said that Richard Robinson was exceptionally wonderful towards us and genuinely loved the band while striving manfully to assist in any way humanly possible. How he lives on in our memory now that he has passed away. His ability to sense the band had potential together with the fact that despite his cruel and restrictive disability he often came to see them play live was undoubtedly a great morale booster. Fortunately, he was ably assisted by his right hand man Nick Lloyd who also proved to be a source of tremendous and unstinting help. Nick, who was a character in his own right, seemed to know everyone in the business as well as most of the Soho wide boys, the police, and everyone on the label. Tall, strong, and determined, he was the perfect link man and how we appreciated him.

Within a few weeks, Shaun Murphy had signed **Ian Dury & The Blockheads** to the resurgent Raft label. An inspired signing? In retrospect you can certainly say it was, although it took another five years and a different label (Stiff Records) before his most prominent and memorable single "Hit Me With Your Rhythm Stick" charted at No 1 for fifteen weeks in Dec 1978. ("What a Waste" charted at No 9 six months earlier, also on Stiff) One night, **Beckett** were playing at their customary Marquee residency to a capacity crowd when Shaun suddenly walked in. On seeing each other we shook hands after which I bought him a drink in the full knowledge that this was to be the acid test. Would he like the band and change his whole perception of rock music, I wondered? Only time would tell although I was fully aware of the importance of having him on board. While conversing, I couldn't help noticing he had a habit of smiling whenever I said anything which I found rather unnerving. Whether the smile was sincere or not was open to question, but I had my doubts, although I remained outwardly unruffled. Despite my unease, I consoled myself with the thought that it was better than a grimace and at least it indicated that he was listening. Meanwhile, what mattered most was that the group played well and that he was personally there to witness it. I recalled how human emotions are undoubtedly a strange animal. They can encapsulate all manner of things including ambition, joy, sadness or distrust. That night at The Marquee, I was experiencing all of these and more as I noticed the group looked quietly confident and relaxed. Fortunately, this helped instil some self assurance, knowing it was a vital factor if they were to impress as the pressure began to build. I thought back to the people who buy a single, album, or CD, before placing it on the turntable in order to sit back and enjoy it. Right then, how I wished I could too, but a live appearance is vastly different when a band's future career hangs in the balance. Knowing **Beckett's** first single hadn't exactly been a monumental success, I urgently needed Shaun to not only like the band, but also to positively enthuse about them which would encourage him to release a single as soon as possible. Finally, the group hit the stage whereupon the resultant and overbearing tension made me feel as if I was strapped into an electric chair, having had my last fateful appeal overturned. Standing there with a mixture of nervous apprehension and hope, I felt helpless knowing there was nothing I could do but watch, and yet in a strange and compelling way, it was incredibly exciting to think of what was about to take place. Minutes later, I realised my innermost worries had proved to be needless as up on stage I witnessed the group unleash a display of unrestrained brilliant and inspired rock. There were no ifs or buts, just sheer elation and warmth at the rapport between them and a wildly appreciative audience. Conquering heroes is a term often used lightly and perhaps I'm guilty of it here. However, it is the only applicable term for what I personally witnessed. Afterwards, Shaun eagerly shook my hand. Smug, self satisfied and cocky? At that moment I could have been accused of all three but I kept my thoughts to myself. However, irrefutable evidence had now been placed before him that would surely give him cause to change his lukewarm and off handed perception of the band. Inwardly I felt good. Hamburg was now just a distant memory but it had undoubtedly honed and polished them into a cohesive unit which had unerringly refused to accept failure or mediocrity. Soon, Terry breezed over and smiled. It was the captivating sort of smile that never failed to win female hearts, as well as instilling confidence in whoever he met. The world was his stage and with a major record contract already in the bag together with a packed Marquee, he was revelling in his new found starring role.

A few weeks later he was to meet a glamorous London model called Olga who became his "steady." How steady only he knows because he seemed to distance himself from the group whenever she was present. Tramps nightclub wasn't too far away and very conveniently she turned out to be an honorary member although how she achieved this lofty status, I was never to find out. One night she invited Terry and me to join her on a visit there where she introduced us to Jack Nicholson and suddenly, I was in another world. On looking around I could see two of the Rolling Stones drinking quietly at the bar while Bianca Jagger and Aimee McDonald, a beautiful television celebrity and dancer, stood only a few feet away. Inside, I found it was dark, extremely comfortable and pleasantly civilised. There was no pushing, overcrowding, or unmannerly behaviour and I liked that. Later, I learnt that Olga had once been on a yacht with Jack together with a retinue of other pretty girls. I continued to look around as more celebrities walked in before sitting in one of the comfortable chairs dotted around its interior. Quietly taking it all in, I remained calm and unruffled, not that there was any reason not to be. Before long, Jack smiled over at our table. He had obviously had a few drinks and appeared to be eyeing Olga in an attempt to renew her acquaintance. I smiled back. Whether it registered with him I was unsure but Terry remained confidently assured and unconcerned. Although Terry was young, lithe and possessed irrepressible charm, I began wondering what the outcome would be if Jack who had international fame, money and a Hollywood mansion decided to wander over in order to renew her acquaintance. Would Terry be able to compete, and more importantly, who would Olga leave with? Her red shoulder length hair and slender yet voluptuous figure certainly looked tempting as Jack made his move before casually wandering over. After being introduced to him and shaking hands he sat down at our table and was most friendly. It soon became noticeable that he was engaging Olga in close conversation with more than a hint of friendly overtones. Shortly afterwards, it was time to go as Olga finally stood up and placed her arm around Terry in a loving embrace, before they left together. Jack looked at me and smiled as if realising his was a lost cause. Was Terry a rock star in the marking? I certainly hoped so.

Earlier that evening, Shaun had enthusiastically informed me how much he had enjoyed the band's performance. Fortunately, there seemed to be a considerable shift in his attitude. To call it seismic may be an exaggeration, but it wasn't far short. The next morning on entering Raft Records I was warmly greeted both by him and his wonderful secretary Jane. It seemed as if they couldn't do enough to help and this was undeniable confirmation that we had finally been accepted into his warm and welcoming arms. A few minutes later I bumped into John Darnley, **Family's** manager, who had a purpose and energy about him, together with an effervescence which I greatly admired. Perhaps it was because his group were already big and were due to play a string of lucrative headlining dates throughout the country. "The group were excellent last night," he happily informed me. "Thanks," I replied as he hurriedly dashed out of the office in an attempt to keep pace with his busy schedule. Despite the previous night's success I was fully aware that there was still a long way to go. Soon, Al Clark, the newly appointed publicist promised to try and get the band some urgently needed music press. Quiet by nature, by no stretch of the imagination could he be called outgoing or dynamic. Countering this however was his sincerity and way of tackling things. Methodical, and highly intelligent, he never became angry or lost control, and yet, I found myself wondering if it would be better if occasionally he did. We often chatted about music and his likes and dislikes, while giving me an insight into his way of thinking. In later years he was to join Virgin Records and work with **The Sex Pistols** who were undoubtedly one of the best groups in the world for generating self publicity. Being able to rub shoulders with people of such vast experience helped add a different perspective to one's own viewpoint in order to assist in the aims of the band. A few days later I walked into the Marquee. Jack Barrie, the manager, smiled before welcoming me with open arms. In doing so I felt that I was finally being accepted into one of the major citadels of British rock music. From then on in, it became my first port of call whenever I visited London.

"Geoff, can I have a word?" asked Bob Barton. I recognised a serious concern in his voice with an inflection which seemed out of character for such a quiet and dedicated musician. "Of course, what is it?" I questioned. "I need a new guitar because this old one doesn't give me the sound I'm looking for," he informed me. "What sort do you want?" I inquired, as alarm bells started ringing. "Actually, the one I want is a hand made one. There's a guy in Soho who makes them called Grimshaw and I've heard they are excellent." "Make some inquires and let me know how much it will cost," I replied, with a certain reservation clearly apparent in my voice. A week later, he came to see me with an anxious look on his face. "It'll cost about £400," he calmly informed me. "Four hundred pounds," I gasped (it was 1974). "You can get a really good Fender Stratocaster for £250, how come it's costing so much?" I asked incredulously. "Well, I want mother of pearl flowers inlaid into the shaft. It will look beautiful and help to give it the right "karma," he said. "That's far too expensive, especially as the group haven't sold a record yet," I stammered. "I also want a new amp and speaker cabinet," he continued. "There's a French chap called Claude Venet who makes them to order. I've already spoken to him and he knows exactly the sound I want." In many ways I must have appeared to be a rabbit that had become frozen in headlights as I became speechless with the sheer audacity of the request. Looking back, it seems that common sense had all but deserted me. Perhaps it was because any qualms I may have held were dispelled by everyone repeatedly telling me how excellent Bob Barton and the band were. Backing this up were noted luminaries such as **John Peel**, while Alan Jones a noted music writer for The Melody Maker, later to become editor, was also very enthusiastic. Pete Erskine an NME feature writer was also very complimentary. As dates and tours were coming in thick and fast, it seemed only a matter of time before they became huge. However, with the money from the advance having long run out, I still had to finance them from my own hard earned funds. Within days, I reluctantly agreed the money for Bob's new guitar. The saying "there's no fool like an old fool" somehow didn't seem to apply as I was still comparatively young. In retrospect, perhaps I was suffering from a huge surfeit of blind enthusiasm, or alternatively, an incurable mental aberration. Nevertheless, I realised it was important to keep the band happy while remaining absolutely determined that nothing would impede or deter us from reaching our intended goal.

One day, while driving back to Newcastle from London in a carefree mood, I was presented with a bill by Keith Fisher the drummer. "What is this for?" I inquired. "It's for £220 pounds to pay for an aluminium drum riser which my dad is making," he replied nonchalantly. "Are you joking?" I questioned. "I haven't sanctioned this and if you want a drum riser, pay for it yourself because I'm not going to," I replied angrily. A disquieting argument then ensued as the atmosphere became decidedly frosty. Unfortunately, this was to be the forerunner of many other such disagreements. It must also be pointed out that when things go wrong the group invariably blame the manager. After experiencing these highly unsettling and disturbing disagreements, you are forced to retreat into a solitary and unwelcoming world of your own, friendless and depressed. A few days later, one of them decided to ring. "Why haven't you been in touch?" he questioned. "We've been rehearsing a great new song and we think it's definitely a hit" he regaled with undiminished enthusiasm. "Why don't you come and have a listen?" he implored. The conviction in his voice sounded passionate and overwhelming as I threw aside all doubts and began eagerly looking forward to hearing it. A hit single? The mind starts to race as you begin to fantasise about the possibilities. If it does enter the charts, the bookings will pour in; their appearance fees will escalate while my musical judgement will have been completely vindicated. As I ready myself for the impending adulation of the screaming fans, it's an intoxicating and heady thought. Dreams begin to merge into a welter of idealistic possibilities knowing the group had to come good sometime. "Top Of The Pops." Everyone knows it's a hugely influential TV show with millions of viewers only this time it will be different. I can visualise it now and instead of the weekly pilgrimage to watch it on television, the group will actually be part of it. The glamorous "Pans People" will also be dancing and who knows, one of them might just notice me. Can you imagine that? **Beckett Hit The Big Time.** Apart from the above possibilities, the huge headlining words that Andy Bone had written in the local press (The Sunday Sun) had also remained indelibly stuck in the dark recesses of my mind. It may have taken a little longer than he envisaged, but surely it was all behind us now. For some strange reason, I recalled one of my schoolteachers remonstrating with me for not listening. "Docherty, stop daydreaming and pay attention or you'll never make anything of yourself," she warned. At the time her words seemed harsh, reflecting the power she had to humiliate, especially as the whole class was listening. But who is daydreaming now I asked myself?

Next day, on entering the rehearsal room, I was warmly greeted. Within seconds I could sense a feeling of expectancy and camaraderie in the air as they began to play the new song live, entitled "Little Girl." It certainly sounded catchy and with a bit of luck, it could even be a hit I thought. Afterwards, the group awaited my reaction and were clearly delighted when my enthusiasm spilled over to them. Soon, Richard Robinson the record company head had heard it and liked it, before agreeing to release it. As I walked out of his office, I bumped into Sean Murphy. I realised that by no stretch of the imagination was is it an avant-garde piece of music which would enthral him or his followers, but it did have possibilities. "Robbie likes the new single and is going to release it," I eagerly informed him. "Yes, I know," he replied in an indifferent and cold manner. Having shrugged off his lukewarm reaction I walked over to speak to Bernie, the attractive company secretary. Whether it was to seek solace, or just an excuse to engage her in conversation I wasn't sure, not that it mattered. "Love the tape of the new single," she enthused, accompanied by a warm and engaging smile which would melt any red blooded male's heart. It must also be said that Bernie's photogenic face was constructed in such a manner it was impossible not to stare, however bad mannered it may have appeared. Unfortunately, John Darnley the manager of **Family** had noticed her too and before long they had formed more than a passing friendship. Still, you can't have everything. A hit single and Bernie would have been too much to expect. Soon the group were in the studio to record the new single. Martin Rushent, (later, to produce the **Human League**) the producer did a fantastic job. It had taken three days to record and on release, early expectations were most enthusiastic. Within days, it started to get Radio 1 airplay, while later that week, **John Peel** played it on his show. It was a heart warming sign giving it credibility as well as a clear indication that things were moving in the right direction. Now, it seemed only a matter of time before it started to sell.

Chapter 5

Now that the single was finally out there and getting extensive radio play, the burning question was would it chart? One day I turned the radio on to find Noel Edmonds, the influential Radio 1 DJ had made it his record of the week. It was undoubtedly excellent news when suddenly the group was booked for television's "Top Of The Pops," which I knew would showcase them in front of millions of potential buyers. My head was reeling with unconcealed excitement knowing that any group who appeared on it usually went straight into the charts. All I could say was thank heaven for John Logie Baird whose years of painstaking work leading to his unique invention would now help the group to create huge public interest. Outwardly I remained cool, knowing there would no longer be the necessity to relate optimistic stories about the bands potential as it would be there for everyone to see. Finally, it seemed all the hard work and frustration was about to pay off. Amidst all the jubilation and euphoria, later that day the telephone rang. It was a routine happening and gave me no cause for any real concern as I calmly lifted the receiver. "Is that Geoff Docherty, the manager of **Beckett?**" inquired the voice on the other end. "Yes it is," I cautiously replied. "It's the producer of Top of the Pops here. I'm sorry to tell you this but we have decided to put **Cliff Richard** on instead of your group. His single is selling a lot more than **Beckett's** and everyone here thinks it will go straight to No 1." His words proved to be absolutely devastating as well as cruel as I put the phone down in sheer exasperation. To be taken to the summit of the hill only to be unceremoniously pushed back down again certainly isn't a prospect to be relished. At that moment it felt like a kick in the teeth and one which may well prove to be terminal where the band was concerned. Later, the inclination to stand upright and step smartly out became impossible under the burden of the news. In the past, I had become familiar with the heartache and vagaries of life which I hoped would help prepare me for any eventuality, but not this. Once again, an immense surfeit of self pity seemed the only safe haven in which to retreat, but it was to no avail. By now I was in deep despair and to cry openly seemed the only emotional outlet. Alternatively, I knew that to sulk is to show the world how much it is hurting and to disappear could be misconstrued as a form of moral cowardice. Suddenly, I found I had inadvertently become afflicted with all three. It seemed to the entire world that Pans People, Noel Edmonds, Sean Murphy and the record industry or anyone associated with it had become my arch enemies. The following week I was to learn that once again we had failed to be selected. On hearing the news for a second time, I could sense dark and doom laden clouds hovering just beyond the horizon. Days later, with five boys hungry for success and a manager who was in a state of shock I realised there was no longer any room for complacency or self pity. Ironically, and unknown to me at the time, it was to be over twenty seven years before I finally arrived on the Top Of The Pops set. However, this time it was to be as the guest of Chris Cowey the producer at the time and was even invited into to the heady heights of the "Stars Bar." Still, they say all things come to those who wait.

London, Warner Bros, Oxford St, **John Peel** and the music pres had all been reeling around in my head in a never ending spiral of optimism, but have you noticed what is missing? Yes, it's the great British public as it soon became apparent that the single wasn't selling in big enough quantities to chart. On entering the record company it was noticeable that heads were beginning to drop, together with a marked deterioration in enthusiasm which had previously been such a powerful driving force. Suddenly, a barely perceptible nod instead of a welcoming smile became the norm. It was hurtful as well as depressing and to say we were back in the doldrums would be to understate the case. Within days I had become apprehensive about the future, despite being all too aware that to instill the slightest self doubt into the band could be highly demoralising. Nevertheless, I felt it remained essential that they were made fully aware of the situation, while at the same time emphasising the importance of maintaining a certain and unqualified degree of optimism. Fortunately, it soon became obvious that my worries were groundless as the group appeared to take the setbacks in their stride. Collectively, they drew inspiration from each other while continuing to retain an irrepressible determination to make it. Despite these setbacks accompanied by certain lethargy, the group and I continued to feel the prize was too alluring and too big to allow any disquieting thoughts of giving up. Indeed, we had no intention of doing so. Despite the failure of their first single, the fact that **John Peel** had played it on his show helped create enough interest for the band to be allowed the task of recording their first album. After one concert at Sheffield City Hall where the group had supported **Ten Years After**, Alvin Lee, their famed guitarist, had approached me backstage in a highly enthusiastic manner. "I think the group are excellent and I'd like to produce their album," he began. I looked at him and smiled appreciatively knowing he was already a big star in America and a wonderfully talented guitarist. But unknown to him, I already had my heart set on Roger Chapman of **Family**. Why you may well ask? There was no real reason except that I held such a deep respect for him as **Family** had been the first major group I'd ever promoted, kick starting my whole musical career. To have him in the studio would be great, I thought to myself. Soon, the group began recording the album at Island Studios in Basing St, London. As I walked into the control room and looked over at the mixing console where **Traffic, Free** and a whole host of other groups had recorded their big selling albums, it gave me an immense thrill to know that we were following in their footsteps. A few days later, the drummer and I walked into Warner Brothers to see the newly designed album cover, before flicking it over to look at a collage of the band's photos on the back which had only recently been taken. Just then, the drummer spoke out in what appeared to be a highly charged and contentious manner. "I don't like my photo," he protested. "What's wrong with it?" I asked. "My grandmother won't like it," he replied. A look of incredulity crossed my face knowing that in all my years in the rock business I'd never heard of anything so ridiculous. The Warner Brothers promotion lady looked aghast, while I just wanted the earth to open up and swallow me. I looked contemptuously towards him knowing that thousands of other groups were desperate for the chance of a similar record contract. At the time, he was already aware that there was a frenzied rush to get the album into the shops in time for a possible 22 date tour with **Slade**. It also had to be considered that it had cost Warners hundreds of pounds to have them taken by a professional photographer which made it appear he was ungrateful. After a brief yet heated discussion and not wishing to hold things up, I quickly informed the promotions lady that the album cover was fine. Sensing my embarrassment, she diplomatically left the room and the offending photo remains on the album to this day.

A few days later, I walked into Island Studios and what I saw was mind boggling. There in the studio were approximately twenty members of the London Symphony Orchestra playing their hearts out to a **Beckett** track. As no one had informed me of this and knowing it would almost certainly be sending the album way over budget, I was deeply disturbed but remained discreetly silent. Experience from speaking to other major bands had taught me that marrying an orchestra to a rock band is not only an expensive process; it can also lead to damaging accusations of grandiose pretentiousness, or even foolhardiness. "Whose idea was this?" I later questioned. "Kenny's," came the reply. I immediately approached him in order to speak to him. "What are they doing here?" I asked concernedly. "It's always been my ambition to have them play on one of my songs," he calmly informed me. As I pointed out earlier, ambition is a prime requisite for anyone aspiring to reach greater heights. Experimentation together with creativity and a sense of adventure is also to be highly applauded. Nevertheless, it must be tempered with realism and I sensed that somewhere along the line a heavy price could well be exacted for such untimely ideals. Two days later, at my invitation **John Peel** visited the studio. On hearing the track he pointed out that he was no great fan of orchestrated music where rock bands were concerned. My heart immediately raced, knowing they might listen to his words with far greater attentiveness than they had mine. Unfortunately, this too was to be of no avail, adding greatly to my frustration. Was the "Machiavellian" figure behind the band losing his grip? It certainly appeared so, especially as I sensed that familiarity was breeding contempt.

During the recording of their debut album the first major problem arrived. It began when I got wind that **Slade** were about to start a major tour of the UK. At the time, they were absolutely massive and had had a string of hits including six No 1s. Previously, every group who had supported them had made it big, due to the high level of national exposure it afforded them. **Status Quo, Alex Harvey** and **Thin Lizzy** being three that spring to mind. It was far too good an opportunity to miss so I quickly initiated a meeting with Chas Chandler, their manager and John Steele, his assistant. Fortunately, as they had both played in **The Animals** they were from my part of the country which I hoped would help the group to acquire the all important support slot. On meeting them, they listened to my plea with a certain degree of sympathy, but soon informed me that whoever they chose would have to pay £3,000 towards the cost of the PA and lights. In those days it was a huge amount and came as quite a shock. "We have a number of other groups who are willing to pay it and we will decide in the next few days who this will be," they casually informed me. Eventually, I left in a sad and disillusioned frame of mind. £3,000 and the cost of hotels, transport, petrol, roadies' wages and other incidentals seemed a heavy price to pay. Nevertheless, stardom beckoned causing me to immediately rush to Warners in order to speak to Richard Robinson. Sitting there in his large office I quickly outlined the urgency of the situation before putting the financial implications to him. There was an intense passion and urgency in my voice as I pleaded and cajoled with every last ounce of energy in my body in order to persuade him. After listening to my exhortations he seemed astonished at the huge cost and immediately rang America. "The person I need to speak to isn't there so I can't make a decision until I've spoken to him," he pointed out after a lengthy wait. His face remained impassive while his words remained agonisingly non committal, as if allowing himself leeway to reject my proposal should it be necessary. Finally, I trudged wearily out of his office with the knowledge that, unknown to the group, I was beginning to harbour serious doubts about their ability to come up with a credible single. Countering this was the deep conviction I had in their live ability, while at the same time, I recalled how they had delivered so many times, even after suffering the indignity of rejection on more than one occasion. It was a difficult decision as

I pondered the possibilities knowing that if I was to leave them it would be a dereliction of everything which I held precious. I was also aware that I would be unable to live with my troubled conscience or the consequences if I did decide to abandon them.

The following day I telephoned Richard Robinson now known to us as "Robbie," in the full knowledge that without his financial backing the opportunity would almost certainly be lost. "Why don't you come in and see me," he replied in the same impartial and uncommitted voice I had earlier experienced. A few hours later I walked into his office before flopping into its huge leather settee with mixed forebodings. "Do you think this will work if we come up with the money?" he asked concernedly. It was time to be positive as I immediately assured him that judging by the standards of previous groups who had done so, success was virtually guaranteed. "But if we do it, we will need posters, badges and stickers, reliable transport and help with the petrol and hotels," I calmly informed him. He leant back with a worried look on his face as the true cost which appeared to be spiraling ever upwards, became all too apparent. For a few moments he paused as I realised he was in deep and contemplative thought. Fortunately, he knew only too well how much I loved the band, how hard we had all worked, and how much it meant to us. "This comes to around a minimum of seven thousand pounds, possibly more" he pointed out in a highly concerned voice. "You'll get it back in album sales," I confidently assured him as he picked up his pen in order to do more calculations. Watching him, the suspense was unbearable as he glanced at me with a face wreathed in a multitude of worry lines. All the while I remained silent knowing that to break the stillness of it could disturb his concentration or possibly unsettle him. As the seconds ticked away his decision was absolutely crucial and I realised that if he said no, it was tantamount to thrusting the group into a barren and desolate wilderness of broken dreams, heartache and rejection. Conversely, if he agreed, it would surely signal the release of momentous and joyful celebrations long into the night. Minutes later, the silence was broken as he spoke. "Okay, we'll go for it," he informed me. I immediately jumped out of the chair in excitement as his dramatic and joyous words hit home. Having seen my ecstatic reaction he immediately began easing his wheelchair towards me before shaking my hand as I heaved a huge sigh of relief. Fortuitously, another major obstacle had been overcome, but we weren't there yet as I realised there was no time to waste. The next hurdle was to convince Chas Chandler to choose us from the myriad of groups desperate to be on the tour. Meanwhile, Robbie saw how delighted I was and after wholeheartedly thanking him, I promptly arranged a meeting with Chas to be held the next day in a spare office at Warner Bros.

As I walked in twenty four hours later, there he stood. The man who had discovered and managed **Jimi Hendrix** was tall, friendly and unassuming. He was accompanied by his assistant, ex **Animals** drummer, John Steele. After exchanging the pleasantries of the day, I eagerly informed him that we were able to come up with the money. However, due to the pressure I'd felt over the previous days, fresh doubts soon began to emerge. What if he informed me I was far too late and he was considering allocating the slot to another group? A deep sense of apprehension immediately enveloped me as I began dreading that everything could fall apart at the last moment. It seemed a strange paradox knowing that the two people immediately in front of me had unquestioned and momentous power to change the course of six lives for ever. Meanwhile, they both appeared completely relaxed and carefree, secure in the knowledge that **Slade** were selling monumental amounts of records faster than they could manufacture them. By now the tension was unbearable as I awaited their decision with time dragging inexorably on. Outside, barely a few yards away, I quickly glanced down at Oxford Street, which was awash with cars and pedestrians. I tried to remain cool in an effort to give the impression that we weren't that desperate for the support slot. However, I soon realised they were far too experienced to be thrown by such an obvious and overstated gesture. After some small talk about the band's hopes for the future, Chas suddenly broke the ensuing silence. "We'll let you know our decision as soon as we can," he told me. His words were accompanied by a warm and encouraging smile, but unfortunately, it signified we remained on hold and there was still everything to play for. Minutes later, as we parted, the one thing which remained uppermost in my mind was that all important support slot. It must be said that desperation is never a good bedfellow to accompany long held dreams as it can create tension and heartache from which there appears to be no respite. Nevertheless, all I knew was that we just had to be on that tour knowing that whoever they chose would be billed as "special guests," and would in all probability "make it." As an added bonus, being described as "special guests" seemed far more refined and classier than "support group." Either way, it didn't really matter. All that did was that they chose us. After two days of agonising uncertainty Chas finally rang to inform me that after great deliberation he had decided to choose **Beckett** causing me to jump for joy with delirious and unrestrained happiness.

In the past I recalled how I'd promoted many major groups which had undoubtedly been high points in my musical career. However, this proved to be just as exciting despite it being an emotional high of an extremely different kind. Now that I knew we had finally been chosen, I realised how excited the group would be on being informed. Suddenly, it appeared to be the final and magical piece in the jigsaw. From Annabel's Club in Sunderland via a major record contract to a lengthy and extensive tour of the UK concluding with three consecutive nights at the Hammersmith Odeon was proving to be just reward indeed. Having finally clinched it, the band's name would be up there in lights, only this time I'd make sure they saw it. Meanwhile, who would we put on the guest list? While appearing to be an innocuous task, we were aware of how important it was to remind ourselves that no one must be overlooked. Within minutes the band and I began conjuring up names. The friendly and very helpful Pete Erskine from the NME was a must. Then there was Robbie himself and his right hand man, Nick Lloyd. There were others too, although we were only allowed so many guest tickets. Times were now tremendously exciting, while in comparison, sleeping in vans, disagreements, poorly attended gigs, greasy motorway food and punctures, coupled with a multitude of other problems, immediately faded far into obscurity. Suddenly, a new found sense of purpose and elation had entered the fray which was proving to be highly infectious while at the same time radiating untold happiness. Now, nothing seemed too much trouble as the group prepared themselves for the tour. Optimism reigned supreme coupled with a grim determination to succeed. In a lighter moment I looked up at the heavens, safe in the knowledge that surely their destiny was about to be fulfilled. I could not only sense it, but could feel they were about to hit the big time and how we all relished such a long awaited prospect.

A few days later, a major and most upsetting problem occurred when I learned that our wonderfully talented bass player had decided to leave having been enticed away by Paul Thompson, **Roxy Music's** drummer. Their offer included trebling the wages he was presently receiving and the lure of immediate stardom. Unfortunately, we were about to start the twenty two date tour of the U.K. supporting **Slade** and Warner Bros had had 5,000 top quality colour posters specially printed for the tour. Regrettably they had now become obsolete overnight as the group's five faces were prominently displayed on them. Later, I walked into the record company offices and couldn't help staring at the huge wasted piles of them now languishing under a bench. Capitulation, defeat, lethargy and frustration all began to fight for space in my depressed thoughts. Not only were the posters now defunct, we also had no bass player with which to tour. To say we were shocked is certainly no exaggeration and it was an undeniable setback. Nevertheless, loyalty is a nice rounded word which has a comforting feel to it and conjures up images of a lasting or lifelong friendship. Any fair minded person has to be prepared to return it unselfishly in equal or even far greater measures. Dad used to have a saying about someone who thinks they're smart without having the foresight to see how selfish or obvious such an action is. "They've got a lot to learn son," he would advise, which was his way of trying to offer solace should something of this nature occur. "Didn't you have a contract with a clause which included the words "jointly and severally?" I was asked on several occasions. I certainly did as I rushed to check and found the clause was most definitely there which was very reassuring. However, and to my deep consternation, a hitch quickly surfaced. I found the specialist music contract lawyer I had contacted wanted £100 (now valued at around (£500) for the initial interview in order to instigate proceedings. After paying it, as I originally feared, he warned that if it went to court and I lost, it could cost me thousands. To be told this in a meeting which has only lasted a few minutes is certainly not something you savour with unrestrained delight. I swallowed hard and stared at both him and the ceiling as it seemed a steep price to pay in order to exact justice. When something of this nature occurs, it seems that everything you and the rest of the group have worked for is being wantonly and disrespectfully torn apart at the seams. Inwardly, the anger and frustration I felt was beginning to reach boiling point until eventually, a feeling of utter helplessness began to overwhelm me. Fortunately, these feelings were soon brushed aside by a deep and fierce determination not to meekly accept the inevitable. Those long hard drives through Germany and Holland in a cold and battered transit van for a mere pittance came to mind. However, so did lots of other things while being used as a mere stepping stone in order to satisfy someone else's cravings for immediate stardom, merely added insult to injury. With an ever increasing resentment rapidly building up, coupled with a determination to prevent an injustice being so callously perpetrated, I felt it was time to act. I thought long and hard about how he had joined **Beckett** at a later date, after the group had already succeeded in obtaining a major record contract. Also, how the group had bought him a Rickenbacker bass when he first joined as well as a small electric piano he had always yearned for. Talent, oh yes, I reminded myself how he had that in abundance and that's why it hurt all the more. I tossed and turned the problem over in my mind while the raging fire burning inside me stubbornly refused to subside. It seemed that Robbie and Chas Chandler, as well as the group and I had all been wantonly cast aside in the indecent haste for money and stardom. But what could be done to redress the balance? Inside, I was spitting blood and remained determined to obtain some sort of meaningful and lasting retribution.

Still angry about the underhand way he had been approached, I decided to ring **Roxy's** manager. "Hello, is that David Enthoven? (now co manager of **Robbie Williams** and previously co manager of **Tyrannosaurus Rex** in partnership with Mark Fenwick.) "Yes, what do you want?" he questioned. "You've just stolen our bass player without even having the courtesy to ask. What's the big idea?" I fumed. "Well, Paul Thompson our drummer approached him and he's agreed to join," he said. "Oh has he, and what about

Beckett? They are just about to start a 22 date tour and I also have a valid management contract on him." "Well I'm sorry, but it appears he has agreed to join us," came the reply. "Oh no, he's not," I protested angrily, with obvious and unmistakable venom in my voice. "Is there any way we can pay you for his services?" he inquired having adapted a more conciliatory tone. "No there isn't," I replied in the strongest possible terms, determined to impress upon him that there was no chance of a deal. "We desperately need him to play bass on our upcoming tour supporting **Slade**," I informed him vehemently. "Well it's up to him," he replied in a somewhat casual and uncaring manner. By now, I was absolutely livid and immediately threatened to go round his office and create havoc if they carried out their plan. "Have I ever interfered with any of your bands?" I inquired. "No," he replied. "Well, don't interfere with any of mine," I riposted. Finally, and to his credit, on realising how bitter and angry I was, he thought better of it and assured me that he would drop the idea immediately. Later, Paul Thompson, a so-called friend, approached me in The Speakeasy and profusely apologised. "Is there anything I can do to make it up to you?" he asked dolefully. "Yes there is. If you can assure me that you will never approach him again or play in the same band as him then that will be the end of the matter," I replied. With a nervousness clearly apparent in his voice he immediately agreed and we both shook hands. He smiled and seemed relieved that the problem had been amicably resolved and so was I. Around two weeks later, the bass player rang to ask if he could have his job back, not having received the lucrative cheque he had been expecting from **Roxy Music's** management. "You're too late," I replied. "We already have a replacement." "I should have put my head in a bucket of s   e (it rhymes with light and is a colloquialism I would never dream of using) for doing what I did," he informed me in a voice tinged with deep regret. On hearing this I felt good at having taught him a salutary lesson while at the same time having expunged a large and unappetising portion of my pent up frustration. On reflection, forgiveness is a truly admirable and worthwhile trait. However, to allow someone to walk all over you while standing idly by turned out to be far too an unsavoury prospect for me to stomach. Furthermore, given the same set of circumstances again, I would act exactly in the same manner and still sleep soundly.

Within a few days, our errant bass player had been replaced by Ian Murray who had previously played in one of my earlier ventures, **This Years Girl**. He was a quiet and unassuming chap who proved to be more than capable of creating some excellent bass lines and it was a pleasure to have him on board. Rehearsals now became fast and furious as the atmosphere and expectations quickly reached new and untold heights. Once again, with the **Slade** tour rapidly approaching, I could sense the big breakthrough was just around the corner. Soon, pulsating thoughts of stardom began floating around in my head once more, in a never ending whirl of undiminished excitement. Later, I walked into Lloyds Bank in Fawcett St which was always a bastion of friendship to withdraw cash for their wages, with a quiet confidence that was difficult to conceal. Even though we weren't there yet, I could finally feel the hypnotic and enticing smell of enduring success deep in my nostrils. The cashier smiled showing teeth which were spotlessly white and seemed to reflect the bright sunlight shining through the windows as she handed over the money. She was pretty too, although with a big reinforced glass partition separating her from the outside world, contact was brief and minimal. In life, we all need a purpose to work towards, which in reality is a form of ambition, and a group trying to "make it" is no exception. Unfortunately, through the very nature of the task facing them they are unmistakably forced to put all their eggs in one basket. To an outsider it may appear risky and in many ways, foolhardy. However, it creates a challenge which acts as a tremendous driving force when setting out to secure that all elusive stardom. Fail and everyone is left with a multitude of heartaches together with a sense of a cruel and undeserved injustice tempered by the invaluable experience they may have gained. Ironically, having encountered failure, with a young determined group, it serves only to increase their appetite for the next venture. Confused? So are thousands of others. But I can assure you, the thought of such a prospect doesn't deter them from trying.

Finally, the group were about to start their third national tour as special guests of **Slade**. Having already played eighteen support slots to **Captain Beefheart and His Magic Band** culminating in two nights at the Rainbow Theatre in Finsbury Park and thirty three slots supporting **The Sensational Alex Harvey Band**, the group had undoubtedly a wealth of experience to draw on. The vibrancy and excitement which was now present permeated into every group member's thoughts, instilling a quiet confidence that this time things would be vastly different. Being so close to success lulls you into a hypnotic feeling that you could reach out and actually touch it, but unfortunately, you can't. You know it's there and can sense it's a very real possibility. However, in reality, it remains enticingly elusive. Suddenly, the telephone rings. This has an uncanny knack of being chillingly nerve wracking as all sorts of worries begin to enter into your head. Has someone had a change of heart culminating in the tour being cancelled? Then again, is one of the band ill or could it be the bank saying one of the paying in cheques has "bounced" again. Fortunately, it's none of these and I heave a huge sigh of relief on finding it's only someone asking where the band are playing next and enthusing about how much they like them. As each day passes there's a vice like grip on your emotions which keep reminding you of what is at stake. To be supporting one of the most popular bands in the country at a major venue in London after a twenty two date national tour was presenting the group with an opportunity to enter the rarified and much sought after singles and album charts. During one conversation, Kenny Mountain had dared to utter the phrase "tax exile," which in itself was a staggering and exciting possibility. Was he dreaming, or were his words a true reflection of where he thought the group were heading? Rehearsals became ever more frantic as the band's determination to finally rid themselves of being the eternal support band clearly began to emerge. Through all this, I watched and waited with a mixture of anguish, frustration, and undiminished optimism. Did the group have what it takes? We were about to find out.

Soon, the opening night of the **Slade** tour was upon us at Bradford St George's Hall. Before the gig, Chas and **Slade** held a reception at the hotel with free booze and a buffet laid on to enable both bands to meet each other and hopefully cement a lasting friendship. As expected, the whole tour had been an immediate sell out and wherever **Slade** appeared there were always hundreds of screaming teenagers waiting outside to greet them. Being a part of something like this is a strange and compelling experience as you find yourself being constantly surrounded by overwhelming success, adulation and ever rising hopes. However, would the astounding success of **Slade** rub off and finally launch **Beckett** into the higher echelons of the music business? It was an intriguing thought which was to consume every passing minute. It's difficult to describe what it's actually like for six working class lads to be given such a rare and golden opportunity. Tax exiles, stars, limousines, adulation, hero worship, TV appearances and America, all for doing something you enjoy. They say the pleasure is in the giving and the group was certainly dispensing it in great abundance wherever they played. Can you blame them for becoming more than excited? While quietly observing them, I couldn't help noticing they looked relaxed, confident and assured just as they had been on that first fateful rail journey to the Marquee. In true Hollywood style, all I could do was wait and patiently watch from the wings. With the group's equipment unloaded and on stage, everything was finally set for the opening night. Just then, Ian Carruthers and Billy Bones, **Beckett's** two roadies approached me backstage. "Geoff, can we have word?" they requested. "Of course, what is it?" I asked. "We want a wage rise," they brusquely demanded. "We can't afford it. I'm losing money while this tour is costing Warners a fortune and you agreed the wage when you took the job. I'm sorry but it's impossible," I hastily informed them. "In that case we're both leaving," replied Billy Bones. "When?" I inquired? "Immediately," came his terse reply. "You mean you are not going to help us load the equipment back into the van at the end of the night or drive it for the rest of the tour?" I asked in astonishment. "Not unless we get a pay rise," he replied stubbornly. At that moment I looked into his eyes, which appeared to be a mixture of steely determination and heartless indifference as if being fully aware that he had me over a barrel and I would be forced to capitulate. "This is blackmail," I angrily replied as the horrendous logistical problems became all too apparent. "You may call it that," he replied in a sarcastic tone which was proving to be highly offensive. "I must warn you that if we don't get a pay rise we are definitely leaving," he reiterated in a smug and cocky manner. Suddenly, I detected what I can only describe as a superior and overbearing manner accompanying each threatening word. "How will we get the equipment on and off stage and complete the rest of the tour?" I asked in amazement. "That's your problem," he replied with a contemptible coldness which was highly objectionable as well as disquieting. By now, the domineering edge to his voice, which by any reasonable standards I was finding extremely intolerable, was beginning to seriously concern me. As they stared long and hard at me I had to think fast. Here they were jeopardising everything we had worked for, and suddenly, it all seemed to be falling apart. Blackmail is a cruel and hideous weapon which can be mind numbing as well as frightening. To have it thrust into your face under such extreme circumstances is even more so. Having been boxed into a corner and being confronted with an intransigent and unhelpful attitude, a flash of unrestrained anger suddenly overcame me as I instantly sent a right hook into his jaw. Peace loving people will call it an act of unjustifiable barbarism, but I wholeheartedly and unapologetically call it poetic justice. To me, it was clearly apparent that they had carefully chosen this moment to spring their blackmailing trap, regardless of the possible consequences and I had reacted. Fortunately, Bob Barton quickly stepped forward to restrain me while a shocked Billy Bones hurriedly disappeared down one of the backstage corridors with blood oozing from a cut on his face. A few moments later, one of **Slade's** roadies hurriedly approached me. "What's happened?" he asked concernedly. After quickly explaining the circumstances, I inquired if they would be so kind as to carry our backing equipment in their van and load it on to the stage for the rest of the tour. There was air of desperation and urgency in my voice as I painstakingly appealed to his better nature. Fortunately, he looked at me with both sympathy and understanding having realised that I had been boxed into a corner and the pressure I was feeling at that moment was tremendous. As an extra bonus I immediately promised to pay **Slade's** roadies the same money I was paying our two roadies, to which they quickly agreed. Fortuitously, the problem was solved and ironically, saved us the cost of two bed and breakfasts for the rest of the tour. Meanwhile, each night while

Slade were on stage playing their hearts out, I would sneak outside and place **Beckett** stickers on the four hub caps of the big black Rolls they were using. Within days, a concerned looking Chas approached me. "Those stickers of yours. The kids keep putting them on our hub caps and I wish they'd stop as they seem to be everywhere," he protested. I smiled, but said nothing, knowing it was my job to get the band into the public eye and it was undoubtedly great publicity.

Halfway through the tour, I received an urgent and what was to be a fateful telephone call from Warner Brothers Records. "Richard Robinson here Geoff. Can you come in to see me as soon as possible?" he requested. I couldn't help noticing his words seemed hurried, while sounding ominous and at odds with his usual friendly manner. Suddenly, I sensed danger. What it was I had no idea, but knew it was imperative to find out. "Come in Geoff, take a seat," he instructed when I reached his office. There was a faltering tone clearly audible in his voice as I entered and sat down. In the few seconds left before he spoke, I noticed he seemed hesitant and incapable of looking me in the eye. This wasn't the Robbie I knew and loved. I swallowed hard, preparing myself for the worst. What could it possibly be? I wondered. All the reviews during the tour had been ecstatic and we certainly hadn't gone over budget. Had there been some sort of accident or unexpected hiatus over which he had no control? I wondered. As every possible scenario crossed my mind, suddenly he spoke. "Warners are disbanding the Raft label so you no longer have a record contract," he told me. His face saddened as if unburdening the news was too much for him to bear. Physically I stiffened but didn't react mentally. When just a baby I'd been brought up in homes and had been in some tricky situations, but this time I knew it needed a cool head as there were five hungry mouths to think of as well as myself. "But why?" I questioned. "The record sales of the groups on the label don't justify the costs. It's an American decision so it's out of my hands," he answered. Each word cut a cruel swathe through my shattered pride, together with all our hopes and ambitions. It was as if the world had stopped and once again I'd fallen from a dangerous precipice into an unknown and dangerous chasm of interminable darkness from which there appeared to be no escape. Saddened and weary, twenty minutes later

I found myself unceremoniously thrust back into Oxford St amidst the mad maelstrom of onrushing people clearly intent on achieving their own destinies or long held desires.

Soon, my own thoughts and the consequences of a hasty or irrational judgment in joining the label began to flood my troubled mind. So the multitude of people who had enthusiastically tipped us for the top had all got it horribly wrong. I walked aimlessly through the crowds, unsure of what to do. In his haste, a stranger bumped into me and quickly apologised. There was no physical pain as I subconsciously looked down at my feet which seemed to be tiring of the burden which I had constantly thrust upon them. My heart was heavy and my mind numb as I thought of Bernie in her warm Warners office and the now defunct Raft Records. Why hadn't I accepted Chris Wright's lucrative offer and signed to Chrysalis Records when I had had the chance? Unfortunately, regrets and mistakes are all part of life but in a situation of this nature, they fail to take away the searing and heartrending pain. However, it was too late now, knowing I had unwisely turned him down and taken the group on a different and ultimately faltering path. Still walking along Oxford St, I couldn't help noticing **The Hare Krishna Temple** chanting in complete harmony with each other while seemingly at peace with the world. I continued to observe them with a certain degree of admiration which sent a surge of unrepressed hope racing through my mind. Whether it was thought transference or just good vibes was incidental. What mattered was that it lifted my spirits and a heightened sense of optimism immediately began to take root. The time had now come to think fast as we were in freefall and I was at the helm. Meanwhile the group took the news calmly which rather surprised me. Having been through a lot together we all appreciated this was no time for anyone to show weakness or the slightest sign of uncertainty. They looked at each other with an unwavering and determined resolve despite seeming oblivious that it was me who was paying the bills. Nevertheless, we had come too far to give up and in the finest tradition of show business I had already decided that the show must go on. Failure and rejection are heavy and devastating burdens for anyone to carry, especially when accompanied by an awareness that they have been cruelly and unsuspectingly thrust upon your shoulders. Fortunately, **Beckett** possessed a deep and admirable strength of character, together with an abundance of moral fibre, which I fervently hoped would see them through. I'd also been taught that if you think about a problem long enough, you will eventually solve it. Bearing this in mind, I immediately thought of Phil Carson the label boss of Atlantic Records in the UK. I had previously met him through promoting **Led Zeppelin** three times and had once had a meal with him and Peter Grant in Cranks health food restaurant just off Carnaby St. Somehow, I knew had to get him to a gig and encourage him to sign the group as I was fully aware his label were doing amazingly well with **The Rolling Stones, Led Zeppelin,** and **Yes** among others. "Okay, I'll come to The Hammersmith Odeon and see them," he assured me after an urgent telephone call. His voice sounded positively encouraging as well as immensely powerful, which he undoubtedly was. However, knowing this I became nervous. They say the bigger they come, the harder they fall. Well, we'd fallen all right and it hurt, but it hadn't proved to be terminal, not yet anyway. Could the group pull it off one more time? Everything now depended on them, while a myriad of doubts continued to surface. Were they tiring? Was the constant struggle sapping their enthusiasm? Had the shock of being dropped weakened their resolve? All of these questions needed to be answered in an authoritative and convincing manner. Just then, I looked at Terry. I could see his eyes had remained bright and clear as well as alert. As I began outlining the task ahead, to my great relief there was no outward signs of tears, histrionics or regrets. Through all this, Kenny remained silent which epitomised his reclusive type nature whenever he was confronted with a difficult or seemingly insoluble problem. Being the two vocalists, I knew it was vitally important that their voices didn't falter or weaken on the night. However, I also knew the rock business has a way of exacting its own demoralising and demanding price. Ironically, it seemed none of this would matter. The unpalatable and frightening fact was that for 45 minutes they would be on trial and if they failed, there was nowhere left to go.

Chapter 6

Earlier in the tour and with the pressure still on, it was time to visit Wolverhampton which happened to be **Slade's** home town. Only a few miles away was RAF Cosford where I had once been stationed as a boy entrant in order to train as an electrical and instrument engineer after leaving school. During our initial training, a bullying and highly oppressive Sergeant Cullen appeared to take great delight in giving me a dog's life and to this day I still don't know why. Fatigues, "jankers," doubling around the square with a rifle, public humiliation and scornful derision were just a few of his harsh and uncompromising ways of instilling his type of discipline. Fifteen years old, tiny, and a long way from home, in order to be able survive in an environment such as this, you have to learn fast In Wolverhampton that night, it all came back to me as I thought of **Beckett** and how they would have to do likewise if they were to survive the night's possible onslaught. Despite **Slade** being absolutely massive throughout the country, Wolverhampton remained a whole different and possibly frightening proposition. Being their home town they were positively idolised and I was fully aware that any support group could at best be ignored, or at worst, jeered off stage to a cacophonous and never ending series of catcalling and boos. Before **Beckett** were due to go on, I had a quiet word with them. "Listen lads, if you are booed or someone throws anything at you, ignore it and just keep going as the last thing I want you doing is walking off stage in a tantrum." As the group listened, I couldn't help wondering if instead of rallying them, I was instilling a disproportionate sense of apprehension and fear into their minds as well as shattering their already shaken confidence.

Soon, it was time to go on as they hit the stage running with the irrepressible Terry cavorting and twisting his lithe and sensual body to the music while hitting the high notes with a confidence that was positively awe inspiring. At this, the crowd cheered and I couldn't believe it. At the end of each following song they cheered even louder as the group's confidence began to grow ever stronger. Finally, at the end of the set, the ecstatic crowd demanded an encore but that proved impossible as under the agreed rules of the tour, **Beckett** were not allowed to and were obliged to come straight off. Backstage, the group were delighted and it seemed all my precautionary words of warning had been completely unnecessary. The following day, I picked up an early edition of the local paper and there staring me in face, was a highly complimentary review which enthusiastically tipped them for future stardom. In one sense, it was just a local review. But being out on the road with one of the biggest draws in the country, it did untold wonders for mine and the group's morale.

Finally, it was time to hit London for the last three nights of the tour knowing everything now hinged on the group's performance in front of Phil Carson. In the record business, it was well known that in signing for Atlantic Records you were undoubtedly entering a new and far bigger league. It was an exhilarating thought which made my mind race at the distinct and very real possibility of it actually happening. It was also well known that they maintained high standards and rarely had a failure. Soon I began fantasising about the possibility of supporting **The Rolling Stones** and meeting Mick Jagger at last. "Hi Mick, not a bad gig you did there. Could you pass me another glass of Dom Perignon please as this one seems to have gone a bit flat while I was discussing the band's appearance on the Ed Sullivan Show. I'm sorry but I'll have to hurry. We've been invited to Hugh Hefner's playboy mansion and he's promised us a really good time and you know what that could mean. Here's a hundred dollar tip for your roadie seeing as he did a really great job of looking after the vocal monitors. Tell him we're thinking about using him for our next tour as well. Please accept my humblest apologies, you know how it is Mick, I must leave. Thanks for offering us a lift but Hugh has sent his personal stretch limo round for us and the driver is waiting to go. Don't wait up for us because we'll probably be late. Oh! By the way, don't forget to tell Keith I like the new song that you've just written. It's called "Satisfaction" or something isn't it? I think it could do well. Incidentally, that tall blonde at the side of the stage that you brought was giving Terry and me the eye, don't worry, you know I wouldn't pull a stroke like that on you. See you at tomorrow's gig, bye."

Back to reality and it's cold outside the Hammersmith Odeon while inside it's nice and warm with **Beckett** posters and stickers seemingly everywhere (where I had placed them earlier). Soon, Phil arrived and I quickly greeted him inside the packed and bustling foyer. In the past I'd met most of the big names and can honestly say I was never overawed. However, human emotions being what they are this was proving to be completely different as he held all the aces while keeping his cards close to his chest. Meanwhile, I shifted uneasily knowing this was the last and final throw of the dice. I was out on a limb and felt all alone and highly vulnerable amidst the jollity and excited chattering of the arriving fans. I glanced purposefully at Phil who was tall and never spoke much, which somehow seemed to make it easier for him not to apologise or give any reason if he turned any aspiring group down. After all, it was part of his job and one more refusal would surely mean nothing to him. I clenched and unclenched my fists which were hidden from view behind my back. It seemed the only tangible way I could ease the tension, while appearing to look outwardly calm and relaxed. Ironically, in many ways I recognised a potential record deal with Atlantic would be a quantum leap from the obscurity and uncertainty of Raft Records. It appeared we now had the indisputable and tantalising prospect of going from a heartbreaking funeral to a joyful and celebratory wedding. However, if the group failed now it would undoubtedly be devastating news, especially as they were so close to achieving the next major step. Tension, which can affect your whole life, is something which none of us ever savour. In a situation such as this, it eats into the very fabric of your soul, leaving you drained of all hope or expectations. The stomach tightens; the mouth becomes dry, while the eyes are unable to transmit anything except the extreme nervous tension racing throughout the overworked brain. The spectacle of realising the next forty five minutes involved all our future careers was a daunting and nerve wracking prospect. Within minutes the group were due on stage and I couldn't help wondering what they were thinking. For better or worse, they were now out on their own and with everything in the balance, there was nothing I could do but quietly observe the drama that was about to unfold.

Soon, the band was up there strutting their stuff, looking relaxed as well as confident and being applauded after every song. While watching and worrying, I couldn't help recalling that fateful night when they played their first London gig at The Marquee and "Berkesy's" superhuman dash in order to get there. Meanwhile, on stage the group were young, energetic and playing with no apparent fear, which is something I have always admired in a band desperately striving for success. Unfortunately, the same didn't apply to me. All the while, Phil appeared strangely aloof and mysterious as if to prematurely air his considered opinion in public would somehow be detrimental to his standing as the head of a major record company. I glanced towards him and forced a smile, only to realise that he was far too experienced to be swayed by such an obvious tactic. However, what other means was there of conveying my friendliness, I wondered? Finally, and with the tension holding me in a vice-like grip the band finished their set to rapturous applause whereupon the lights immediately went up. Within seconds, Phil turned to me and quietly told me that he would come again the following night. There was no apparent sign of enthusiasm or compelling words of criticism, just a faint nod of the head and he was gone. I swallowed hard as it was a huge disappointment, but I consoled myself with the thought that it wasn't an outright rejection. But what was it? In reality I realised we remained stranded in no man's land as if walking on a tightrope amidst a minefield of untold and mysterious possibilities. On the other hand, there remained room for cautious optimism that there was still a chance of reaching a successful conclusion. A troublesome mixture of conjecture, hopes and theories all abounded as he quickly disappeared into the darkness of the night, his taxi inexorably taking him further away from my desperately puzzled and apprehensive thoughts.

Twenty four hours can seem like an eternity and it was never truer than the following day which proved to be both long and tortuous. Finally, the evening arrived as the band looked at me and I looked at them. Backstage, and with the tension rising, there was nothing

I could say. Their homes were 300 miles away while their young unlined faces didn't seem to have a care in the world. Having returned to the foyer, Richard Robinson turned up with his trusty right hand man Nick Lloyd carefully pushing his wheelchair. Robbie smiled warmly as if signifying he wanted to give us his wholehearted moral support, while feeling guilty at having to discard us in such a brutal and off handed manner. Suddenly, my heart began to race. Seeing him was certainly a morale booster knowing that everything he did was clothed in genuine kindness and understanding. I couldn't help thinking back to the fateful day of our parting, which I knew he hadn't desired or wanted, but had been reluctantly forced upon him. At The Hammersmith Odeon that night, we shook hands. Ironically, this was the very hand that had signed all those cheques which had enabled the group to be on this very tour. He knew it and I knew it and he'd come to see it through, right to the bitter end. I looked down at him as he smiled again while my respect and admiration immediately soared to even greater heights remembering how patient and helpful he had been. "Phil's coming Geoff, I spoke to him on the telephone," he informed me with a perceptive air of heartfelt encouragement. "I know," I replied. "Good luck." A tear came to my eye as coming from him, those two words meant everything. Just then, and with the group about to appear on stage, Nick gently pushed his wheelchair to a suitable vantage point as if they were both wholeheartedly willing the group to succeed. Having gone down amazingly well the previous night, everything now hinged on this final and possible career enhancing performance. The lady manning the small confectionary stall in the foyer smiled. I immediately smiled back knowing she had her own life to live and probably had some loved ones at home who were just as important to her as the night's event was to us. Meanwhile, **Slade** souvenir tour posters were selling fast as parents continued to drop their children off before they excitedly made their way to their seats. Finally, Phil arrived, offering me the obligatory handshake before casually positioning himself at the back with me nervously accompanying him. Minutes later, **Beckett** appeared on stage and quickly hit full stride as a confidence bordering on arrogance began transmitting itself to **Slade's** young and appreciative audience. I held my breath which was all I could do. Suddenly, the spotlight shone on Bob Barton's guitar, highlighting the expensive mother of pearl inlay he had insisted upon. Kenny, who was the oldest, looked cool and unperturbed, probably due to a mixture of experience and the cannabis he insisted on smoking before going on stage each night. Soon, his lilting and distinguished voice settled over the audience, soaring and diving with even greater intensity as if calmly guiding the others through uncharted, shark infested waters. At this point, Terry swung the mike stand before darting across the stage causing the young girls in the audience to become transfixed as he pirouetted, teased and manipulated them into a conscious state of uninhibited admiration. Sensing this, and with the stage appearing to be his natural home, he was revelling in the adulation, especially as he had previously supported **Rod Stewart & The Faces** and had observed **Robert Plant** at first hand. Now he was emulating them in his own inimitable style. Ian Murray remained motionless and quiet, which he was happy to do whether on or off stage, complimenting the front three. I shifted uneasily knowing it seemed to be going all too well as Bob began to sing one of my favourite songs (which he had written) entitled "Life's Shadow." It proved to be highly emotive and with a third vocalist of this quality demonstrating both his vocal and guitar prowess, my hopes began to soar.

Halfway through the set, Phil Carson, later to become manager of **Robert Plant,** turned and gestured me towards the exit. I recalled years previously when Syd Simpkins had uttered the immortal phrase, "it's the brush off" at The Ellis Wright Agency. His words immediately came to mind as I dutifully followed Phil. Suddenly, a whole myriad of unanswered questions began racing through my mind. Was he bored and intent on leaving as quickly as possible? My heart sank at such a thought as I had mistakenly assumed he would have had the courtesy to stay and see the whole set, but it wasn't to be. I swallowed hard at the thought of rejection as it seemed we were failures and I would soon be burdened with the humiliating and heartbreaking task of informing the group. Suddenly, Phil's authoritative words broke the silence. "Where can we talk because I want to sign them?" he questioned. My heart immediately raced with gushing and outlandish pride, knowing all the heartache and setbacks of the previous weeks and months were now finally behind us. I hadn't begged prayed, or even cried, but now the electrifying moment had arrived. In the corner of my eye, tears of sheer elation and bliss were gathering as I discreetly fought to hold them back. Hearing those enduring and unforgettable words was one of my most exciting moments in rock and meant everything to me. In a few magical moments, pride and unstinting enthusiasm had been restored, and this time, I really could think of America.

"I'll give you a further £10,000 advance (£100,000 today), two guaranteed meaningful tours of the States with a major band and a top name to produce their album in a quality studio." As I sat listening in a quiet pub just around the corner, his words were tumbling out in what appeared to be a torrent of magical bribes and promises. However, this was no empty or false bribe. It was for real and I was staggered. Within minutes the deal was done and finally, apart from actually signing the contract, we were on Atlantic Records, one of the most prestigious labels in the world. Now, floating on air, I re-entered The Hammersmith Odeon and informed an ecstatic band that once again they had a major record contract. It was a defining moment and one I'll never forget. Kenny smiled. It wasn't a broad smile; it was more a triumphant one which reflected his immense relief. For Terry, it was particularly satisfying knowing that Ahmet Ertegun, one half of the brothers who had first founded the label in America had previously tipped him for super stardom after seeing him perform at the Marquee. "That singer's a super star in the making," he had said. It is difficult to describe my own sheer and unbridled elation. That dark day as I walked along Oxford St after being dropped by Raft Records should have been just a fading memory, but it wasn't. The pain and anguish of outright rejection had stubbornly refused to free its ever marauding and hurtful words from my thoughts as well as acting as a potent and everlasting warning. Fortunately, it was all behind us now as I allowed myself the luxury of contemplating a bright and momentous future within the safe confines of a prestigious and highly respected record label.

In the calm light of the following day, amidst the heady dreams, there remained new horizons to be conquered, new goals to be achieved and a lot of hard work facing us. Inside, my mind was racing with excitement on realising how the group had, with a little luck, finally played themselves into the big time. After a few minutes I walked back inside to watch **Slade** make their final appearance knowing that such a lot had happened during those 22 dates and somehow, I felt a deep sense of gratitude towards them. Their ecstatic audience remained transfixed and cheering every song. I looked around and could see pubescent teenagers just starting out on the road to the maturity that would hopefully go on to broaden and expand their own musical tastes. But for now, they were thoroughly enjoying themselves and, without **Slade**, I was fully conscious that we would have been denied such invaluable exposure as well as the fantastic opportunity of being signed to a major record deal.

A day later, having reached calmer waters, I took stock as I contemplated the future amidst an inward feeling of outright euphoria. A major record contract, an excited group, respect from the music press and praise from **John Peel**. It had all come together like a dream and to cap it all, I had a young experienced band that I fervently believed possessed genuine talent that had the ability to go all the way. Being handed a cheque for £10,000 is also a strange sensation. It endorses a reassuring faith in the band which is a clear indication that someone other than you has genuine and unerring faith in their talent. In those wonderful and unforgettable heady days, peace and love was at the forefront of the musical revolution rapidly taking place. Ulterior motives, and a desire to possess material things seemed non existent and unworthy of such meaningless considerations. **Scott McKenzie's** "San Francisco (Be Sure To Wear Some Flowers In Your Hair)" which had been at No I for 17 weeks in 1967 seemed to encapsulate everyone's feelings towards each other. While attending gigs or music festivals, it was wonderful to meet people whose perceptions in life were not of greed or selfishness, but of helpfulness, sharing and compassion, together with a genuine affection for each other. Music was more of a hobby than a business and it was gratifying to know and feel that **Beckett** were already a part of this. **The Incredible String Band**, the wonderful and highly intelligent four "freakers" from my home town, **Roy Harper** and **Dot Fisher** the receptionist from the Bay, together with **John Peel** and Glastonbury Festival had all helped to engender this feeling of togetherness in the hope of a better world.

Were we naïve daydreamers or simply optimists who had lost all sense of reality? In light of the present day, it seems strange that we ever imagined it could all come true, but we really did. At festivals, people sang and played acoustic guitars as we all gathered round camp fires to listen. Joss sticks were lit while no one felt like a stranger and everyone became your friend. They were undoubtedly immensely carefree and heady days and how joyous it is to recall them.

Unfortunately however, darker clouds were hovering just over the horizon. **Country Joe** was back in America having succeeded in waking people up to the dangers of a futile war in Vietnam. There was real concern in his voice and a potent message in his lyrics. "What Are We Fighting For?" he had asked of the politicians. We listened and no longer felt helpless as his message reverberated around the whole world. But good intentions, together with a warm heart, are no match for the desires which materialism and a lust for power bring. In later years, with these roots having already become firmly embedded, it was to be a rude and timely awakening which ignominiously pushed aside the hopes of even the most optimistic of faithful followers. Despite these unwelcome constraints, music remained a collective and calming antidote from the ever increasing tensions of day to day living. Festivals such as the Isle of Wight and **Bob Dylan** were on everyone's lips. Young people listened and learnt which allowed their minds to become even more enriched on hearing such meaningful and passionate lyrics. With this knowledge firmly entrenched in their thinking, mercifully, and against all the odds, youth continued to nurture and retain its own irrepressible way of expressing itself. Such thoughts and observations had been the very foundations on which the British music scene had flourished. Now, would it be possible for **Beckett**, to practice, uphold and encourage these ideals? I certainly hoped so. The following day, I walked into the Ship, a well known watering hole in Wardour St, to find the band surrounded by friends and pretty girls. With a major record contract about to be signed it was noticeable that there was a spring in their step, together with a new-found confidence rapidly seeping through their every deed. Atlantic Records. It rolls off the tongue just like **Aretha Franklin's** high and seemingly ever lasting notes.

Soon, the group had a gig to play and their new Mercedes van was parked in the narrow street at the back of the Marquee. It was the roadie's job to keep an eye on it and its contents, but suddenly I became worried at the thought of all their comparatively new stage equipment being stolen. If so, it would prove to be catastrophic to say the least? I decided to check and having reached the van I peered in to find "Berksey" fast asleep with both doors locked and the equipment intact. Relieved, I made my way back to "The Ship" to find Keith Moon had walked while the group were staring in admiration. For a few moments, **Beckett** looked overawed but quickly snapped out of it. Hadn't **John Peel** said they were the best band on at Reading Festival right up until the Saturday evening? Just then, Terry stood up. Tall, young and confident when he wriggled that slim athletic body of his, he was sexy too. As usual, Kenny Mountain who was the main song writer, seemed non-plussed and appeared to be taking it all in his stride. Watching him, he seemed to possess an air of inner confidence knowing that in a short while he would be on stage and doing what he loved best. Shortly afterwards, due to the constraints of time, I left and hurriedly made my way to the Marquee to check the guest list. Having entered its illustrious portals, Pete Erskine of the NME turned up, whereupon I happily bought him a drink. On first impressions he seemed a nice chap, but then again, he hadn't seen the band for quite some time. I already knew he was not afraid to write a vitriolic or unfavourable review should he feel so inclined. Meanwhile, I continued to remain nervous as I insisted on buying him another drink, having realised that trying to solicit a favourable review can be very expensive. Terry, who was always outwardly full of confidence coupled with a friendly personality which everyone seemed to like, then breezed over. Soon, it became noticeable that he and Pete were chatting like old friends which relieved me of the responsibility of explaining the history and hopes of the band. Finally, the group hit the stage and went down fantastically well to a packed and highly enthusiastic Marquee. Later, I was to learn that Pete Erskine loved them while Alan Jones of The Melody Maker had failed to turn up. Still, one out of two wasn't bad. Back in the dressing room I found Kenny relaxing with his usual "joint" accompanied by a succession of giggles whenever anyone approached him. In retrospect, it proved to be a joyful and exciting time which instilled renewed hope and excitement into everyone's minds. Inevitably, an unending series of backslapping congratulations and enthusiastic reactions led to a sense that the musical world was finally about to become aware of their emerging presence. Once again they had effortlessly conquered London, or should I say The Marquee? **The Stones, The Who, David Bowie, Jimmy Page, Jeff Beck, Jimmy Hendrix, Eric Clapton, Led Zeppelin,** and hundreds of others had all played there in their early days before going on to major success. Knowing this made it all the sweeter as I and the band unashamedly revelled in the atmosphere.

Earlier that day, I'd been reading a critical article about a Machiavellian figure who was orchestrating a group's every move, while being accused of stifling their natural creativity. Being sensitive, this set me thinking. Could I inadvertently be falling into the same trap under the guise of desperation, or even ignorance? The fact still remained that we were in urgent need of a hit single and the band seemed unable to write one. Looking back, I'd been fortunate enough to have had some great hit singles on the Bay Hotel jukebox while working there. The first thing I noticed was that there was an immediacy and credibility about them which appealed to all cross sections without being lightweight or meaningless. After listening to hundreds of them over a period of six nights a week for five years, the natural rhythm of their underlying soul creeps into your bones. Add to this knowledge a multitude of progressive thinking bands that I had promoted enabled me to expand the parameters of my thinking while allowing a more balanced picture of what is good or bad to emerge. Of course it still remained only my opinion but at least it was an experienced one. Meanwhile, having previously faced rejection, without that hit, problems had quickly began to intensify. Nerves had become frayed, patience at times was exhausted and the band had begun to lose heart. Times such as these inflict mental scars which are not readily healed while heated exchanges become more common as excuses proliferate and fail to paper over the cracks. Fortunately, all this appeared to be behind us now. With a major record contract firmly in the bag, the future was stunningly bright and it had all become very exciting. Back in Sunderland and still in a heady state of euphoria, a few days later I received a call from Bob Barton asking if he could come and see me. At the time his voice sounded normal and gave no real indication as to what he wanted, so I remained unconcerned. I liked Bob. In fact, I positively admired not only his playing ability, but his hard work and dedication. This, together with his easy going manner, meant he was a joy to manage. With all this in mind, once at my flat, I listened as he began to speak. Suddenly, and without prior warning, there was an urgency and seriousness in his voice which immediately made me feel apprehensive as well as uneasy. "I want to leave the band and start one of my own but I still want you to manage me," he calmly informed me. I reeled back in shock realising it was a crazy as well as a reckless suggestion. A sense of utter despair quickly overcame me knowing we were about to sign for Atlantic Records and start on a whole new and exciting venture. "You can't do it Bob. It will dilute the talent and jeopardise the record contract," I warned with more than a strong hint of desperation in my voice. "I don't want to be in the group anymore. The only way I will stay is if I am allowed to travel separately from the band," he said. "But that's ridiculous. The group need to travel together so you can discuss things, go over new songs, and most important of all, arrive together for the second checks while maintaining the necessary camaraderie. Anything else would be a nightmare, and anyway, the rest of the band wouldn't like it," I pointed out in a panic stricken voice. "I don't want to travel with them. I think Terry is getting too big headed and the group aren't as professional as they should be," he continued. "He's not big headed, he's just confident," I assured him. "Take that away and you destroy what is there naturally. Don't you realise you are jeopardising everything we have worked for?" I cautioned. He remained calm, as if detached from the gravity of the situation and how ridiculous his suggestion actually was. "I want to form my own band," he repeated in an emphatic and stubborn manner. His words sounded ominous, cutting deep into my shattered and alarmed feelings as well as all our hopes and ambitions. I took a deep and exasperated breath as I realised that perhaps he had been given too much too soon and it had all come too easy for him. New guitars, a new amp and speakers, major tours, a record contract, and unparalleled praise needs to be accompanied by a balanced and level headed attitude in order to keep a person's feet on the ground. Inside, I found my frustration and resentment welling up as I wondered could this really be happening? Unfortunately it was and had come totally out of the blue. Despite my immense admiration for Bob, there was no question of allowing him to dictate the policy of the group as well as undermining its new found spirit. I pleaded, cajoled, and just about begged before explaining what seemed like a thousand times why it was so important he stayed. Unfortunately, it was all to no avail, as unbowed, and unmoved, he finally stood up to leave. I'd never expected such an unforeseen impasse to come between us and within seconds he was gone. I glanced around the room where I had previously held so many joyous and blissful parties. Now, it seemed sparse and cold as well as bereft of any visible life form which could resuscitate the abject despair which had now overtaken me. A few hours later, I informed the group of what had taken place. They looked shocked as well as disappointed, but to their immense credit, were determined to soldier on. "We will just have to get someone else," suggested Terry. "What about Arthur?" queried Kenny. At the time, I was still bemused by it all and felt the group needed a few more days in order to consider their next move without rushing into any cul de sacs or panicking into making the wrong decision. Inside I was hurting. To be cast aside in such a reckless and inconsiderate manner is not only highly disquieting and irregular, but soul destroying as well. Nevertheless, the group had shown more than an abundance of moral fibre in the past. Now it was up to all of us to show that it was still there as circumstances urgently required it.

A few days later I walked into Phil Carson's office to discuss the finer points of the new record contract. Inwardly I was distraught but determined not to show it as I prepared to put on a brave face in order to appear unruffled and calm. "Our guitarist has left, but don't worry, we'll soon have a new one as there are lots of excellent players in the NE," I began. "He's what? He's left just when we are about to sign you. In that case the deal is off. If he hasn't got the enthusiasm to stay, then I haven't got the confidence to sign them," he exclaimed in a heightened and disbelieving voice. Once again I pleaded with all the urgency and passion I could possibly muster, but it was all to no avail. To say I was absolutely crestfallen and distraught would be to put too fine a point on it. To say I was in utter despair would be much nearer the truth. The pain and anguish etched deep in my face told its own demoralising and unbelievable story. But it was no use. The much lauded deal was off and despite a triumphant nationwide tour with **Slade**; we were now back in the wilderness. To have the prize snatched away when it is actually within your grasp, I can assure you is heartbreaking, while to recall it brings me no joy. After leaving his office, in a moment of abject self pity and shock, I began to reflect on everything that had happened and knew I'd learnt a valuable lesson in life. How I wished I'd never sacked Arthur, especially as he had formed the group, was totally dedicated to its success, and was a really genuine and smashing person. Ironically, he had also helped to get that first major record contract and in my haste to supposedly improve the group, it seemed I had inadvertently destroyed it. Malaise, ineptitude, a disproportionate sense of self pity, a lack of motivation, laziness, inability to listen, a sad and disconsolate recluse, lack of appetite, both physical and mental, all insidiously enveloped my body as if anaesthetised by a drug far more powerful than any previously discovered. Failure is a cruel and unrelenting tormentor. The eyes feel hollow and the mind numb as the body's breathing becomes laboured in an unending search for a solution. Such an affliction, while not being a disease, or even terminal, is however deep and wounding.

Fortunately, despite profound regrets, time is a great healer, allowing that deep driving and underlying urge to gather renewed momentum. Soon, the battered remnants of a hastily destroyed enthusiasm began to take root. In a situation of this nature, to constantly dwell on a setback, no matter how damaging or hurtful, seems tawdry, wasteful and self limiting as the body instinctively and resolutely dispatches it into the realms of a dark and long forgotten era. Meanwhile, the group and I had a major problem. With no guitarist and no record contract, the music world had suddenly become a desperately sadder and more lonelier place. Sandy Saddler, a highly revered world famous featherweight boxing champion from years previously who eventually became penniless was once famously quoted as saying, "First your legs go. Then your title goes. Then your money goes, and then your friends go." Even though I'd never held a title, right then, I could certainly empathise with his sad and telling sentiments

"Beckett Hit The Big Time." The once enthusiastic headline in The Newcastle Sunday Sun would now have to be amended to **"Nearly Hit The Big Time,"** or alternatively**, "All Washed Up."** These despairing thoughts came to me as I wondered how I could possibly extricate the band out of the seemingly bottomless pit we now found ourselves in. Unwanted personnel changes are a nightmare at the best of times and I was now tiring of the logistic and financial responsibilities which I had allowed to be inadvertently thrust upon me. Driving up and down the motorways through snow and sleet, gigs being cancelled, working for so little reward accompanied by petty arguments and failure are no incentive to prolong such misery. Robert the Bruce had reputedly watched a spider successfully crawl across a broken cobweb after a defeat, which gave him the incentive to go on and savour victory. Unfortunately, I could see neither a spider nor its web. A few days later I glanced upwards and saw dark clouds gathering as it began to rain, while the wind freshened and brought its own form of discomfort to my exposed face. My mouth felt dry, my muscles leaden and my heart ached, but looking at the past three years realistically, it had been a huge gamble which had failed. Nevertheless, there had been a number of hard earned compensations along the way. I'd gained invaluable experience, learnt a lot about managing bands and also met some interesting people. Here, it must also be pointed out that a disgruntled musician is a formidable adversary and one not to be taken lightly. Should he become a leading light in his band, he possesses power far beyond that which can be considered as fair and equitable. In reality, it's an inflated ego, and as a manager you have the unenviable task of trying to suppress or deal with it. On occasions, a more sensible and restrained member of the band may intervene and restore calm. But why tolerate such selfish or childish behaviour you may well ask? However, in reality you have no choice. In a last desperate effort to placate the aggrieved member you agree to buy him better and more expensive equipment in a vain effort to appease him. This is rock & roll at the sharp end and when a band is struggling, there is no respite. There are hungry mouths to feed, gigs to play, and hopefully, a renewed determination to succeed.

Back home, a few days later, the telephone rang. "Geoff, Terry here. Arthur has agreed to rejoin the band." he informed me happily. The words struck home with touching simplicity and immediately lifted my sagging spirits. With Arthur back I immediately realised unity and empathy would almost certainly be restored. As he was always such a driving force, enthusiasm would also be rekindled together with a new sense of purpose. Ironically, it was also a chance to redeem the deep hurt I'd previously caused him and maybe, just maybe, he might see it in his heart to forgive me. After the short conversation with Terry, I put the phone down and began a series of deep, thought provoking questions. "Could we come back? Could they do it and could I muster the energy to make one last attempt at making it? I thought of the five thousand wasted posters lying in Warner Bros when our much vaunted bass player had left and had resolved never to put photographs of the band's faces on a poster again. However, I also realised that any new attempt would be more than just about posters. To me, it seemed that we would be attempting to climb Mount Everest in bare feet without Sherpas or oxygen. Also, it seemed we'd driven down the motorway that often, even the cafeteria staff knew how many sugars we all took in our tea. Days passed and I was still undecided even though I hadn't actually left and fortunately, neither had any of the remaining members of the group. In reality, we all needed a rest or perhaps we should have called it a day. However, an underlying conviction kept telling me the prize was too big to be allowed to slip away so easily. The carrot and the donkey is the only analogy which seems apt although I never did learn if the donkey ever succeeded in finally achieving its aim. Unfortunately, it was now happening to me as temptation and determination were still proving to be an immense and powerful driving force. The prize remained tantalisingly in front of me as I took a deep breath while wondering if I should reach out and attempt to grasp it. If I did, it would mean another gig, another demo tape, another record company and yet more heartache. But had fate other ideas? What then is the motivating force that keeps driving you on? Is it greed? Is it an unrealistic assessment of the group's talent, or just bad luck? Yes, you've guessed it. Your own vanity or ego reassures you that it's just bad luck as myriads of other possibilities are quickly dismissed. Others are consigned to the bin marked "record company lacks foresight," or "light years behind where we are at." Nevertheless, the driving force which has all but consumed you continues to wantonly cast aside any doubts which may have resurfaced. Having become steeped and deeply entangled in the throes of a mad and single minded determination to make it, it is time to soldier on.

With Terry' persuasive voice still ringing in my ears, I drove through to rehearsals, which Arthur had organised before gingerly entering the room. He glanced towards me but remained silent, while I had deep pangs of guilt burdening my conscience and was at a loss as to what to say. As usual, he had his trusty guitar in his hands and quickly reeled off a few searing notes. Sooner or later I knew we had to speak. Being acutely aware of this, I also knew that a sincere person has to truly believe what he is saying. Yet, how could Arthur possibly believe anything I said and furthermore, why should he? Suddenly, the band broke into a song entitled "Rain Clouds." Everyone had said it was a hit, including my brother Leo, but I honestly never thought so. It seemed too slow and over orchestrated, while lacking any excitement and failed to portray any positive direction. Nevertheless, the fact that they were playing it showed they still had that independent and rebellious streak which is something I had always admired in a group. Terry smiled. Carefree by nature, he always did and today was to be no exception. "What do you think?" he asked. A manager's job is to encourage, cajole, and be constructive as well as being honest and supportive. However, being 300 miles from London while everyone else was settling into a self satisfied groove is no substitute for the harsh realities of a demanding or ruthless record company. "Let me hear a few more numbers," I requested. Moments later, the band broke into "Little Ada," a real rocking number that Arthur had written which in my opinion had "hit" written all over it. Unknown to the group, this was the moment I decided to rejoin the fray. Meanwhile, I had to think fast. A group down on its luck needs a deep and determined resolve to come up for air and try again. Having decided to go ahead, Shakespeare's words came to mind. "Uneasy Rests The Crown." How apt. But having accepted it, it was time to plan and engineer some new strategy which would lead to a successful conclusion. In bed, I tossed and turned, constantly reliving where we had gone wrong, but it seemed there was no way forward. Despite this, "Little Ada" was a song which wouldn't go away. It possessed an energy and naturalness about it and to think Arthur had had this up his sleeve all the time. How ironic. Was the quietest man in the band making a statement by clearly spelling out how wrong I had been? If so, he had certainly succeeded in hammering the point home.

Chapter 7

Now that I had once again agreed to be committed to the cause, I had to think fast. I began wondering how I could possibly elevate **Beckett** into the rarefied atmosphere of the big time. However, I remained under no illusions that this time would be any easier. In the rock world there are only so many avenues to explore and if a group are failing to sell records, word soon gets around. Fortunately, in the euphoria of the late sixties and early seventies, worthwhile music didn't have to rely on entering the charts with a hit single as the music itself was judged on its own merits. However, the unpalatable fact was that everything was beginning to change and not having a hit meant in the corporate and money driven record business we were now entering, a minefield of endless and insurmountable problems faced us. Being aware of this, after careful thought, what I considered to be an inspirational idea suddenly came to me. Reading Rock Festival, the most important one on the calendar at the time, was coming up in a few weeks. Jack Barrie, who organised the event, was a friend of mine and I knew it was far too good an opportunity to miss. Should I succeed in getting the group a spot and they played well, there was no telling what might happen. Sure enough, after a quick call he immediately agreed to give them a slot, and suddenly, we were back up there among the big boys. Approaching Reading and seeing the horde of musical devotees with their rucksacks on their backs, eagerly making their way towards the festival, proved to be a very pleasant and exhilarating sight. Immediately noticeable was the wonderful sense of camaraderie and togetherness clearly prevalent in the air, with their inherent love of music the sole reason for being there. Soon, the music started and over the next three days the groups you have spent the whole year reading about were up there and strutting their stuff. To be managing a band that is actually playing on its exalted stage is, I can assure you, an even bigger thrill. Nevertheless, there remains a certain tension hanging in the air. Will they play well? Will the crowd take to them, and more importantly, will it lead to bigger things? Around an hour before the group were due on stage, I glanced into the small tent that **Beckett** were sleeping in, only to find it empty. Knowing it was undoubtedly a big day for their future hopes and aspirations, I finally located them in the backstage bar. After acknowledging each other's presence I realised it would be completely pointless to give them any last minute words of advice as by now they were far too experienced to warrant it. Soon, it was time for me to gingerly make my way out into the festival itself in order to watch them perform. As I did so, my mind began to race with a mixture of enthusiasm and fear. Finally, having reached my chosen vantage point, I realised it was another make or break moment for all of them.

It was late Saturday afternoon when they finally hit the stage to pleasant but restrained applause. Having positioned myself out front, I now found myself feeling extremely apprehensive in case anything should go wrong. Could they cut it and pull off a minor miracle? Watching quietly from the side of the stage was **John Peel,** who at times could be a deep thinker as well as being quite humorous and witty. However, as always, where he was concerned, there was no sitting on the fence which meant you could never take him for granted. Credibility in any field is a precious asset for anyone who cares about their chosen profession, and the slightest endorsement from him, no matter how minor, would be like manna from heaven for the group. Unfortunately, all I could do was watch and wait as the tension began to build. Here it must be said that forty five minutes up on the main stage in front of a huge crowd can be very intimidating for a group who are relativity unknown. Luckily, it had turned out to be a warm sunny day as I quietly surveyed the crowd while shifting uneasily with a certain tension still hanging in the air. As I looked up at the group they appeared to be relaxed but I certainly wasn't. One guest slot to decide your whole future is not the recommended medicine to entice relaxation. All the while, myriads of unanswered questions were racing around in my head in a never-ending and desperate search for answers. Atlantic Records, Bob Barton, The Top Ten Club in Hamburg, the group themselves and "Berksey" had all played their part, but that was all in the past. Backstage in the VIP area people were contentedly relaxing on their deck chairs while enjoying the sun together with a carefree drink. All I wanted to do was run towards them in some crazy or demented manner before screaming "the band are on" in the vain hope of acquiring much needed support and publicity. Unfortunately however, such histrionics were patently impossible.

Meanwhile, up there on stage, their rendition of **Neil Young's** "Southern Man" came up. As the crowd listened in a respectful and awe struck manner, it seemed as if it was tailor made for Terry's voice. Suddenly, Kenny and Arthur came in on harmonies. This song cried out for subtlety together with an expressive lead guitar, giving it the respect such a brilliant song deserved. Realising this, Arthur stepped forward and unleashed a delicate and reverential solo which could be heard above Kenny's instinctive and pulsating rhythm playing. As I continued to watch, the band looked cool and professional reminding me of their halcyon days in Hamburg. At the beautiful and lilting end of the song, the crowd cheered wildly and I began to relax. There was no denying it was a proud moment, knowing that they were my boys up there, tackling the unknown while wholeheartedly and defiantly proving that they were far from being a spent force. Over the previous years I'd been to lots of Reading Festivals as a privileged guest, but this one was certainly proving to be vastly different. As the set progressed, the audience became ever more appreciative and I could tell by their mannerisms that they were gentle and refined, eagerly soaking up the vibes of both the music and the warm rays of the sun. Ironically, it somehow reminded me of a **Van Morrison** concert I'd once promoted at Newcastle City Hall. In fact, I've never forgotten it and it seemed the crowd who had come to experience his wonderful voice had been specially flown in from heaven. I recall how appreciative and well mannered they were as they smiled while listening with a deep and reverential admiration. Peace and love is such a wonderful sentiment which readily conjures up an inner beauty all of its own. Just reading or saying the words conjures up its own beautiful and calming serenity. In reality, it's what we are all looking for and at Reading that afternoon, I was both witnessing and experiencing it. As I continued to watch, there remained a calm and confident assurance about the group's playing. At moments like this, managing a band brings a tremendous satisfaction and exhilaration which is difficult and impossible to quantify. Their performance certainly became an indelibly unique and never to be forgotten memory "That was **Beckett**, give them a big hand," urged **John Peel** (who was the resident DJ) on completion of their set. The unrestrained and lengthy applause continued unabated as I proudly dashed back stage. On seeing me, Terry smiled, his body soaked in sweat, his face a picture of uninhabited happiness. For some reason, I instinctively turned to Arthur as he carefully placed his guitar back into its case. Meticulous as ever, he wasn't looking for or expecting plaudits, just making sure his beloved instrument was safely back where it belonged. "Excellent gig," said Steve Winwood to Terry. Terry looked at him in awe. Here it must be said that there's something about Steve Winwood which sets him apart from other musicians. It's not just his talent or his wonderful impassioned voice. It's also his sincerity which has a naturalness about it and commands great respect from his fellow musicians. **Spencer Davis, Traffic, and Blind Faith** are three of his previous groups whose excellent and expressive songs have unfailingly stood the test of time.

Later at the backstage bar, Pete Erskine said how much he had enjoyed the band. "Thanks." I replied, delighted to receive such a compliment from one of the main feature writers of the New Musical Express. "I'd like to interview them sometime soon, can I have your number and I'll give you a ring?" he requested. As I said earlier, he could be a fearless and harsh critic if he felt a group warranted it while his words meant everything as I began to sense we were finally on our way back. The following week I bought the music press including the NME and Melody Maker. To my great surprise, **John Peel** was a guest writer reviewing the festival and there in startlingly bold letters was his wonderful and unsolicited endorsement of the group's performance. "The best band on up till the Saturday night," it stated. I read it and re-read it as if to reassure myself that it had actually happened. In terms of publicity it was a priceless endorsement and one which I felt the band richly deserved. However, what would the reaction of the record companies be? Would they think likewise and be only too eager to contact me? Over the following days, whenever the telephone rang, I raced to pick it up with an increased air of expectancy. Unfortunately, the hoped for call we desperately needed never came, as I fretted and wrung my hands in exasperation, wondering why. Later that week I realised it was time to strike. The new editions of the music press were due out in a couple of days and I knew that unless I acted promptly, in all probability we would soon be last week's news. Unfortunately, the rock business is like this. It evolves at a fast and unrelenting pace while remaining indifferent to anyone who is failing to sell records or capture headlines. Last week's news. It was a chilling and frightening prospect and not one I wished to dwell on. With indecision and procrastination being its own worst enemy, I decided to ring CBS Records to extol the virtues of the band's startling success at Reading. Having done so, I was invited in for a chat at their head office where I was later to learn that Alan Bown the ex lead singer who worked for them in A&R had already seen and recommended the group. Previous experience had taught me that having entered a record company meeting of this nature, it is most important to convey a deeply held conviction to the person sitting on the other side of the desk that it would be catastrophic if they failed to sign the band you represent. Having successfully instilled this fear, it is time to attack. To falter at any reservations he may express about signing them is tantamount to abject failure. In employing these tactics, there is real pressure knowing the group desperately need that record contract while the record company won't have any sleepless nights if they decide to turn them down. Nevertheless, despite your own innermost fears, it is important to stay outwardly strong as you owe it to your protégés as well as yourself.

A few days later I was invited into a meeting with Paul Russell, a qualified lawyer who was head of A&R ("artistes and repertoire," or talent scout) at CBS Records in London. "I've had some good reports on the band," he began. I smiled approvingly having recognised that it was a good start while being fully aware that tactically, it was important for him not to appear too keen. On the other hand, I was also aware that if he failed to show a reasonable degree of enthusiasm, there was always the possibility that I might go elsewhere. Conversely, and this is the tricky bit, if I appeared overwhelmingly desperate to sign, the terms and royalty rate could suffer. "Would you like a coffee?" he asked. I immediately recognised this was a good sign and meant I wasn't being hurried out. "Yes please," I replied as I noticed how confident and assured he looked, having every right to be. After all, he held the purse strings and if he didn't like what he heard, he would still receive his pay cheque at the end of the month. After a short while, at what I thought was the optimum moment, I placed the opened Melody Maker on his desk and enthusiastically pointed to **John Peel's** article. Have you read this?" I inquired. "No, I haven't" he replied. I paused before allowing him to read it and having done so, sensed the power base was beginning to move in my direction.

In many ways, his office was like a courtroom. Sitting in front of me was an experienced company lawyer and at times, I felt I was in the dock as he fired a series of searching questions at me from across his polished wooden desk. "What sort of terms for the group are you thinking of?" he questioned. It was now time to be positive. "£10,000, and a ten per cent escalating royalty rate depending on sales," I replied. After a series of further questions, he finally agreed and was about to shake hands. Oh! there's one other thing," I casually informed him. "What is it?" he inquired. "We desperately need a decent car to travel in. Surely CBS must have a reliable spare company one lying around somewhere." His body stiffened, and his face reddened as he leant forward before pressing an intercom button. Within seconds, a younger colleague of his entered. "Have you heard what this manager wants?" he inquired. "He thinks we're a garage. Will you tell him that we're a record company and he's got his wires badly crossed?" His friend immediately laughed in a highly dismissive and disparaging manner which was clearly intended to humiliate and crush any last vestiges of my confidence. However, unknown to them, I looked and felt a certain pity towards him and his outlook on life. Had it reduced him to being merely a grovelling sycophantic mentor of his boss who curried favour by concurring with everything he said, no matter how ridiculous or inappropriate the suggestion? I wondered. I took a deep breath knowing that two powerful record company executives ridiculing me while openly chuckling or guffawing to each other was an obvious tactic to shame me into an abject and fearful submission.

However, unknown to them, I was determined to remain strong, resolute, and unabashed. As I have previously explained in an earlier chapter, I knew the importance of getting a group to its gigs fresh. If they set off in a much slower van as opposed to a car, it could add tiresome hours to their journey, ultimately reflecting itself in that night's stage performance. The room fell silent as I continued to dig my heels in. I then strongly and unerringly outlined the above reasons why it was such an important item. "Get me a car and then we'll sign," I assured them. "Okay, but only if we get your song publishing rights as well," interjected Paul Russell. For a moment, I hesitated before speaking. "The group's publishing is already signed to Lionel Conway at Island Records. Let me have a word with him and I'll see what I can do," I prompted. The following day I was in Lionel's office in Oxford St to find Carl Wayne of **The Move** sitting in reception. I couldn't help remembering their hit songs, all of which had been on the jukebox in my earlier days at the Bay Hotel. "I Can Hear the Grass Grow," "Flowers in the Rain," "Blackberry Way," and "Fire Brigade," all had an immediacy while not being too highbrow or overstated. I sneaked a second glance, having never previously met him. Suddenly, his eye caught mine. I may have blushed slightly knowing it was bad manners to stare as I quickly turned away. In reality I had just wanted to shake his hand in order to tell him how much everyone at The Bay had enjoyed his group's music. Unfortunately, it was not to be and now that he is no longer with us, I have always regretted not doing so

Moments later, I was ushered into Lionel's office. After a quick exchange of pleasantries, I got straight to the point. "Lionel, I need a really big favour." The man who had once worked for Dick James Music and had first signed **The Beatles** to a song publishing deal, looked at my imploring face. He'd also once managed an unknown **Elton John** in his earlier days and I'd been one of the few people to agree to book him for £50 when Lionel was desperate to find him gigs. Ironically, only a few weeks earlier, I'd eagerly accepted a cheque for £3,000 from him and now I was hoping to rescind the deal.

"Lionel, if I get you the full amount of the money back, will you agree to release us from the contract?" I requested in an imploring voice laced with a mixture of humility and serious concern. "If you do, CBS have promised to sign us to major record deal and will provide the group with a suitable car to travel in. They will also send the cheque over to you immediately we sign for them," I assured him with as much sincerity as I could muster. Fortuitously, Lionel also managed The Island Record Company football team for which I played at the time and felt I always gave 100%. I also knew he was a really nice chap who had never done an underhand deal to anyone in his life. Anyone else may have possibly become enraged, but fortunately, his human and caring side immediately surfaced. He listened and pondered, while his face remained concerned and friendly. Somehow, I could sense he wanted us to have that car, especially as he was the man who had first recommended the group to play at the Marquee in front of Warner Bros executives. "Okay, if it helps you, I'll do it," he assured me. On hearing his words I heaved a huge sigh of relief and broke into a broad smile. "Thanks Lionel," I replied with as much gratitude as was humanly possible to convey. It was an emotional moment as I sensed the group were about to be thrust into the excitement and maelstrom of a third major record contract.

Forty-eight hours later I was back in Paul Russell's office and immediately informed him that we were now free to sign for song publishing as well. Okay, give me a few days and I'll see what I can do about the car," he replied. A few days later, as instructed, I called in to see him. "I've got you a nice Austin 3 litre executive car, how does that sound?" he asked. "Sounds smashing," I replied. "But have you insured the group to drive it?" I inquired. At the other side of the desk, he went ballistic. "Are you crazy," he shouted. "We've got you a car and now you expect us to insure it as well." Here, please allow me to explain the logic of why it was so important. Trying to insure a young pop group to drive a car with fully comprehensive insurance at the time was horrendously expensive, if not near impossible, especially if you wanted to insert an any driver clause. However, I knew that CBS Records with its huge fleet of rep cars could easily bury it in their annual insurance policy. Having explained all this to him, he finally saw the sense of it and relented. I liked Paul Russell. He was a tough negotiator who for some reason didn't fit the archetypal image of a lawyer. His dark curly hair on top of a reddened face (which appeared slightly weather beaten) hid a worried look, which seemed to be a permanent feature of his quiet demeanour. Nevertheless, I found him very friendly, that is, until some unforeseen difficulties arose. Days later, having completed the official signing, the group were now up and running and looking forward to the huge challenge which lay ahead. Around a month later, the telephone rang as I settled comfortably into my flat in Sunderland. "Geoff, Arthur here." "We're at Norwich University for tonight's gig but Terry and Kenny haven't turned up. We left them at the CBS Studios in Whitfield St, London and travelled down in the Mercedes van. They said they wanted to stay behind to mix the tapes and would follow us later in the car but haven't arrived. We are due on stage in a few minutes and the social sectary is becoming very concerned. I'll put him on because he wants to speak to you." "Hi, I'm the social secretary. Where are your other band members?" he inquired. "I don't know, but they should be there any time now," I assured him. After replacing the receiver, twenty minutes later, it rang again. "Your other two band members still haven't arrived. It's too late, now even if they do," he informed me in an irate and disillusioned manner. Crestfallen, I apologised and immediately offered him a free date in the future. "No thanks," he replied with an unqualified disdain before putting Arthur back on. "Geoff, we may as well set off for home now as there's nothing we can do. We just about have enough money for petrol," he said. Next morning, I was still furious. Prestigious university gigs were extremely hard to come by and the loss of the much needed £100 fee only added to my frustration. Terry and Kenny never did make it and instead, had taken it upon themselves to stay and mix the album tapes in the studio. Two days later I called a group meeting with all its members present. I glowered at Kenny and Terry as my deep anger and frustration knew no bounds. Managing the group had proved to be a long and tortuous journey as well as a costly one and I now felt it was time to get everything off my chest. "I'm leaving," I hurriedly informed them with a certain degree of bitterness and sadness. In doing so, there was no great histrionics or threats, just a cool determination to extricate myself from the disillusionment and frustration of it all. "Why?" asked one of them in a somewhat surprised and quizzical manner. "These two have just made my signature meaningless," I pointed out while at the same time nodding towards the two offenders. "From now on, if I ever sign another contract people will just ignore it and say it doesn't mean a thing. In effect, you have completely destroyed the credibility of myself and my signature. Also, we desperately needed the money to keep our heads above water. We can't keep relying on the advance or it won't last two minutes," I pointed out in a frustrated and angst-ridden voice. The room fell silent as I awaited their reaction and was soon to find that none was forthcoming and I was deeply hurt. The next day, from their £10,000 advance I withdrew £3,000 and transferred it into my own personal account knowing I had still lost many thousands of pounds but wasn't complaining as that was the risk I had taken. A few days later, with a sad and heavy heart, I went in to see Paul Russell and reluctantly informed him of what had taken place. Here, it must be said that in any walk of life you have to be prepared to take the rough with the smooth and I fully realised his anger would know no bounds. Nevertheless, I knew it was my duty to turn up and personally face his wrath, no matter how savage or vitriolic it might be. On hearing I was leaving his face became ashen with disbelief knowing it was I who had first talked him into signing the band. Inwardly I winced on recalling how he had obtained superb transport, insured it for them, and given them a nice tidy advance. To say he was fuming would be an understatement of gross proportions as I looked down at the floor, feeling wholeheartedly ashamed and disgraced. However, despite this, underneath it all I held a deep conviction that I was doing the right thing. "So you're leaving us holding the baby." His angry and savage words were deeply cutting as he paused for them to register. This was to become one of my worst moments in rock. All the previous enthusiasm and energy on signing had now dissipated into a morass of hand wringing misery and it appeared to any outsider that I was its main architect. I thought of all those years of night-time drives through the snow, the cold dressing rooms, the endless arguments, and the seeming futility of it all. How could he possibly understand as I sat there with head bowed, determined to leave with some semblance of dignity and pride, no matter how readily it would be ridiculed or misconstrued. As I sat there, unknown to him, I was too afraid to reveal that the beautiful car he had provided was, at that very moment, sitting in a garage with a seized engine. "What's wrong?" I had asked the mechanic. "The engine is bone dry, there's not a drop of oil in it. Whoever's been using it has just recklessly run it into the ground," he informed me. As I walked away, I looked at its sleek paint work and cream leather seats and could have cried. This had been the straw that had finally broken the camel's back, or in this case, my very own.

A few weeks later, time being a great healer, in a reckless moment of foolhardiness, and without the group even asking, I decided to return and manage them. Why, I will never really know. In reality, perhaps it was a deep and burning desire of not wishing to be beaten, having sensed that if everyone pulled together, there was still an outside chance of making it. Having rejoined, the first task was to get the group mobile so they could once again tackle gigs throughout the country. After a quick search, I located a tidy looking Triumph 2,000 saloon at a cost of £750 and immediately bought it. The following day I breezed into Annabel's nightclub and happily informed the drummer of what I had done. "What make is it?" he inquired. "A Triumph 2,000," I replied. "Well I'm not travelling in it because we wanted a Volvo," he coolly informed me. I looked at him with a mixture of anger, frustration and incredulity. The reality was the group had yet to sell a record and it hadn't been too long since he had joined, yet here he was making demands which were patently and clearly unacceptable. At that moment, I thought back to when I'd had a short stint as a railway porter after leaving the Fleet Air Arm.. The trains arrived, you carried the passengers' luggage or loaded the mailbags, and at least got some thanks and appreciation. At the time, I had thought it wasn't a worthwhile job, but suddenly, I was beginning to realise just how wrong I had been. "So you don't want to travel in it?" I asked. "No, I don't," he replied. "Okay, you're sacked," I angrily informed him. Within minutes, another band member appeared who was a friend of his. "If he goes, I go too," he warned. It was a chastening moment, knowing that to replace two band members at such short notice seemed highly impractical as well as foolhardy. Three days later in an effort to unblock the impasse that had been imposed upon me, together with a desire to stabilise the situation, I reluctantly swallowed my pride and reinstated him. The fact that later he grudgingly agreed to travel in the car seemed a pyrrhic and unsatisfactory victory. A few more weeks quickly passed and I found I could no longer sustain my hard pressed efforts and left the group for the last time. In doing so the money, enthusiasm and the will to win had all dissipated into a frustrating and futile attempt to salvage something from the wreckage. Here, it must be pointed out that hurt pride of this nature can be very wounding. It carries with it scars which are not readily healed, as well as succeeding in destroying any last vestiges of self confidence. Also, the stigma of failure can be unnerving, debilitating, and as infectious as any known illness, or at least it seems that way. Meanwhile, a feeling of worthlessness and uncertainty soon begins to enter into every thought, rendering them meaningless and devoid of compassion. The well had run dry as nerves had become irreparably frayed. Fortunately, however belatedly, common sense had finally empowered me to act on realising those goals which had proved to be so tantalisingly out of reach had drained the last vestiges of energy from my once unstinting and wholehearted enthusiasm.

Fortunately, despite the heartache, there were certain compensations. With the unburdening of the responsibility of having to worry about five individuals, the shoulders felt unencumbered while the regrets and overwhelming dissatisfaction had left deep scars. Oscar Wilde is quoted as saying that failure is often passed off as experience. In that context, I had irrefutably gained what could be classed as an immense surfeit of it. Meanwhile, and thankfully, the incoming bills from the group had ceased as had the seemingly pointless disagreements, accommodation squabbles, and petty worries. Later a passing acquaintance smiled and said hello. In doing I sensed there was no ulterior motive, it was just the kindness of his thoughts which at a moment like this can be priceless. Fortunately, in the fullness of time, my spirits began to recover and life began to redeem itself as my new found freedom looked for new and more challenging outlets. In the context of rock management, I was now a little more enlightened as well as a lot more cautious. Ironically, I had also learnt an invaluable lesson about the weaknesses and frailties of human behaviour. Having spent over six years in the Fleet Air Arm and travelled all over the world on the aircraft carrier Ark Royal, I had been under the mistaken impression that I was worldly wise, as well as streetwise. Unfortunately, this naïve illusion had been irrevocably and wholeheartedly shattered. Next time, I promised myself I wouldn't make the same mistakes again. However, was there to be a next time? There certainly was. Meanwhile, **Beckett** still had a record contract and set about finding a new manager. Unfortunately, their search proved to be of no avail and months later, they were dropped from the record label without their second album ever being completed.

A few months passed and on visiting London, I called in to see Paul Kossoff the lead guitarist of **Free**, who had played on their world-wide hit, "All Right Now." Paul and I had become good friends from his earliest days in the band which I had been fortunate enough to promote on many occasions. I was also aware he lived in a small mews in Ladbroke Grove, London where I found him in a deep and serious drug induced stupor. To see a young, lovable human being in such a state is heartrending as well as highly emotional. Not being his legal guardian, I was uncertain about what to do as I wondered how I could possibly help. Knowing that seven previous stays in hospital had already failed, (all paid for by his father David), I continued to ponder the dilemma facing me. Suddenly, there was a knock at the door. I watched, as Sandy, his girlfriend shook him vigorously whereupon he literally crawled across the floor in a semi comatose state before recklessly signing a cheque which he handed to a dealer. I immediately noticed his eyes were rolling and he seemed incapable of discerning reality from fiction. Instinctively I smelt danger, as Sandy looked at me with a resigned look of helplessness written across her face. I thought back to first meeting him at The Bay Hotel in Sunderland when he had just come off stage. His cheeky smile, accompanied by a twinkle in his eye after an ecstatic crowd had begged for more, had proved to be an unforgettable experience. That night, it was clearly apparent that he and his group were on the ascendancy and were capable of achieving much greater things. Everyone could sense it and sure enough, it wasn't long before it became a reality. The live album **Free** had recorded at The Fillmore North in Sunderland also came to mind as did many other superb gigs. Now, here he was lying helpless, having slumped back into unconsciousness. Meanwhile, I watched and waited, still uncertain of what to do. I glanced around the room and noticed his trusty Les Paul guitar standing proudly in the corner. However, it was no ordinary guitar and I knew that only Paul could coax his own unique and blistering sound from it. Unfortunately, it appeared to be sad and lonely as if we both recognised its master was unwell and may never be able to play it again. It was a devastating thought as I decided to take immediate action, knowing that while lying there, he was no longer a star, but a human being in desperate need of help. I stepped outside and reached a telephone kiosk, before speaking to his beloved dad. "It's pretty serious. If something isn't done soon, I fear the worst," I informed him with words which sounded both desperate and highly emotional. "Let me take him up to my flat in Sunderland. There are no drug dealers knocking on my door," I assured him with a conviction which needed no second telling. To his credit he listened with great concern as well as alarm and sensed I only wanted to help. "Alright, if you seriously think you can help him, go ahead. But please be careful," he warned. His caring and loving words were underpinned with a deep sadness which I found highly emotional. Right then, I realised he wasn't a famous British film star, but a despondent and desperate father. Replacing the receiver, I stepped outside the kiosk in order to think. What had I done and could I achieve what seven previous stays in hospital had failed to do? One thing was certain. If I couldn't, it wouldn't be for the want of trying. Hours later, I tried to speak to Paul but he just looked at me with rolling eyes which failed to respond. Gently, I led him to the **Beckett's** Mercedes van and sat him between two of its members for the long trip north. Nobody spoke. It was as if he was being given the last rights, but I had other ideas, knowing human life is far too precious to be taken lightly, especially if there is a deep conviction that you can help.

Having reached my flat after a long journey, I quickly set about my task. The first two days proved to be highly fraught, difficult, and worrying. A human being whose life is in the balance is a daunting prospect as well as a grave responsibility. However, deep down, I reasoned that once his supply of damaging and potentially fatal drugs was cut off, the youthfulness and suppleness of his body might just respond. At first, I set about my task by encouraging him to eat small morsels of good healthy food while breathing the nearby fresh sea air through a partially open window, together with some gentle exercise such as walking. I prayed and thought of mother nature in the full knowledge that everything else had failed and it was his and my only hope. Fortunately, I had always striven to eat healthily and had a reasonable knowledge of how the body worked; and its response if treated kindly. The fact that I had often enjoyed the delights of nature, while walking along our magnificent coastline and the nearby Mowbray Park, with its beautiful blossoming flowers, always seemed to soothe a worried or despondent frown. Within time, I hoped to introduce Paul to the same therapeutic delights in order to hasten the healing processes of his seriously drug ravaged and listless body. Having been gently introduced to this new and daily regime of nutritious food and rehabilitation for three months, far from being a helpless like baby, he was now fit and well. It had proved to be a remarkable transformation and it seemed all my prayers and hopes had been answered. One day he looked at me and smiled. His loving mother had just made her daily telephone call to speak to him and each time I could sense the immense joy in her heart. I smiled back. There was a deep inner satisfaction at having brought him from the brink of impending death and this was to prove a vindication of everything I believed in. One night, we both eagerly watched "Top of the Pops." Suddenly, he craned his neck forward as he took it all in and I sensed it had ignited an energising spark within him. From then on in, he became restless while looking for an outlet for his new found enthusiasm. Not long afterwards, unrestrained and full of renewed vigour, he asked me to help him to form a new band in order to allow him to return to what he loved best, playing his beloved guitar. I thought long and hard. I recognised there would be no long struggle for a record contract, or lack of prestigious gigs as he was already a well known name and I started to become excited. A further two months slipped by and after deciding to invite John Glover (the ex manager of **Free)** to become co manager, we were up and running. (This difficult period is explained in greater in detail in my first book, **"A Promoter's Tale,"**) Days later, Terry had joined the band with Graham Bryson (ex **Spooky Tooth**) on drums and Jim Wily on bass. Each night they would rehearse in secret at the Sunderland Bowling Alley starting at midnight. This was at Paul's request as he said this was when he felt truly inspired. Within hours, the band began to gel and I sensed the portents were truly awe inspiring. Within weeks, and unknown to anyone, I had a band who sounded positively inspirational. Knowing this, I rang Johnny Glover and informed him of what I regarded as one of the best kept secrets in rock. My plan had been to keep it that way until all the City Halls throughout the country had been booked. Then, and only then, would the news be released to the press knowing the group would get substantial press coverage. Unfortunately, Johnny Glover immediately invited Paul to stay at his house in Reading, before informing the press that Paul was fit and well and had formed a new band. This was all done without consulting me, and sure enough, Paul and the group (**Back St Crawler**) received full page coverage in a number of music press articles. Once back in London, at Paul's insistence, John Bundrick ("Rabbit," later to join **The Who**) joined on keyboards and quickly became the main songwriter. Rehearsals came thick and fast as I quietly and patiently listened for a song which stood out and could possibly become a hit. Here, it must be pointed out that meaningful album tracks coupled with integrity and credibility are wonderful things to listen to and possess. But unlike the earlier days when it was regarded as "selling out," a hit single had not only become desirable, but in order to get the band off the ground, was a virtual necessity. Meanwhile, time was passing by and as an experienced promoter, I realised the press should never have been alerted until the group were ready to start their first major tour. Then, the press coverage would have been positively invaluable in order to fill seats. A few days later I was introduced to a colleague of John and told he was also to be a co-manager of the band. Suddenly, I now found I was a co co manager and felt the situation was rapidly becoming farcical. Thinking about it retrospectively, "creativity" is a word which appears to constantly crop up, signalling an underlying talent and ability. But what exactly does it mean in the context of a rock band? After all, a group can't just spit out hit singles on request, unless of course you are **The Beatles** and no one expected Paul's new and recently formed group to do so. Nevertheless, idly waiting and watching from the wings was proving to be an extremely frustrating time. I was already aware that stage presence and excitement are certainly prime requisites for any group hoping to be a successful rock band. Fail to possess these, and unfortunately, a sense of apathy soon becomes apparent to a watching crowd. At rehearsals, I could sense something was wrong and that the collective talents of the group had failed to fuse into a balanced and cohesive unit. It was particularly noticeable that the songs lacked sparkle, while Paul's guitar playing was devoid of its once inspiring intensity. Unfortunately it seemed his very presence was unable to carry the group. Earlier, Johnny Glover had obtained a huge advance from Atlantic Records on the strength of Paul's and Terry's name. The figure in 1976 was £200,000 which is about the equivalent of well over one million by today's standards. Meanwhile I soon began to have deep reservations about the band and couldn't help feeling the money was merely serving to paper over the cracks. At rehearsals, I watched and held my breath, fully aware of the proverb, "a wise head keeps a silent tongue." Conversely, only a weak or frightened individual remains silent if he senses the portents of imminent disaster are blatantly staring him in the face. However, in the interests of diplomacy, I decided it would be prudent to remain sitting on the fence knowing full well that in many ways it was a form of cowardice or a lack of inner confidence. In reality there appeared to be no other option as spirits were sky high, money wasn't a problem, and the expectations of the group were at a premium. Only the fullness of time, together with the fans reaction would reveal the final outcome. All I could do was watch and wait in the wings.

Soon, it was time to start their first major tour which had been booked to correspond with the release of the group's first album. After lukewarm reviews and a disastrous tour in which most of the City Halls were more than half empty, we arrived at London's Lyceum Ballroom for the final date. It was mid-afternoon as I walked in to see a multitude of roadies and lightning technicians hovering around the stage. What I saw immediately made me realise that the set up was wrong. In those days, PA systems were extremely heavy and cumbersome, often reaching as high as seven or eight feet. Unfortunately, after the crew had positioned the PA onstage, the lightning system had been placed on its outside. The end result was

The 50,000 ton
Ark Royal, on which
I served for two and
a half years,
entering harbour.

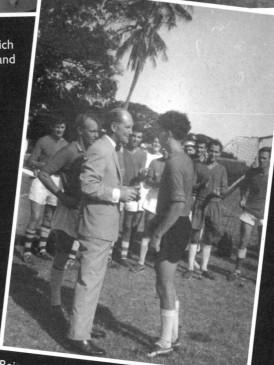

Being presented with the winners cup in
Mombasa by Captain Pollock of the Ark Royal.

DICK JAMES MUSIC LIMITED

NEW YORK
PARIS
SYDNEY
STOCKHOLM

JAMES HOUSE, 71-75 NEW OXFORD STREET, LONDON, W.C.1
TELEPHONE: 01-836 4864 (5 LINES)   CABLES: DEJAMUS, LONDON, W.C.1
DIRECTOR   RICHARD L. JAMES   TELEX: 27135 (DEJAMUS, LONDON)

LC/MC

Jeff Docherty, Esq.,
Bay Hotel,
Whitburn,
nr. Sunderland,   11th October 1968
Durham.

Dear Jeff,

    This is to confirm that the Plastic Penny will
play at The Bay Hotel on Thursday 14th November at the
fee mentioned.

    I will speak to you soon.

    With all good wishes.

Yours sincerely,

LIONEL CONWAY

NORTHERN SONGS LIMITED   MANAGERS FOR
MARIBUS MUSIC LIMITED   METRO MUSIC LIMITED   GRALTO MUSIC LIMITED
                  PAGE ONE RECORDS LIMITED

Bay Hotel — Tonight

★

FAMILY

★   ★

7-12 — Pay at Door 10'6

BAY HOTEL TONIGHT

PRESENTS TOP STARS

PINK FLOYD

7 till Midnight :: Admission 7/6

Plastic Penny charted at
No. 6 with the single
'Everything I am' in 1968.

DISC·O·CHAT

DICK JAMES ORGANISATION   Date:

NEW

PLASTIC   PENNY

CASHBOX

PLASTIC PENNY (Page One 21005)

YOUR WAY TO TELL ME GO (2:39) (Dick James, BMI-Raymond, Murray)

On first listen, this is one of many fine rock efforts
that could crack the best seller ranks; but after a second
and third spin the side takes off all the way in a blistering
beat ballad that carries instrumental and rhythmic excitement
as well as a teen lyric that should make it a top forty break-
out side. Flip: "Baby You're Not To Blame" (2:38) (Same credits)

DICK JAMES MUSIC LIMITED
71-75, New Oxford Street, London, W.C.1
01-836 4864 (5 Lines)

From The Office Of:-
LIONEL CONWAY

TWO MEMBERS OF DEEP
PURPLE IN EPISODE SIX

Bay Hotel TONIGHT

(BALLROOM DISCOTHEQUE NOW OPEN)
Top Recording Stars

EPISODE SIX

All Ages Welcome. 7-Midnight. Admission 3/6.

Bay Hotel THIS MONDAY

Personal appearance of

JOHN PEEL

playing his own selection of L.P.'s   PLUS

VAN DER GRAAF GENERATOR

PLUS

BLACK SABBATH

6 hours non-stop entertainment. ALL AGES WELCOME
Special early start 6-Midnight.   6/6 Adm. 6/6

Clockwise: Mick Grabham, Tony Murray, Paul Raymond & Nigel
Olsson who is now playing drums with Elton John.

Letter received from Dave Stewart after reading 'A Promoter's Tale'.

DAVE STEWART

Dear Geoff,
        I would like to congratulate you on your accurate and highly interesting account of being at the forefront of Live Music in the North of England during that crazy period. I read your book over Xmas again and it brought back fond memories of the "Bay Hotel" gigs and sleeping on the beach at seaburn head swimming with music and the possibility of adventure into the crazy world of Rock + Roll!
        I would love to see a screenplay of your story it would be a cool film
                        love Dave Stewart
P.S. Did you see "Almost Famous"

Dave Stewart has agreed to become music consultant should a film of my original book be made.

Bay Hotel — Tonight
SPECIAL LATE DANCE—LATE BAR
TYRANNOSAURUS REX
★   *Free*   ★
THIS YEARS GIRL
7—1 A.M. PAY AT DOOR 12/6

TYRANNOSAURUS REX

This Years Girl

BAY HOTEL—Tonight

PERSONAL APPEARANCE OF

JOHN PEEL

PLUS

SPIRIT OF JOHN MORGAN

PLUS THE MUSIC OF

JAN DUKES DE-GRAY

6 — Midnight   ::   Admission 6/-

::

★ MONDAY, MARCH 17th — SPOOKY TOOTH ★

★ **LOCARNO** ★

FRIDAY, 23rd MARCH

FILLMORE NORTH PRESENTS

ROD STEWART and THE FACES

ALSO

BECKETT

Guest D.J.   John Peel

LATE BARS TILL 2 a.m.   Commences 7.30 p.m.
Tickets 75p. On sale Sphning Disk, Olive Street,
and Locarno

Faces, Faces everywhere, at least they were in 1973 for John Peel

BEST

THE FACES, SUNDERLAND, 1973

IT WAS the night Sunderland beat Arsenal in the semi-final of the Cup the year they went on to win it. The Faces were always wonderful live anyway and in Sunderland on a night like that... I mean, the entire place was in a state of near-hysteria anyway and The Faces were the perfect band for that. I actually ended up dancing onstage and I'm a man who doesn't dance at all!

On their rider, they had about a crate of Blue Nun so we were each issued with several bottles and a riotous time was had by all.

And obviously The Faces came on hours late as they always did and started kicking footballs into the audience. The combination of football and music came together in a unique conjunction that night.

PICTURE: GARY MERRIN

John Peel
describes his
best gig.

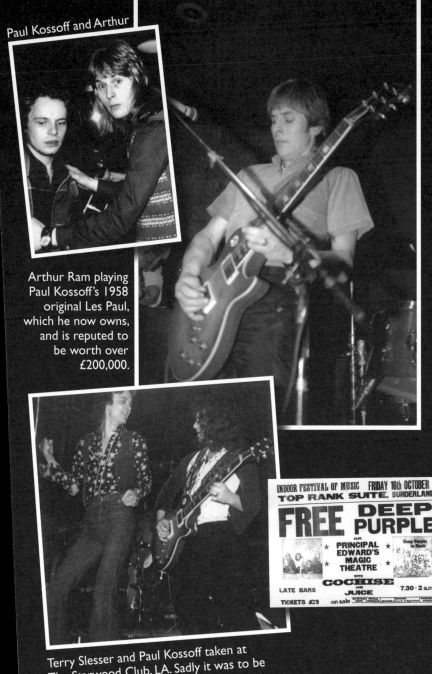

Paul Kossoff and Arthur

Arthur Ram playing Paul Kossoff's 1958 original Les Paul, which he now owns, and is reputed to be worth over £200,000.

INDOOR FESTIVAL OF MUSIC   FRIDAY 16th OCTOBER
TOP RANK SUITE, SUNDERLAND

FREE   DEEP PURPLE

ALSO

PRINCIPAL EDWARD'S MAGIC THEATRE

WITH

COCHISE

AND

JUICE

LATE BARS

TICKETS £1   on sale

7.30 · 2 a.m.

Terry Slesser and Paul Kossoff taken at The Starwood Club, LA. Sadly it was to be Paul's last ever gig.

Celebrity wedding: Geoff, far left, complete with the hairstyle of the era, was a guest at the wedding of Procol Harum's Mickey Grabham in the 70s. Also pictured are Ray Fenwick, far right, of The Spencer Davis Group and Rick Wills (back row, 4th from right) of Foreigner and Roxy Music.

MAYFAIR - FRIDAY, 7 AUG.

DEREK AND THE DOMINOS

FEATURING

ERIC CLAPTON

BOBBY WHITLOCK

CARL RADLE

JIM GORDON

ALSO

WRITING ON THE WALL

TOP RANK SUITE · FRIDAY 7th MAY

(SUNDERLAND)

A FILLMORE NORTH PROMOTION

THE WHO

LATE BARS   LATE TRANSPORT
8-1a.m.   NO DRESS RESTRICTIONS

TICKETS 50p! YES ... ONLY 50p

On sale | BERGS | SAVILLE'S | DISQUE (Newcastle)

50P TICKETS 50P

Dead Pan Joy

Well Well Well pictured on stage at The Marquee.

Paul Rodgers on stage at The Newcastle Arena with Queen, 2008.

Geoff and Paul Rodgers back stage at The Newcastle Arena where Paul was performing with Queen, 2008.

Geoff reunited with Simon Kirke of Free.

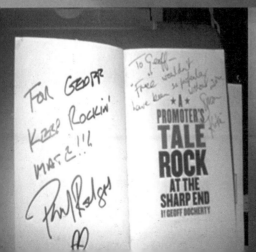

FOR GEOFF
KEEP ROCKIN'
MATE!!!

Paul Rodgers

To Geoff—
"Free wouldn't have been so popular without you"
Simon Kirke

A PROMOTER'S TALE
ROCK
AT THE SHARP END
BY GEOFF DOCHERTY

Geoff presented with Paul Rodgers and Simon Kirke's autographed version of

"A Promoters Tale"

that as the light shone across the stage, the high PA partially blocked it, leaving the centre of the stage in semi darkness. I looked at both sets of road crews and swallowed hard, knowing they looked weary after their long drive and that moving heavy equipment is never easy at the best of times. Nevertheless, as a manager, I knew how vitally important it was for the lead singer to be seen as well as heard. I approached the stage with a heavy heart in the full knowledge that I would receive a highly unwelcome reaction. "I'm sorry chaps, but you'll have to swap the equipment around. The centre of the stage is too dark," I pointed out with as much conviction as I could muster. To a man they looked at me with a horror-struck expression while the shock of what I had said seemed to have frozen them with disbelief. "The follow spotlight will soon light him up," replied one of them. I immediately thought back to the proverb "a lazy person will always find the easiest way," but knew it didn't necessarily mean it was the right way. I smiled, having always admired people who possess a self belief in what they do as well as being prepared to stand their ground. A self satisfied, almost triumphant grin immediately spread across his face as the others gave him an appreciative glance and I could sense their relief at such an astute reply. Unruffled, I pointed out that there was definitely a problem and it needed to be resolved. I further pointed out that as the group had two other backing singers and there was only one follow spot available, the whole of the stage needed to be lit, otherwise it would look ridiculous as well as highly unprofessional. "We're not moving it. That's where we were told to put it when we arrived and that's where it stays," he protested vehemently. I looked at him and felt his words sounded sincere and I firmly believed him, but it still didn't solve the problem. Whoever had given him instructions to place it there had obviously blundered, or was patently incapable of realising how important it actually was. I paused, knowing I had to think fast. This was a prestigious London gig and once Terry stepped onto the stage, it would become more than obvious that something was amiss. In a calculated gamble, I spoke out. "If you don't move it, we'll refuse to pay you," I threatened. They immediately jumped up with a look of alarm and consternation written across their faces and for a moment I sensed there might be trouble. Fortunately however, despite it being a grossly inflammatory statement, after a further discussion, they finally relented before agreeing to rearrange everything into its correct position. Meanwhile, I was worried as I was already harbouring grave doubts about the band's ability to write some decent songs. "Where's my supposed co manager?" I thought. I seem to be the one taking all the flack and could have done with some moral support. Accompanying these feelings was a deep unhappiness at the lack of excitement at their gigs during the previous dates. Was I being impatient or failing to spot their future potential you may well ask? It's an accusation that can be levelled at any manager and I was fully aware of this. However, during the tour, each night I had looked at and noted the audience reaction. In reality, they were the true judges and their response was proving to be extremely lukewarm while it seemed the group were aimlessly soldiering on and hoping it would all come right in the end. Unfortunately, I couldn't see it and was rapidly becoming disillusioned. A few hours later the band was up on stage and playing their hearts out. The material is still weak I thought to myself. Although the songs were well played, they sounded average and lacked any underlying zest or passion. I'd previously been fortunate enough to have promoted **The Who** on four occasions and had been privileged to witness the sheer spectacle of their enthralling and unforgettable gigs. I had also promoted **Led Zeppelin** three times in one year**, Deep Purple, Rod Stewart & The Faces** on four occasions**,** and then there was **Free.** Yet, with **"Back Street Crawler,"** it seemed something was sadly lacking as there was no spark or spontaneity. The longer the group played, the more I became convinced that my earlier doubts meant a long and unequal struggle lay ahead. But where would it all end? I wondered. At some point, someone somewhere had to accept that among the euphoria of signing a mega record deal, failure was a distinct possibility. It may have been just around the corner, it may have been delayed, but to me, it seemed unmercifully inevitable.

When touring with a group, you inevitably become close friends while confiding in each other and possessing the same hopes, aspirations and heady dreams. Occasionally, in an effort to relieve the tension, someone cracks a joke and everyone laughs. But this tour was proving to be no laughing matter as it had been a disaster, both financially and attendance wise. Once up on stage at The

Lyceum, I glanced at the crowd having realised Paul Kossoff and "Rabbit" seemed unconcerned as they steadfastly played on. Tony Braunagel on drums, (later to play with **Bette Middler, Johnny Nash, Taj Mahal** and currently **Robert Cray)** was undoubtedly a superb drummer who never missed a beat, while Terry sang his heart out. As always, an excellent vocalist singing mediocre or lacklustre songs is far from entertaining. As I shuffled my lifeless feet in an effort relieve the tedium, my mind began to wander and there was a certain sadness at witnessing such an unwholesome, uninspiring and monotonous spectacle. Watching the group that night, the famous playwright George Bernard Shaw's alleged quote came to mind. A beautiful young girl he had once met suggested that they have a baby together. "It will have my looks and your brains. It will be a beautiful baby," she had excitedly enthused. "What about if it has my looks and your brains?" was his disarmingly honest riposte. This seemed to encapsulate everything that was wrong with the group. Despite being highly talented, it appeared the sum of the parts didn't have the spell binding magic that everyone had envisaged when they first formed. In reality, Atlantic Records had paid out the huge advance on the strength of Paul Kossoff's name and Terry's previous association with **Beckett**. "That singer is a potential superstar." I recalled Ahmet Ertegun's words after seeing Terry perform at London's Marquee Club. This unsolicited endorsement was from no less a person than someone who had signed **The Rolling Stones, Led Zeppelin, Yes, AC/DC** and a whole myriad of major soul and jazz legends before taking them to international stardom. Knowing this, he had to be taken seriously. However, could he be wrong, or had he made a monumental error of judgement where **Back St Crawler** was concerned? It certainly seemed so, but no one seemed the slightest bit perturbed, despite such compelling evidence.

The Lyceum Ballroom in The Strand. How the memories come back. I'd sat on the floor along with hundreds of others and watched some excellent groups at The Midnight Court held there every Sunday Evening. **Edgar Broughton** and **The Nice** came to mind. "Out Demons Out" was Edgar's famous war cry and how we loved them. Now, I found myself in the dressing room of the very theatre where the Miss World contest was once held while being shown to millions of people throughout the world on TV. My imagination began to run wild at the thought on realising that being backstage with the contestants certainly seemed a more thrilling prospect than being with the group. Wishful thinking, dreams, or even fantasy quickly began racing through my mind. If only I was the golden haired vocalist Robert Plant, the world's most beautiful girls may have seen me in a different light and would surely have come running. Unfortunately, fantasy and reality are worlds apart while the disturbing picture of an unimpressive group rapidly unfolding before everyone's eyes had to be faced. After the gig, the group and I retired to their rented flat in Earls Court. Unknown to them, I felt uncomfortable, not that they seemed to care or even notice. I recalled how I'd once toured with **Free** and thoroughly enjoyed every moment, while walking into their dressing room was always an exhilarating and satisfying experience. Everywhere they played was sold out and they never failed to have flocks of admiring fans eagerly waiting to obtain their autographs at the stage or dressing room door.

Remembering this, it was easy to draw comparisons. Where were **Back Street Crawler** heading, and more importantly, where were the missing fans? During their initial rehearsals near Tower Bridge Johnny Glover had issued some cruel and damning words in front of me and Terry Slessor when discussing Paul Kossoff. "Just keep him alive for one album a year," he had said, clearly indicating that money was the real driving force, conveniently overruling all other considerations. Witnessing something such as this and sensing danger, I was torn between loyalty and common sense. Soon, it was time to make a decision and over a couple of weeks, having realised I wasn't enjoying the job and saddened by the music they were creating, I decided to leave.

After two American tours, supporting Kiss, and playing with **Roxy Music**, recording their album there, also jamming with Paul Rodgers, Mick Ralphs and Boz Burrell of Bad Company when headlining at The Starwood Club, they arrived back in England. Approximately 18 months later, the band was in serious trouble. The money had run out, debts were piling up, and record sales were minimal. Soon, Terry approached me and asked if I would return in an effort to help.

I liked Terry. We had been through a lot together and I felt there was just a chance that I might be able to salvage something from the all enveloping morass of shattered hopes and dreams. Having finally decided to go ahead, the first and immediate priority was to secure a further injection of desperately needed cash from Atlantic Records. With this in mind, a meeting was arranged at The Hilton Hotel in Park Lane London with Ahmet and Neshui Ertegun. Phil Carson, head of the label in London and Johnny Glover the other co-manager were also present as were all the other members of the group. After the initial pleasantries and morning coffee, it was soon time to get down to business. To any right minded person a struggling group invokes a certain sympathy, especially if you feel it is about to implode in an unholy and undeserved mess. By now, sadly, Paul Kossoff at 26 had passed away from a drug induced heart attack and Geoff Whitehorn had become his replacement.

Before entering the meeting, I couldn't help thinking of Paul and how sad his untimely death had been. There were the good times and how he had thrilled the audiences whenever and wherever he played with **Free**. There was also that wry smile of his in which his lips arced slightly upward as he initially looked at you with a certain suspicion before smiling with a wonderful mischievousness in his eyes. I recalled how I'd first met him as an unknown and had been fortunate enough to witness the meteoric rise of his unknown group. I'd also toured with him and **Free** and thought of that fantastic gig at The Royal Albert Hall when, due to audience demand, they had played five encores. Then there was that sad and despairing day when I'd witnesses him at his lowest ebb in his Ladbroke Grove mews house. I recalled bringing him 300 miles back to my Sunderland flat in order to nurse him back to health and weaned him off the deadly drugs that were one day to become fatal. Then there was the callous drug dealer who had knocked on his door the day I was visiting together with my deep regret that I hadn't acted in a more forceful and authoritative manner in order to prevent such a dastardly deal taking place. There were also the good times when we laughed and he would look longingly out of the window of my twelfth floor flat at the pretty girls leaving Annabel's trendy nightclub, situated just below. I also recalled the dark days and how incomprehensible it was to see such a talented guitarist sink so low and to such depths. At that never to be forgotten time, when I was struggling to nurse him back to health, I was desperate for help in order to keep him alive and remembered my innermost thoughts when he was perilously close to death's door. **"Outside, the plants flower, the trees grow, while children in the street laugh and play, but here it's only sadness. I hope I'm doing the right thing. If I fail the summer of life will fade away into the bare trees of autumn's sadness before withering away in the gloomy dark of the wintry cold. There's just the two of us and I can't do any more. Mother Nature, you're the only one who can help and I'm frightened. Are you listening because we don't have much time? I've got to get him better. Please, please help.**

Fortunately, within weeks, it appeared that mother nature had responded to my prayers and after Paul had made what appeared to be a miraculous recovery, he had been enticed back to London. Unfortunately, once there, he again succumbed to temptation. A few months later the telephone rang. It was Terry Slesser informing me of Paul's death. Paul had died in mid air while flying from LA to New York aged twenty five. On hearing the news, tears came to my eyes although I didn't cry despite knowing the happiness, the talent, and the good times, were gone forever.

Now Paul was gone, I was involved in attempting to rescue the group I had once helped him form. His replacement was Geoff Whitehorn, who despite his excellent playing, was unknown to the fans and this was to greatly add to the difficulties. Once inside the Hilton Hotel in Park Lane, across the other side of the large boardroom table sat the whole of the imposing Atlantic hierarchy. Unfazed, and having realised there was nothing to lose and everything to gain, I spelt out the sorry plight the band now found themselves in. However, I was under no illusions that Ahmet and his brother Neshui were undoubtedly smart with sharp calculating brains to match. With their long and successful track record of signing unknown groups before turning them into major stars, they had my utmost respect. With the group's huge advance just about gone, I was aware they had every reason to be cautious, if not highly suspicious. For his part, Johnny Glover remained quiet in the full knowledge that he had handled every single penny of the cash advance. With his huge outdoor swimming pool at his newly acquired house and twelve acre garden, he seemed keen not to rock the boat. In a situation of this nature, diplomacy is of course an admirable trait while silence gives everyone time to think. But unfortunately, an enforced diplomatic silence doesn't pay the bills. With time being of the essence, I felt the moment had come to stress the importance of an immediate injection of cash while realising that to do so in a bombastic or demanding manner would be counter productive and highly unsettling. Nevertheless, I could feel the tension in the air as no one relishes the prospect of having witnessed a million pounds of their money being frittered away for so little reward. Knowing this, I began by outlining their predicament in a reasoned and straightforward manner while stressing the immediate urgency of it. As they sat listening, I sensed I was getting through to them which was an encouraging sign. Soon the tension began to ease as they finally agreed a further cash injection of £50,000, (around £250,000 at today's value). Having secured it, an hour later we found ourselves outside the hotel in a very upbeat mood. Soon, the million dollar question had to be asked. Could the group capitalise on this new found lease of life and come up with some worthwhile material? Unfortunately, within weeks the old problems resurfaced. Once again, the gigs were half empty and after all the overheads had been paid, the money seemed to be disappearing faster than their previous cash advance. For my own personal integrity, I must stress that at no time did I handle or receive one penny of all the advances or transactions that had taken place. In fact, once again, it had been a continual loss making exercise from my rapidly depleting bank account. However, I did eventually receive two small cheques from Johnny Glover my alleged co-manager which unceremoniously bounced on reaching Lloyds Bank in Sunderland. Terry Slessor will happily verify the authenticity of my story. Days later, I held them in my hands and stared at them with a certain nostalgia. For the bank, they were merely another failed transaction. However, for me they represented the failed and unfulfilled hopes of a record company together with the group, and myself. Accompanying it was the tragic story of Paul, the acquisition of a fine country house by Johnny Glover, and Terry who was a great singer that had been fed mediocre songs which failed to sell. Once again, dad's words which were highly appropriate hit home. "In life, you have to pay for your learning son." How prophetic they had proved to be.

Here, it must be pointed out that when managing a band, unstinting enthusiasm becomes the main driving force which enables you to overcome seemingly insurmountable obstacles. Take such an important commodity away and problems quickly become burdensome while life quickly develops an aimless and uninspiring feel to it. With **Back St Crawler**, this was the position I now found myself in. Soon, I realised they seemed to be going nowhere while the initial optimism of once again being involved had rapidly dissipated into a morass of unattainable and lacklustre dreams. Suddenly, I realised that Paul's death had hit everyone harder than anyone had ever imagined. That impish smile of his together with his trusty Les Paul remained deeply ingrained in my memory as I recalled how every time I had entered the dressing room in his presence, there was immediate warmth and I felt he respected me. However, in comparison **Back St Crawler** seemed like strangers who I never really got to know. Sure they were nice chaps but that doesn't necessarily translate into a meaningful or lasting friendship. A few weeks later, having once again realised the futility of being involved in such an unrewarding and uninspiring venture, I again decided to leave. Fortunately, it wasn't a difficult decision to make as the dream of being involved with Paul and Terry while touring the world had turned into a wasteful flight of the imagination. Unfortunately, the bounced cheques, the passing of Paul, and the lack of meaningful or credible songs left a deep regret and sadness within me. Obituaries concerning a band are never enjoyable to recall, especially where nothing has been achieved. However, to have been allowed to take part in what at first appeared to be a wholesome and exciting project did afford me a certain consolation as I'd met some interesting people and gained more invaluable experience. Sadly, around 18 months later they were to finally split for good, with the bailiffs relentlessly chasing them for rent money after being ordered out of their flat in Earls Court. Godfrey Davis car hire group were also pursuing them for unpaid bills which came as a huge shock to the group. A waste of time? An exercise in mismanagement? Lack of stronger material?

Bad luck? Naivety? Or a combination of them all? Take your pick and be warned.

Having arrived back in Sunderland once again, it was time to take stock as a calm and peaceful aura of contentment settled over me. I was to find that failure has its own unforeseen compensations which instil a certain pride in that at least you have tried. To others it's a form of excuse which they may deride and scorn, but such criticism is futile when matched against the inner tranquillity which is soon pumping new found energy into every aspect of your thoughts. Ironically, sceptics can have the opposite effect as unknown to them; they are actually fuelling a desire to find another group to whom you can pass on your hard won experience. Having already decided to do this at some future juncture, there was no imminent desire to rush things as music doesn't work like that. Instead, the newly found peace of mind acts as a precautionary or restraining hand which warns that you need time to recover from the disappointments and setbacks of the past. What could possibly be learned from such an experience that would benefit anyone contemplating being in a band or entering into management? Unfortunately this is extremely difficult to define as each situation has its own complex array of difficult and varying factors. Nevertheless, it would be pompous and highly inappropriate of me to instil fear which might discourage any aspiring musicians to shrink back from entering the potentially exciting and multifaceted world of music. However, there remain certain aspects which appear to arise in every situation where a band has failed. In an inexperienced manager's case, the most common affliction is one of over enthusiasm. As I have said earlier, it is most certainly a vital necessity but must be tempered with a certain degree of realism and caution. Having decided to take the plunge, a natural propensity to spend hard earned cash, make hundreds of telephone calls, and drive thousands of miles, quickly becomes the norm. Then there is the most important requirement of all to consider. Does the group have real or exceptional talent? One's own interpretation of this essential ingredient can be wide and varied as we each have our own impression of what it actually is. However, surely the most important yardstick is that where musicians are concerned, it embraces creativity. Unfortunately, unless they genuinely have it, you are ultimately staring at a bleak and uninspiring future. In assessing whether they do in actual fact possess it, a critical and far reaching analysis is also vital at an early stage. Defer, or cast it aside in the hope that it will magically appear at some later stage does, in my opinion, mean you are unwittingly entering a highly dangerous and precarious future. The other vital ingredient is attitude. Where a group or individual is concerned, once a band member becomes arrogant or too full of his own importance, heated arguments and constant disagreements will undoubtedly ensue. This will of course lead to discontent, dissatisfaction and in most cases, the eventual demise of the group. So why do inexperienced people take up the challenge, you may well ask? I'm afraid it's that one word again, enthusiasm. In most cases they misconstrue this as reasoned judgement and continue to plough a deep and troubled furrow from which there is no escape, just sheer and absolute frustration. This may well sound defeatist but over the years I've met hundreds of failed and inexperienced managers who unfortunately remind me of my own foolish and possibly far too confident self when I first started. Meanwhile, one final word of warning. One learned top music lawyer in London by the name of Gillian Baxter, who has also written a book about TV and film contracts, recently informed me that in her opinion, being a group manager is the worst job in the world and she wouldn't ever contemplate becoming one. Having personally represented managers and record companies in major disputes with group members on numerous occasions, she also adds that it is the most unappreciative and unrewarding task which could ever befall a human being.

Nowadays, launching a group is extremely expensive, as is touring, advertising and other ancillary costs which explain why a credible hit single becomes of such prime importance. **David Gates** "Babylon" and **Coldplay's** "Yellow" are two examples. The **Kooks** entered the charts with an excellent single entitled Oh La which should surely will eventually bring them to a much wider public. **The Kaiser Chiefs, The Zutons, Kasabian** and **Razorlight** have all managed to have hit records while bringing fresh impetus to a potentially moribund music scene. Then of course are a whole new band of female singers such as **Pixie Lott, Florence & The**

Machine, Kelly Rowland and **Kate Perry** as well as the talented and awesome **Amy Winehouse** whose first album "Back To Black" is most certainly a joy to listen to. Going back even further, **Rod Stewart's** "Maggie May," and **Eric Clapton's** "Layla" are others who successfully pushed their international stature to even greater heights after capturing a hit single. In **Rod Stewart's** case his live appearance fee after this one hit rocketed from £500 to £1,500 per night and I should know because I had to pay it. "Roxanne" by **The Police** and **Procol Harum's** "Whiter Shade of Pale" also come to mind. In effect, the latter ones single gave them an international career spanning almost three decades. Finally, even **Pink Floyd** had a hit with "See Emily Play," as did **Led Zeppelin** with "Whole Lotta of Love," which was only released in America. However, behind all the groups who go on to have longevity are those who possess these three vital words. Namely, creativity, attitude, and a patient forbearance towards their fellow man. Here, at the risk of stating the obvious, it must be pointed out that a high percentage of the bands who fail invariably split up because of economic pressure. As I said earlier, another factor which is just waiting to rear its untimely head at the merest whiff of success is ego. In being aware of it, how can it be prevented? If only I knew, or could answer in a helpful or objective manner. Unfortunately, I haven't a clue. In contemplating this issue, another of George Bernard Shaw's quotes immediately comes to mind. "It's a shame that youth is wasted on the young." Unfortunately, a member or members of a group with ego problems are like a rampaging elephant who is prepared to trample and destroy all before him in its desperate desire to achieve its own aims. Where ego is concerned, need I say more?

Incidentally, may I point out something that the burgeoning musician or inexperienced manager may not be aware of. In the euphoria of signing a major record deal such as a long term 5 album agreement, there is a very simple yet highly important clause inserted in the contract. It's called options. To put it bluntly, if the first album fails to sell in large enough quantities, the record company is under no obligation to take up its option and can then drop you. Unpalatable as it may be, when it does occur, and despite the overwhelming euphoria when having first signed, it is not only a shock; it is also a very unpleasant and unsettling experience for all concerned. However, from a management point of view it does possess certain compensations no matter how painful the experience may prove to be. Suddenly, the group who may have become carried away with it all and have prematurely become far too full of their own importance are unceremoniously brought back to earth with crushing and humiliatingly speed. Their reckless spending and irresponsible outlook are finally exposed together with an unflattering reminder of their feeble sales figures being placed before them. Nevertheless, as a manager, it still means that all your efforts have been in vain. It also clearly shows that your initial judgement was sadly and misguidedly impaired. If only. Yes, those two uncompromising words suddenly come to haunt you as they consistently and unerringly remind you of what a futile exercise it all was. The recovery process remains one of unremitting anguish which blunts the driving enthusiasm that was so predominant when first setting out. Laughable? In a brighter moment you could say it most certainly is. Unfortunately, these moments of mirth are overshadowed by the barbed comments of your contemporaries who knew all along that it would all end in tears. Depressed? No. Disappointed? Yes. Learnt anything? Lots.

For those bands who do achieve initial success, you may well ask why there are so many one hit wonders. To climb the mountain only to unceremoniously plummet back down the other side must be even more soul destroying. However, in many cases it's not the artists fault. Personally, like many other people, I'm convinced that luck does play a major part. As I have said earlier, experience, genuine talent, and determination are all vital factors. Nevertheless, if a group fails to receive much needed airplay and are unfortunate enough not to capture national press coverage, then the portals of rock & roll fame may elude them through no fault of their own. At this juncture, having pointed out the reasons for possible failure, you may well ask how then do other managers or groups succeed? It's a reasonable question and one I will attempt to answer. Take the late Peter Grant, **Led Zeppelin's** esteemed manager for instance. He had the reputation of being one of the shrewdest and most successful managers in the world and in terms of ensuring they received every penny they earned, he most certainly was. But let's look a little deeper. When he first started managing the group, Jimmy Page had already had hits and been a huge success in America as well as the UK with the **Yardbirds.** As Atlantic Records were fully aware of this and had spotted their potential, they immediately agreed to sign them to a major world-wide deal. With the golden haired Robert Plant as their front man as well as one of the best rhythm sections in the world, bookings were instant. Once again I should know as I personally booked them for £75 when they first formed but then failed to appear at The Bay Hotel as agreed in the signed contract. The reason being they were off to tour America, the most lucrative market of them all. Virtually from the outset, every gig they did, they headlined, or were high up on the bill. Within a year to eighteen months they had become huge worldwide. There were no long drives up and down the motorways to appear at soul destroying gigs for this band. They were there almost before they started; such was the magic of Jimmy Page's reputation and ability. At the same time, the mega bucks and expertise of Atlantic Records were also behind them. At the 2006 Hall of Fame awards at Alexandra Palace in London (which I was fortunate to attend), after receiving an award, Jimmy Page lamented how sad he was that the now deceased Ahmet Ertegun was seriously ill as he recalled how much his company had helped the group. Years later, Peter Grant was able to repeat this success with **Bad Company.** Once again Paul Rodgers was already well known through his previous group **Free** and their worldwide hit, "Alright Now," (Incidentally, this record is reputed to be played somewhere in the world every seventeen seconds.) Here too, I should know as I personally promoted **Bad Company's** first ever three gigs in the UK at Newcastle City Hall which effortlessly sold out for three consecutive nights. Co-incidentally, once again Peter had Atlantic Records behind him. In between he managed the Scottish singer, **Maggie Bell**, previously with **Stone the Crows.** This time however, things were different as she wasn't as well known and despite a major record contract with Atlantic Records, she never made it, excellent though she was. He is also greatly lauded for his deals, after being the first one to insist on, and obtain, 90% of the gate receipts for **Led Zeppelin** wherever they appeared. Once again, when you are managing one of the biggest bands in the world, promoters were only too happy to pay it for the prestige of promoting them as well as earning an easy 10% from a potentially huge gross. In a situation such as this he had them over a barrel and knew it while still ensuring a good time was had by all. Ironically, two years after they had first pulled out from that £75 booking in Sunderland, I was more than happy to promote **Led Zeppelin** three times in one year in the NE for the same 10% of the net receipts which I was more than grateful to receive. Despite Peter Grant's fearsome reputation, I am duty bound to say I found him to be very fair and he was also very kind to me. One indication of this was the occasion when I promoted them at Newcastle City Hall. Prior to the gig I asked him if I could have permission to sell souvenir posters of the band and he assured me it would be all right to do so. On the appointed night, just before the concert was due to commence, a somewhat belligerent roadie rushed up and started heatedly berating me in a venomous and highly unsettling voice. "What are you doing selling posters of **Led Zeppelin**?" he raged. "I've got permission from Peter," I cried out in an effort to placate him. "No you haven't. Nobody in the world sells **Led Zeppelin** posters but the group themselves." With that, he brushed me aside before hurriedly snatching up the posters and immediately rushing backstage to triumphantly inform Peter Grant of the heinous and dastardly crime I had allegedly committed. All the way there, I followed him while vehemently protesting my innocence, but unfortunately; it proved to be of no avail. Having finally reached the dressing room, a sympathetic and somewhat embarrassed Peter looked at me before hastily informing the roadie that I did indeed have permission. "Give him his posters back," he ordered in an authoritative and somewhat enraged voice. The red faced roadie turned before reluctantly handing them back to me, which readily indicated that Peter was indeed a man of his word. Should that roadie ever read this; I continued to sell them at gigs for months afterwards as this could make all the difference between a profit and loss at borderline gigs.

Here, it must be pointed out that if a manager does succeed in acquiring that elusive and all important record contract, he is not alone. He can then look forward to a multitude of professional people to help him. First, there is the press department who are invariably in daily contact with the music press together with both local and national newspapers. Then there are the promotions department who have innumerable contacts with TV and the BBC, as well as independent television and radio companies throughout the country. Also there is the A&R talent scout who first signed the group. One of his first jobs is to book them into a professional recording studio as well as arranging for a suitable and hopefully, a highly capable producer. Having received all this attention, when the band do release a single, there are professional "pluggers" who are paid by the record company to obtain the all important airplay. The fact that they invariably have excellent personalities and long established contacts within the broadcasting industry is of course a major help. Downloading has also become a very important sales tool as are web sites. Finally, there is the cash advance which enables the band to survive while recording their first album and to buy much needed equipment. From this, it can be seen that there is a vast and well oiled machine waiting and ready to help the band attain that longed for stardom. This however, can be the danger period. With everyone constantly smiling and congratulating the band, they can become extremely difficult and even more egotistical. In saying this, I always think of a remark that John Lennon is reputed to have made to Brian Epstein while the **Beatles** were recording. After making what he regarded as a helpful suggestion, he was told in no uncertain terms to keep quiet and just keep taking his 10%. But where would they have been if he hadn't initially bought those five thousand copies of their first single which undoubtedly helped it into the charts?

Some years later, I got talking to an acquaintance of mine in Newcastle. His name was Peter Gowling (who unfortunately was later murdered in mysterious circumstances at his NE residence). "I've heard a great band from Durham," he enthused. "What's their name?" I inquired. It's "**Stella**," he enthusiastically informed me. "Here's a tape, have a listen and let me know what you think." After doing so, I thought they had potential and quite liked their music. It had a folk edge to it which merged with a free flowing guitarist who proved to be excellent. Within weeks I was managing them having in my wisdom, already decided to attempt to take a short cut to the top. Previous experience had taught me that continually driving up and down the motorways with an unknown group for miniscule amounts of money was soul destroying. Couple this with little or no crowd response and not only was it soul destroying, it was positively a waste of time. One night while sitting in the Marquee, jovial Jack Barrie the legendary manager decided to join me. Not wishing to kick a gift horse in the mouth, I realised it was the perfect opportunity to ask him to showcase them on the bill at Reading Festival, (which he personally organised). "Sorry Geoff, it's impossible. Nobody has heard of them, they won't draw ten people, and the bill has just about been finalised. There are a couple of slots left to fill but I'm keeping them open for major headlining groups," he informed me. On hearing this I looked at him with imploring eyes, but it was to no avail. I quickly realised his words had a finality about them and had proved to be highly discouraging. Nevertheless, undeterred, I decided to press on. "What about **Robin Trower** (ex **Procol Harum** guitarist who played on "Whiter Shade of Pale.") He's become a big draw, why don't you get him?" I inquired. "I've tried, but he doesn't want to do it," he replied in a somewhat downcast manner. "What about if I have a word with his manager, he's a good friend of mine?" I questioned. "There's no chance of him doing it," he reiterated as if suggesting it was a wholly unrealistic possibility. "But if I did manage to persuade him, will you put **Stella** on?" I inquired. He turned towards me with a look of incredulity on his face. Completely unabashed, I assured him I would speak to Wilf Wright his manager, and point out a few things which might help to change his mind. "If you do, and he agrees, then I'll definitely put them on," he quietly informed me. On hearing this, I was buzzing with anticipation at the possibility. Not being one to shirk a challenge, I knew the following day could be a make or break one for the group. I liked going to Reading Festival. Jack would furnish me with a guest backstage pass which would give me an opportunity to see a multitude of upcoming bands and meet friends. Backstage, there was a bar, record company tents, a restaurant and lots of friendly people. Underneath the main stage was a walkway leading to a small enclosure where you could see the bands in relative comfort. Jack, in his own inimitable style, called it "the annual garden party for the rock business." Sitting in the open grassed area backstage on a sunny day seemed to epitomise this description and it proved to be a very relaxing way to enjoy the festival, especially as you could still hear the groups who were playing. However, to be actually involved while managing a band, it was not only the excitement; it was also the invaluable exposure the group would obtain which was most important.

"Hi Wilf, Geoff Docherty here. Why don't you let **Robin** play this year's Reading Festival? You've spent a lot of time in America and people here in England are desperate to see him. I've been speaking to Jack Barrie and he's very keen to have him on at the festival and you'll be able to pick your slot," I informed him with as much enthusiasm as I could possibly muster. "I'm not sure. Maybe he needs a rest as he hasn't had much time off this year," replied Wilf in a non committal manner. "He'll go down really well, especially as his last album has gone platinum," I urged. "Do you think so?" he questioned. "Definitely. We've both worked together for a long time now and if I didn't think so, I wouldn't suggest it. One other thing Wilf, if you do decide to do it, Jack has agreed to put a band I'm presently managing into a support slot on the Friday. It's the only way I can get them on," I informed him in a somewhat desperate tone. "Let me think about" he replied. "I need to know soon Wilf otherwise the slot might go and it will be too late," I warned. Forty eight hours later, he rang me. "I just want you to know that later today I'm having a meeting with Jack and if the money and the stage times are okay, we might give it a go," he informed me. The following day, he rang to confirm that it had been agreed that **Robin** would in fact be headlining on the Sunday. On hearing this I jumped for joy before wholeheartedly thanking him. Seconds later, with my pulse racing, I rang Jack Barrie. "I've just heard the news from Wilf that Robin has agreed to do the festival so I hope you are going to keep your promise," I reminded him. "Of course," he replied calmly. "**Stella** will definitely be on." After replacing the receiver, I allowed myself a self-congratulatory sense of satisfaction. The plan was now in place as I knew that most of the record companies would be there as well as the music press and thousands of music lovers. It was undoubtedly a gift wrapped opportunity and if they seized it, there was no telling where it would lead. Backstage on the day of the festival, I wandered around the field to where **John Peel**, (who was there as a guest DJ) was having a kick about with a ball as I eagerly joined in. Inside, my excitement knew no bounds as I thought there was a realistic chance that there would be no long struggle for this band. In being selected to play at the festival, they had leapfrogged thousands of others and would soon be strutting their stuff. At moments like this, I can assure you rock & roll is tremendously exhilarating. It possesses an unparalleled magic which is impossible to quantify and seems to take over your whole life. Suddenly, a jauntiness which can quite easily be misconstrued as cockiness becomes deeply embedded in your psyche. You begin to smile at strangers, and in doing so, make new friends. Where's your pass, asks a security guard as you make your way out to the main public arena. "You're supposed to hang it around your neck," he curtly informs you. Little does he know that I think it's a form of big headedness which appears to make the wearer look superior compared to others out front who have paid. I fumble in my pocket before producing it as he waves me through, whereupon I quickly return it to its previous location and settle in to watch the band. Meanwhile, at the appointed time, they gingerly clamber up on stage. "Ladies and gentlemen, please give a warm welcome to **Stella**." **John Peel's** distinctive introduction comes out loud and clear over the PA, reverberating around the festival crowd. His calm and reassuring voice has a genuine stamp of authority, giving the group a certain credibility as well as untold confidence.

Having plugged in, the band broke into their first song. On finishing it, there was little or no response and I quickly began to feel a distinct sense of unease. At the end of the second song a plastic bottle full of urine arced through the air and just missed the lead singer. Undaunted, he shrugged it off before bravely beginning the third song. A few bars in, a whole fusillade of plastic bottles begin raining down on the hapless group. At this, the lead singer's voice faltered as his face became ashen with fright and he seemed unsure of what to do. Just then, someone booed as I looked helplessly up at him. Seconds later, a whole chorus of them erupted while he was attempting to sing. Suddenly, I began to feel for him knowing he wasn't just a singer; he was also a human being who was being subjected to a cruel baptism of mass venomous disapproval. A few feet away, someone stood up before throwing an unidentifiable missile towards him. Incensed, I began to hurry towards the miscreant with the sole object of confronting him as he quickly sat down. Just then, common sense prevailed. This was Reading Festival and who knows whether such an altercation could have started a riot. I was also fully aware that Jack certainly wouldn't like that and the end result would surely mean I would never again be given a guest pass. By now, the lead singer was becoming increasingly flustered and unsure of what to do. With his lack of experience and confidence in shreds, he looked a pained and pitiful sight. Realising the futility of continuing, he stormed off with the group following behind. It was a desperately sad moment as I hurried backstage to the tuning up tent. Once inside, I found Eenie their brilliant guitarist looking highly perplexed. It seemed my attempt to short circuit the system and elevate their group to immediate stardom had been an unqualified fiasco. A week later, disillusioned by their response, they split up. With the fullness of time, I can laugh about it, realising that I'd learnt another valuable rock & roll lesson. Never put a completely unknown and inexperienced band on at a major rock festival. However, should you choose to disregard this advice, please ensure they are wearing crash helmets together with full body armour before attempting to do so.

Soon, it was Sunday night and **Robin Trower** was due on stage. "Would you like to join us on stage?" asked Wilf in a considerate and friendly manner. As I did so, Robin stepped up to receive a warm and tumultuous welcome. On conclusion of the first song, the crowd cheered wildly while the atmosphere was electric and one of expectancy. Dusk soon came whereupon the light show was switched on, creating a magical and fairy-like setting for the rest of the set. After one and a half hours and three encores later, it was finally over. Backstage, Wilf, Robin and Jack Barrie were ecstatic as they collectively smiled at me. I don't know what Robin's fee was but I was confident it would have been pretty hefty, Wilf's economics degree obtained at Hull University would have seen to that. Later, **John Peel** approached me. "That guitarist in **Stella.** He's pretty good, you should keep your eye on him," he advised. I nodded in agreement, but sadly and as far as I am aware, he has disappointingly faded into the dark recesses of musical obscurity. Fortunately however, I was able to stay and enjoy the rest of the three day festival despite a highly disillusioned **Stella** immediately leaving for home. A few weeks later, Durham police rang me. "Are you the owner of a Mercedes van, they asked? "Yes," I replied. "I'm afraid there's been an accident and it's now lying half submerged in the River Wear at Durham. A chap who says he is the bass player from a group called **Stella** has crashed it through the stone wall of Framwellgate Bridge and it has ended up in the river. It's a bit of a mess I'm afraid." "How is he? Is he alright?" I asked concernedly. "He's fine. There's not a scratch him," he assured me. "Anyway, will you make arrangements to have it recovered?" he asked. "Yes, I'll do that right away," I assured him. Unfortunately, as the group had split up, I had allowed the insurance cover note to lapse. It had seemed pointless to spend more money to renew it thinking it was safety parked outside the bass player's house. Later, on questioning him, he admitted that he had taken it without authorisation to go to a party. The fact that he hadn't passed his driving test only added to the problem. Later, I drove through to Durham to see it lying half submerged near the water's edge. When purchasing it brand new, I'd insisted on a costly, bigger engine to minimise the risk of it breaking down. I'd also had a coach building firm fit seats which could be folded into bunk beds while on the move, at an extra cost of £300, (now around £1,500) so that if any group members were tired, they could have a restful sleep on the long journey home after a gig. Ironically, only a few days earlier, I'd agreed to sell it to Windows Record Store in Newcastle Arcade for £1,750. Unfortunately, this had now become a non starter as it was a total write off. Still, it's only rock & roll.

Being philosophical about failure leads to some strange conclusions. As I've said earlier, music, as well as being an art form, is in itself a potent drug. Once hooked, it's impossible not to yearn for more in whatever capacity this may be. Meeting interesting people and participating in the challenge of helping someone "make it" is assuredly an unusual and fascinating occupation. In doing so, and without at first realising it, you have placed your whole future in their hands. However, in the case of an inexperienced and unknown rock group, it's all a question of a person's own values. Unless you are extremely fortunate, I can assure you, yours will differ greatly from theirs. Initially, those rose tinted spectacles which everyone appears to see through are a delight to wear and each person appears to be extremely happy at the arrangement. However, sooner, rather than later, that old proverb comes to mind, "familiarity breeds contempt." Whether this is just cynicism on my part is not really the issue. What is, is that you become fully aware of it, and however unpalatable, must realise it will inevitably occur. Meanwhile, **Humble Pie**. What an apt name for a group. Get used to eating it or as a manager you won't get past the first hurdle. Then why do it in the first place? Despite everything, it's still disarmingly exciting. That little clock ticking away inside has its own inbuilt driving force which appears to have an insatiable capacity to shrug off setbacks while demanding greater effort. Slack for just a moment and it becomes a hard and uncompromising taskmaster. The magical thought of "making it" stubbornly remains there day and night, constantly reminding you that with even greater effort, it could all come true After each successful gig, blind optimism succeeds in burying its roots deep into your thoughts while spirits soar and the goal you are desperately seeking seems ever closer. Soon, the pace and workload begins to increase. It has to in order for you to stay in the race. To disregard the absolute necessity of maintaining it is to accept or encourage failure. To ignore it, is failure itself. During all this, it is important to remember the group also possess their own ambitions and emotions while their problems become your problems. Pride, self satisfaction, a happy group and an appreciative audience are a much needed tonic. It inspires fresh hopes, bringing with it a whole raft of new and heady dreams. Successful nights such as this are the exciting end product of a group desperately trying to succeed, and suddenly, it feels highly emotionally gratifying to be part of it. However, does this actually constitute success, or does it merely indicate a false dawn? "There Are None So Blind As Those That Cannot See," is most decidedly an apt proverb whose intuition is uncannily telling. Having successfully obtained three major record contracts for bands I have managed, I look back on those wise and unforgettable words of wisdom and believe I have an inkling of their true meaning. It may be fun, it may be cruel, but it's definitely rock and roll at the sharp end.

Chapter 8

After experiencing failure, the challenge is to shrug it off and resolve to do infinitely better next time which is far easier said than done. Nevertheless, with man being an eternal optimist, it is natural that at some juncture, he will be only too eager to re-enter the affray and try again. These are the thoughts I found myself with one sunny afternoon in the early eighties while wandering aimlessly through town. In doing so, I bumped into a well known vocalist known affectionately as "Pud" who had previously played in many local groups, but unfortunately, had failed to "make it." Despite the apparent lack of interest from record companies, he possessed an excellent voice as well as taking a keen interest in any new bands together with their music. "Geoff, I saw an excellent group the other night called **The Showbiz Kids**," he began. I could see his enthusiasm was running extremely high as I continued to listen. "Their lead singer is amazing and I think they could go all the way. They're playing at The Londonderry pub this Saturday, so why don't you go along and see them?" he suggested. After a brief conversation, I went on my way deep in thought. **The Showbiz Kids.** I liked the name and it set me thinking. The beauty of the rock business is that you can be a failure one minute and the next; you can be signed to a lucrative recording deal and be heading for the top. Bearing this in mind, the following Saturday I quietly breezed into The Londonderry in order to check them out and soon the place was packed. Minutes later they were up on stage and quickly began strutting their stuff. By now, the punk revolution had gripped young people's imagination and they appeared to be a cross between a rock and a frustrated punk group. I also noticed they were young, energetic, and outwardly vibrant. As I continued to watch, the lead singer commanded the stage as if it was his rightful home as well as possessing an imposing and awe inspiring presence. Being restless and still possessing visions of "making it" while touring the world with a successful band; I became excited by their energetic and fascinating performance. However, in the light of previous experiences, I felt that certain questions still needed to be addressed. Firstly, and most importantly, did I have the capability to take them to the top and did they have the songs to get there? At the time, I was still labouring under the constraints of caution together with the added fear of losing even more money in a fruitless and time wasting exercise. I also had to exercise prudence and seriously consider whether it would all end up in heartbreak once again. However, one thing was for sure. I needed to see them again before having a chat with them in order to gain an insight into where their heads were at and what their intentions were.

A few nights later, I watched them for a second time and once again the lead singer's stage presence was thoroughly absorbing as well as highly enjoyable. Soon, I was to subsequently find out that his favourite artist was **John Lennon** which added a certain credibility allied to his already impressive stage persona. Within weeks, having been suitably impressed, I had signed them under a management contract before setting out to acquire that all important record deal on their behalf.

Later, it transpired that the lead singer's name who had so impressed me was Robert Coyle (later to join **Dr Feelgood**), while the guitarist's name was Pat McMahon. Their line-up was a standard four piece, all of whom turned out to be highly intelligent, which augured well for some credible music as well as interesting interviews should they ever occur. However, experience had already taught me that intelligence doesn't necessarily make someone streetwise or hardworking, although it's certainly a plus. Within weeks, owing to my continued friendship with Jack Barrie, the group was given a prestigious monthly residence at London's Marquee Club. My intention was to have them gigging in London as often as possible, hoping their name and music would quickly reach the ears of influential people. Other recognised venues they played at in London at the time included The Hope & Anchor, The Nashville Rooms in Kensington and The Greyhound in Fulham. Unfortunately, sleeping in the van often became a necessity due to lack of funds, but at least it was character building, or at least I hoped so. In order to prove that I was just as willing to endure the discomfort as they were, I also accompanied them having realised the importance of keeping costs down. A few months later, armed with the knowledge that by now their London exploits had made them the biggest local band in their home town, I decided to showcase them at Sunderland Locarno where I had previously promoted many major groups. Having set up the date, I decided to contact two friends of mine at Chrysalis Records. They were Chris Briggs, head of A&R (talent scout) and Stewart Slater, head of media operations there. After listening to my enthusiastic and unrelenting entreaties, they finally decided to fly up and see them. On the actual night in question, to my absolute astonishment, 3,000 people were crammed in and I couldn't believe it. In many ways I still can't, but it's absolutely true. Halfway through the set, Neil Johnson, a local boutique manager and an acquaintance of mine, now resident in Australia, enthusiastically rushed towards me before uttering his unforgettable words. "These are going to be as big as **Led Zeppelin** Geoff." On hearing such a wild and expansive assessment of their potential, I looked at him with a mixture of scepticism and bewilderment. Ironically, **Led Zeppelin** had previously played on that very stage and were undeniably capable of filling any stadium in the world. However, being completely realistic, it must be said that a local group filling a gig in their hometown is light years away from achieving such global eminence. Being fully aware of this, I looked at him and smiled, knowing there was nothing else I could do. Nevertheless, everyone is entitled to their opinion and for a fleeting second, I wondered what would happen if his prediction was to ever come true? Meanwhile, up on the balcony the two record company executives watched as the group went down fantastically well. Three encores later it was finally over as I invited Chris and Stewart to Annabel's, a nearby local nightclub. Once inside, I bought them a drink after which I eagerly sat down to discuss the record contract I was supremely confident that the group were about to be offered. Sitting there, I felt completely relaxed as well as highly elated on recalling how everything had gone like a dream only hours earlier. Furthermore, two top record company executives who had personally witnessed it were sitting right beside me. While awaiting their offer, raging and undiluted optimism together with dreams of stardom began spinning around in my head in a never ending spiral of hope. Inside the darkened club, the music pounding out from resident DJ John Harker's turntable was noticeably atmospheric as well as highly innovative. On glancing at the dance floor, couples could be seen blissfully and shamelessly shedding their inhibitions in an effort to escape the realities or pressures of their everyday lives. All around, seemingly impervious to watching eyes, there was laughter, kissing, and wandering hands, all searching for a comforting embrace as they continued to enjoy themselves. Amidst this carefree and alcohol induced merriment, I patiently awaited the offer of the major record contract which I felt sure was about to be forthcoming.

Before long, the silence of my two companions began to become unbearable. The passing minutes seemed like hours as the ever rising tension continued to build. Despite this, my mind was racing in anticipation of the exciting news I would soon be able to relay to the band. After what seemed an eternity, Chris Briggs turned to me with an implacable look clearly visible on his face as I strained to hear his words above the music. "I'm sorry, but we're not going to sign them. They aren't for us," he exclaimed. To say I was staggered would be an understatement. In all my years in music, I can honestly say it was one of the biggest shocks I had ever experienced. During my days of promoting, groups not turning up, **Led Zeppelin** finally agreeing to play, **Steppenwolf** pulling out, **Free** becoming massive, all paled into insignificance in comparison to that night. I swallowed hard. "Don't count your chickens before they're hatched" is a well known proverb. But optimism, allied to experience, together with a 3,000 sell out crowd had given me every reason to feel this way. "Why not?" I sheepishly inquired as the shock waves continued to race through my brain in a surge of complete disbelief. Chris nonchalantly shrugged his shoulders in a forceful and non committal manner while at the same time appearing to struggle for any satisfactory explanation. Having astutely sensed how much it was hurting, he declined to elaborate as I slumped back into my seat. Seconds later, I became numb and felt as though rigor mortis was about to set in. Defeated, and demoralised, I found myself at a complete loss for words. I glanced at the packed club with people still happily gyrating on the dance floor and couldn't help noticing how carefree, energetic and full of life they seemed to be. In contrast, I was grim faced, disillusioned and utterly bewildered with confusion racing through my thoughts. Suddenly, nothing seemed to make sense and it was as if a wild rampaging bull had run amok, trampling everything in its path. Just what do you have to do, I wondered? However, the inescapable fact was that the group weren't being signed and I was inexplicably being forced to accept the reality of a painful and total rejection. At that moment, overcome with shock, the rock business appeared to be a cruel millstone of shattered dreams hanging aimlessly in the air. Grown men aren't supposed to cry, but right then it seemed the only real alternative. At the end of the night, on the long walk towards the exit, someone smiled and stopped to bid me goodnight with natural and heartfelt warmth. Fortunately, it succeeded in penetrating the deep inner gloom that had hastily enveloped me in self pity. Suddenly, I sensed that in receiving such a simple kindness, all was not lost. Nevertheless, facts, no matter how unsavory or unpalatable, had to be faced. Was it the end and were they consciously telling me something that I hadn't foreseen or been able to grasp? It certainly seemed so. However, despite this setback, I was still convinced the lead singer had star quality, which in the light of what had just occurred seemed a contradiction of what others thought. However, tangled emotions, recriminations, and critical analysis all seemed to lead to one glaring fact. The group can't have been that good otherwise they would have signed them. Amidst the confusion, I was completely at a loss as to which direction to take. "Don't ever give up son." I recalled Dad's caring advice when any untoward difficulty arose which always proved to be an invaluable source of strength as well as an inspiration. After hearing him say it a number of times as a young boy, there was no denying it had become irrevocably ingrained in my psyche. In the meantime, I was again faced with the grim task of informing a group that their hopes of securing a major record deal was in tatters. Having done so, I looked at their weary and dejected faces and felt an inner sadness that I had to be the bearer of such soul destroying news. Only hours earlier, young and fresh faced, they had energetically strutted across the stage to an ecstatic audience in the full belief that they could do no more. Now, their expressionless faces and limp bodies painted a sad picture of cheerlessness and abject disillusionment.

The following day I walked along the nearby picturesque beach deep in thought as the gentle crashing waves brought solace and an inner comfort to my troubled mind. Each lungful of air was proving to be invigorating, helping to exorcise the ghosts of the previous night's failure. At each step, the self recriminations which had descended over me like a cloud of hungry locusts, slowly began to dissipate. Just then, a seagull swooped overhead as its wings guided it effortlessly through the air. Nearby, a fisherman had cast his line from the promenade in order to savour the fruits of the temperamental and impatient North Sea. I glanced towards him, more out of curiosity than any inherent urge to join him, before quickly recognising that he too had his own hopes and ambitions. Inwardly I smiled, knowing that tranquillity and peace of mind together with the comforting sounds of nature possess their own calming influence.

As a manager of an unknown band trying to make it, as each day passes, dreams of stardom float enticingly around in a vision of superlatives inside the brain. Conversely, axiomatic to such heady dreams, reality refuses to be brushed aside. Its defiant barbs and stings constantly prod and probe in order to remind you that failure is not only a distinct possibility, but is highly probable. It also reminds you that managing a group is a perilous occupation which has few parallels and should a band fail, there are no safety clauses or hand rails to cling onto. A few days later, I was talking to one of the band about the possible reasons why they had been rejected. "You brought the record company up too early in our career," he pointed out in a scathing and highly unappreciative manner. Ironically, when I had first informed him that a major record company was flying up to see the group, he was positively ecstatic. Now, because they had failed to impress, it was me who was to blame. If only he had realised how lucky he was that they had taken the time and trouble to come and see the band, he may have thought differently.

Having overcome such a huge disappointment, it was now time to take a deep breath and try again with the past having been unceremoniously consigned to the deep archives of experience. At the next Marquee gig, Rob Coyle introduced his version of **John Lennon's** "Cold Turkey" which, without doubt, was positively mesmerising as well as charismatic. Coupled with his boundless energy and innovative stage theatrics (which were breath-taking) the group behind him steadfastly drove the song along at a fierce and awe inspiring pace. There was no let up as the crowd became totally captivated by his unique and exceptional stage presence. To this day, it lives long in the memory and will surely never be surpassed. This was the measure of the young singer and somehow I felt I still had a superstar in the making. Another memorable song of the group was entitled "White Africans." This was about apartheid and his hatred of its hypocrisy and everything it stood for which was highly relevant at the time. His face would contort with unrepressed anger as his raised voice spat out the lyrics in a torrent of complete cynicism and unrestrained outrage. To hear it was spellbinding while to realise he had written the lyrics, was awesome. A third song he co wrote was "Freedom" which showed a depth and sincerity which never failed to captivate the audience as well as myself. Unique songs of this quality weren't "hits" in the normal sense, but nevertheless, were truly unforgettable. To be able to marry theatrics and rock and turn it into such a superb spectacle was a unique talent which gave me the incentive to try even harder. A few weeks later, the band supported **Chris Rea** at Redcar Coatham Bowl. Afterwards, I wandered into his dressing room to say hello having never previously met him. "I really liked the group," he informed me. "Thanks," I gratefully replied. In reality, I hadn't been looking for praise as I just wanted to meet him and found him refreshingly friendly. Nevertheless, an unsolicited endorsement from such a respected figure was most welcome as well as immensely encouraging.

Having taking on the task of promoting groups at The Seaburn Hall on the sea front in Sunderland (where I had previously promoted **The Jam** on the opening night), I put on a local group by the name of **Straw Dogs** as support to **The Saints** two weeks later. While watching them, a diminutive guitarist by the name of Olga immediately caught my eye. Bouncing non stop around the stage, he appeared to exude a confidence which was most unusual, as well as refreshingly eye catching. This, together with his cheeky smile, certainly livened things up as I watched with increasing intensity. Suddenly, an intriguing thought occurred to me. What if he was in **The Showbiz Kids** playing rhythm guitar? It would certainly improve things, I said to myself? But would he join, and more importantly, would the group accept him? On approaching them, at first they were reluctant. However, the stark reality was that by now most of the major record companies had turned them down. "It needs a new approach," I pointed out. "We can't keep going down to London and banging our heads against a brick wall. Sleeping in the van is no picnic either." Thankfully they listened and finally agreed. Within days, Olga had joined and after a series of rehearsals was ready to make his debut. As I watched the new line-up for the first time, the group now had two outstanding front men, each with their own contrasting but complimentary styles. At their first gig, watching the crowd's reaction, I immediately became excited on realising how they loved and appreciated them. Suddenly, I could sense a new found purpose in the band, together with a renewed on-stage energy which augured well for the future. Soon, full of hope, I took the new line-up down to London in order to showcase them. However, it proved to be a hard slog as I sensed Olga was surprised as well as extremely disappointed at having to sleep in the van. In Sunderland the group were big. However, once past Scotch Corner on the A1, I was fully aware that they meant absolutely nothing. It was certainly proving to be a baptism of fire for him and to find they were being paid so little also came as quite a shock. Late one night I arrived back at the van to find Olga fast asleep with the top half of his diminutive and skeletal, almost Belsen like frame, half exposed to the chilling cold of the night. I looked at him and felt protective as I carefully pulled the blankets back over his pale and seemingly underfed outline. In doing so, I secretly had immense and hopeful thoughts of my own. If we keep this line-up, it won't be long before we can afford decent hotels, I said to myself with a certain degree of excitement coursing through my veins. By now, my expectations had risen dramatically. Surely, there isn't another group in London with two such charismatic figures that appear to be destined for stardom, I thought. With the live act now finely honed into an absorbing and highly innovative stage presence, all they needed to give me was just "three minutes of magic" on a tape and I was confident I could get them a deal. As I quietly slipped into my sleeping bag, I found myself in the unusual and rewarding position of being immensely happy and extremely contented. On awakening the next morning, it was time to eat a cheap "fry-up" breakfast in a nearby local café. "If you're hungry son, you'll eat anything." Unfortunately, Dad's words were running true as what appeared to be an excess of murky engine oil surfaced on my plate. As I wiped my lips I couldn't help thinking of the horrendous Torrey Canyon oil spill and it seemed I was being used either to absorb or dispose most of it. This, and the indignity of hurriedly searching the streets for a public toilet in which to wash was all part of the group's and my own character building. Ironically, in some strange and inexplicable manner, it actually seemed to be what is known in musical terms as "paying your dues." Nevertheless, there was an underlying purpose to it all in which the group was finally showing an immense resolve to "make it."

Now that they were regularly gigging London, I started to introduce Olga to influential people, namely members of the music press, record company executives, and London promoters in order to gain publicity as well as notoriety for the band. At a Newcastle University gig I introduced him to Malcom Gerrie who was a noted TV executive at Tyne Tees Television. After seeing the band, his enthusiasm knew no bounds and I felt it was another career defining step in the right direction. Criticism at what appears to be a pre pubescent stage for a band can be very damaging as well as hurtful. Conversely, praise and the chance of building a worthwhile following are the very foundations on which a struggling band's hopes are built as well as nurtured. London is however, a fast moving city especially as hundreds of groups a night are playing within its vast boundaries. For an unknown group, an empty or sparsely attended gig is a soulless and dispiriting place to play. Far from being character building, it rapidly crushes their hopes into an unsettling miss mash of confused and disenchanted emotions. In experiencing it, they are quickly and ruthlessly confronted by the sheer spectacle and hopelessness of the task facing them. Afterwards, slumped in the dressing room, they can prove to be a sorry sight. Outside, the hurriedly discarded advertising flyers, which earlier had been so patiently and energetically given out, are wantonly strewn over the roadside. Later, having suffered the indignity of playing to only a handful of people, it's time to begin loading the equipment into the back of the van. It's dark and cold as no one speaks or smiles and it's as if fate has already decreed they are wasting their own and everybody else's time. Behind them, the sound of the gig doors being slammed shut reaches their ears without even a token goodbye from the promoter or a member of the sparse audience. Soon, more dispiriting news is relayed to them as I inform them that after all their efforts they haven't been invited back. Fortuitously however, every cloud has a silver lining. It's one less gig to play, one less gig to phone, and an extra day to rehearse. As I said earlier, London moves at an unremittingly fast pace. For a struggling group, it seems to be too fast. If only it would stop or slow down just for a moment in order to listen to the band. Meantime, they are tired and hungry, knowing the bright lights have stubbornly eluded them and success appears to be as far away as ever. The following day, **The Rolling Stones** are playing at Earls Court. Unfortunately, the tickets are too expensive and I can't get them on the guest list as once again it hits home that they're nobodies, and it hurts. However, tomorrow is another day and another gig which means there will be a whole new set of flyers to hand out, together with frozen fingers and a desperate search for petrol money.

Now that Olga appeared to be firmly entrenched in the band, there was a new resurgence of hope and having shaken things up a little, it certainly appeared to be working. Within weeks, as I had fervently hoped, people were beginning to notice and talk about them. As each week went by, the favourable comments together with the wholehearted and enthusiastic feedback made me sense that I was finally onto a real winner. A few weeks later, amidst the euphoria, the telephone rang. It was Olga's attractive girl friend who at the time was chairwoman of the local young Conservatives. "I just want to let you know that Olga is leaving the band and you are no longer his manager," she curtly informed me. On hearing her middle class voice, which had a patronising and superior tone, I quickly forged an immediate dislike to it, however premature my assessment may have been. "I have a management contract on him that includes the clause, "jointly & severally." Do you know what that means?" I questioned. "It doesn't mean anything because we've taken legal advice and we've been advised the contract he signed isn't worth the paper it's written on," she replied in the same superior and patronising tone. I swallowed hard before eventually replacing the receiver, disillusioned and angry, but not surprised. In rock, all sorts of people attach themselves to impending success at the merest whiff of it and I recognised that reflected glory from a potentially rising star is better than no glory at all. Nevertheless, to be treated so indifferently by someone so young who had not yet experienced the vagaries of life was deeply hurtful. However, one thing was certain. To act in such a manner, you have to posses a callous and selfish disregard for the hopes and welfare of your fellow human beings. The fact that Olga had enlisted the services of his girlfriend in such a cowardly fashion was also highly disturbing, giving an insight into his own grasping and selfish persona. On reflection, realising lawyers cost a fortune; I decided not to fight it. Legally and morally, I felt his girlfriend was wrong, and yet in one respect, she was right. If a band member wants to leave then it is pointless trying to keep him, unless of course he is a major star who is shifting monumental amounts of records.

Before long, while at a loose end, I began working for a major leisure company. Two brothers who were its owners approached me and informed me they were opening a Rock Café in The Isle of Man. The year was 1982 and it was to be based loosely on the Hard Rock Café in London. A good friend of mine named Peter Edge was to manage it and I was to be his assistant. A few months later, with Peter having returned to England, I became its new manager. How can I describe this period in my life? All I can say is that it was fun all the way. Parties, good music, and celebrity Radio One DJs who visited the Island, all made there way there. The famous Tourist Trophy Races, better known in the motor cycle world as the TT, was particularly memorable. Visitors from all over the world came to see it and it was a wonderful spectacle to witness which certainly defies comparison. Brian Johnson of **AC/DC,** Paul Thompson of **Roxy Music,** and John Coughlin of **Status Quo** were all in residence while I was there as it is a tax haven. They were also frequent visitors to the café which was named simply Joe's, a Peter Edge inspired name. Without wishing to sound too self congratulatory, it quickly became the "in place," on the island. With no dress restrictions, good music, excellent food, and a perceptive crowd, it was a pleasure to work there. Characters such as Sally Hardy Jackson, Patrick-De-Bott, Gerard McQuillan, Trevor Baines (a retired banker) together with many others, inspired a feeling of togetherness which I thought had long been lost from earlier experiences. Fortunately, I'd been well schooled in the art of making someone feel welcome from my Aunt Anne (who I have subsequently learnt offered to take me in as a baby when my mother died). During my visits there, nothing was too much trouble and I have steadfastly tried to emulate her. The friendly smile, the food and sincerity, together with the caring attention to every need made it a joy to visit her. Please allow me to mention her four lovely daughters who are exactly the same, Nancy, Betty, Aida and Joan, who all reside in Washington, Tyne & Wear.

Ironically, having formed his new group (whose name was **The Toy Dolls**), Olga brought out a single entitled "Nellie The Elephant." The year was 1984 and as I said earlier, luck undoubtedly plays a very important part. The single appeared to be going nowhere until **Anne Nightingale** decided to play it on her Sunday Evening Radio One show. Within weeks it had entered the top thirty and went to No 4, staying in the charts for 12 weeks. Suddenly, Olga was a huge celebrity, especially locally. The single then went on to sell a quarter of a million copies while the **Showbiz Kids** manfully struggled on, unable to secure that all important record contract. Locally, Olga continued to strut his stuff and it seemed to all the world his ruthless streak had more than handsomely paid off. Embarrassed, bitter, or jealous? Not in the slightest. Disappointed, definitely. But getting to the top and staying there is another matter. Once again, as I said earlier, it takes real talent in which song writing and creativity remain major factors. Quietly, and without fuss, I watched from the sidelines as his career progressed. "Sounds." an important music journal at the time interviewed him in a major article, but unfortunately it lacked any real depth. Here, it must be said that you can only talk about superficial things for so long. To be well schooled, you need to be streetwise and well informed. To have read the daily papers, watched the TV news and documentaries, visited the local library and nurtured friends who are capable of drawing you into stimulating and worthwhile conversations while broadening your horizons. However, if a person is unable or unwilling to incorporate any of the above into their own lifestyle, one dimensional thinking quickly takes root. Before long, it leads to disaffection among those who were initially gullible enough to listen, while discerning music lovers look to more interesting records in order to indulge and satisfy their tastes. By now, punk was deeply embedded with young people dressing and rebelling against virtually everything that society held dear. The Terry Wogan TV show (which was family orientated at the time) was a prime example. One night, **The Toy Dolls** appeared on it and went on to blow their credibility right out of the window. **The Sex Pistols, The Clash,** and **Siouxsie & The Banshees** were all major groups who would never have dreamed of appearing on it at the time. Why? Because they had genuine belief in what they were railing against. Of course some people just want to be entertained rather than educated and I must admit that Olga was certainly good at that. However, to stay at the top you need to have depth and acquiring it is a lot more difficult than just idly watching it from a peripheral vantage point. To attain it you have to live and learn from it. In doing so, I firmly believe discerning people are not easily fooled. It is substance, honesty and humility, allied to genuine talent which fills concert halls, sells records, and stays in people' memories. Unfortunately, in the mad and destabilising rush for success, it can be conveniently thrust aside. Olga is very big in Japan I was constantly told. But what is big? It is a word which is open to a whole host of misleading interpretations. However, record sales are usually a good indication, if not the defining factor. Take it from me, if a promising English band are big in Japan, word quickly reaches the ears of the major record companies and a major signing becomes imminent. With Olga, over twenty years later, I'm still waiting.

Meanwhile, I still had **The Showbiz Kids** to think about. Rob Coyle performing Cold Turkey was certainly an asset, but unfortunately, time seemed intent on proving it wasn't enough. What we desperately needed was a fresh spark of inspiration or something which would lead to a step up from the mediocrity of constantly playing on small stages in the back rooms of licensed premises. Here I must qualify this apparent criticism, as it must be said that these establishments gives a group time to hone its skills while providing invaluable experience for hundreds of bands. Nevertheless, there comes a time when new and greater horizons have to be contemplated and this was **The Showbiz Kids** aim. In order to achieve this I felt it was now time to move the band to London as their live stage performances were still excellent and at the same time, I hoped they might be capable of establishing a following once they actually lived there. It was a calculated gamble, but in my opinion, one well worth taking whereupon 181 Sutherland Avenue in Maida Vale became our new abode. Six single beds in one room, plus a lounge with one shared bathroom wasn't too much of a hardship, although it certainly couldn't be construed as luxurious by any stretch of the imagination. Having arrived, their eager faces were full of hope while the possibility of making it was an encouraging sign. They laughed, they smiled, they rehearsed and occasionally they gigged. At the time, Prince Charles and Diane were about to be married and London was awash with visitors from all over the world. On the actual day they married, there was a huge firework display in Hyde Park whereupon everyone unashamedly held hands as well as being amazingly friendly. It proved to be the catalyst for an intense and joyous occasion, and as I walked through the massed crowds, I couldn't help thinking of the bands future and what it might hold for them. The extremely passionate and joyous revelry which had descended on London at the time created a sense of unlimited optimism and high hopes of a brighter future together with a whole myriad of positive thoughts.

As I said earlier, when a band enthusiastically unloads its equipment onto a venue's stage and come the evening, only a handful of people are there to watch, it's an immensely sad spectacle to witness. Repeat this scenario on a number of occasions and you begin to feel a sense of desperation creeping in. As a fully committed manager waiting impatiently in the wings, you pray that somehow they will come up with that all important killer song. In the event that it proves beyond them, it becomes a testing time causing the band to lose momentum, as well as heart. Sleeping late, rehearsing less, and for some members drinking more becomes the norm. While the whole idea of moving was to make it, at times the possibility of it ever remotely occurring seemed as far away as ever. Soon, a laxness began to envelop them which was bordering on terminal apathy. Suddenly, the offer of a gig comes in causing spirits to soar but unfortunately it's only temporary.

Desperation becomes a constant bedfellow which hangs ominously in the air. Fortunately, youthful and ever eager bodies seem to take it all in their stride, as if having already realised that obduracy and tenacity are inbuilt and essential requirements in order to make it. Nevertheless, despite the hardships and doubts, the mystifying and resolute will to make it remains unbending as the fight steadfastly goes on. As a manager, from time to time, you take stock in an attempt to evaluate if it's worth continuing. Ironically, St John's Wood (which contains **Paul McCartney's** house) wasn't far from where we were living while Glen Matlock the ex bass player of the **Sex Pistols** frequented the pub at the end of the street. It seemed fame was all around and being aware of this, it felt as if anything was possible. Decca Wade, the effervescent diminutive drummer with the **Angelic Upstarts**, began to call round. They'd already had several hits and he was undeniably funny as well as being a character with an engaging personality. One night I met him in The Ship, a pub in Wardour St to find he was drinking with a bevy of young shapely strippers from Raymond's Revue Bar. Luckily, he was always allowed in free as one of their guests after giving them a few of the latest albums he'd acquired from EMI who had recently signed them. Seeing him was always fun and looking back, the girls were certainly a pleasant distraction. Unfortunately however, a year later, sadly disillusioned and still without a record contract, it was time for the group to return home. Ignominious defeat is always unpalatable and to dress it up as anything else would be stretching credulity too far. Years later, one member of a major group went on to state that they had had the most fun when they were first struggling to make it. In many ways he was right, and yet, in others, he was decidedly wrong. Having successfully achieved stardom, he could afford to look back with a certain fondness knowing that it had all been worthwhile. But when a group hasn't achieved what they should and could have, I can assure you it's a completely different story. Ultimately, there are misgivings, blame, and recriminations as well as regrets. However, that's rock & roll and if it was easy, there would be hundreds more groups who would make it, while lacking any real sense of achievement

By now, having arrived back in Sunderland, it was patently obvious that **The Showbiz Kids** needed a songwriter who could provide that missing spark of inspiration. With this in mind, I recruited a local keyboard player named Stephen Clifford who had previously attended Music College in Newcastle. Talented, and with an engaging personality, he appeared to be ideal. Within months, two of his colleagues from the college had also joined the group, a bass player and drummer. Soon the band were gigging and going down really well. With the charismatic Rob Coyle still present as the front man and some fresh songs, things began to sound most promising. New names for the group began to emerge and after a couple of false starts, they finally settled on **Well, Well, Well.** Personally, I thought it a totally unsuitable name as at the time a new group from Scotland called **Wet, Wet, Wet,** were fast gaining a name for themselves. I pointed out to them that the group's chosen name was far too close to it, but unfortunately my deep misgivings were contemptuously brushed aside. Within weeks, the keyboard player seemed to have taken over as he gradually introduced his own songs while two of my particular favorites, namely "White Africans" and "Cold Turkey" were promptly consigned to the rejection bin. However, some of his songs sounded really promising and as the previous group members had seemed incapable of producing any of their own, I allowed things to progress. Soon they were gigging on a regular basis including headlining at The Marquee in London. After each successful gig, the all too familiar roller coaster of high expectation and excitement began to build and it seemed only a matter of time before they were signed. At each Marquee gig, being important as always, I knew I would have to work extremely hard to try and ensure it was full. In order to help me achieve this aim, Jack Barrie had kindly given me a print out of every residential college in London as well as a multitude of nurses' homes. Armed with this information, and prior to each gig, I had a thousand flyers printed each admitting the holder and a guest free of charge. In order to assist me, Robert Coyle would painstakingly write out the addresses and I would post them off. On the night, as they were eagerly handed in, I asked the receptionist to discreetly hide them so it would appear to any outsider as though everyone present had paid. During one appearance, in order to help give the impression that the group had become a huge draw, Jack placed an A board outside saying "Sorry Club Full," even though there was still room for a few more. Here, it must be pointed out that a completely unknown group attracting a full house at The Marquee Club in Wardour St quickly got people talking, and even more importantly, got them noticed. As an experienced promoter, I sensed it wouldn't be too long before word reached the ears of a major record company. But would the strategy work? Everything now hung in the balance as I certainly hoped so. Around this time, an exciting new rock show known as "The Tube" began being aired on national TV. The show soon established a name for breaking unknown bands such as **Sade, Frankie Goes To Hollywood,** and **Fine Young Cannibals** among many others. As "The Tube" assumed greater national importance, I requested that the band be given a chance to appear on it. "I'm sending Chris Phipps to see them," Malcolm Gerrie the producer informed me. "He's our A & R guy and depending on his assessment, we'll decide whether or not to showcase them." On hearing this, I was in turmoil, knowing the show was being televised from Newcastle and everything now hinged on Chris Phipps opinion. Realising its importance, I began to look for any inherent weaknesses the band might possess. Were the songs strong enough? Would the guitarist break a string? Would the sound be all right? Finally, and most importantly, would Rob hit the right notes and be his usual confident self? On the night the gig finally arrived, I tried not to worry. Nevertheless, pressure of this nature seems to make each minor concern outweigh its actual importance. Shortly, what turned out to be an important but inoffensive looking figure sidled over before introducing himself. "Hi, I'm Chris Phipps. "I've come to see the band." His softly spoken words had an air of friendliness and warmth which immediately put me at ease. He then proceeded to shake hands while I quickly recognised was no ordinary greeting as it signified a possible TV appearance together with a route to the top in double quick time. I smiled and nodded approvingly as if to dispel any misgivings he may have held. For some inexplicable reason, my confidence began to sag. In reality, there was no reason why it should. However, I felt apprehensive as I began wondering if I was subjecting myself to needless worry. Finally, after a scintillating set, the audience applauded the last of the two encores as I began to question what would come next. Moment's later Chris Phipps began to amble towards me in a somewhat restrained and casual manner. Each fateful step seemed to take an unbearable amount of time as I nervously awaited what could be a momentous decision. Just then, he spoke. "I'm going to recommend them for the show," he told me. His words hit me hard as I heaved a huge sigh of relief. A grateful and joyous band immediately surrounded him with faces wreathed in smiles. However, would it lead to a major record contract and eventual stardom? It seemed that as one mountain was climbed, another always appeared to loom. Right then, I realised they were in with a real and genuine chance of stardom? Once again, I began to dream about the possibilities. Heady aspirations soon began to emerge accompanied by a whole profusion of wild and invigorating thoughts. Stardom and success are basically the same thing especially if followed by longevity and credibility. "The Tube" now offered this tantalising and exhilarating prospect. Forget **James Brown, Elvis, The Beatles, The Rolling Stones, The Animals Jackie Milburn and Charlie Hurley,** the illustrious centre half of Sunderland fame. Chris Phipps had now become our new local hero and to this day, he is someone I have never forgotten or failed to appreciate.

Soon, the band were filmed on location inside an aircraft hanger at Usworth Aerodrome on the outskirts of Sunderland, (now the site of The Nissan car factory). The song they had chosen to showcase was entitled "Possession or the Run." In my opinion it sounded excellent and I was feeling quietly confident it would create a highly favourable impression with any watching record company and television viewers. Here, it must be pointed out that a major record contract signifies far more than it may appear to any interested outsider. Initially, it's not just about selling records and becoming worldwide stars. In the early stages of being signed it is imperative to establish a toe hold which will help introduce the group to a much wider audience. As I said earlier, this is where a major record company can make or break a band with their press and promotion department together with their A& R talent scout all using vital contacts and energy to promote the group to a much wider audience. Amidst all this are the major agents who book the band into universities as well as the major festivals in both the UK and Europe. Unless you have acquired that all important record contract they are highly unlikely to take you on to their books. Each one of the above has their own particular part to play. As members of a cohesive unit employed to wholeheartedly back a newly signed band, the benefits are incalculable. Finally, a word about a record producer. In many ways he is the most important person of all. A group with a well written song which has potential is obviously the starting point. But a good producer with years of studio experience behind him, coupled with an excellent musical insight in how to enhance the sound of the song, is absolutely invaluable. The difference between a band's demo and a finished production of the song can be immense. Take **Frankie Goes To Hollywood** for example. The difference in quality between the "Tube" appearance of their first big hit, "Relax" and the finished release was incredible, thanks to the genius of Trevor Horn. Other examples are **Simple Minds** and **U2**. Both have at some time been produced by Steve Lillywhite who was instrumental in giving each band a unique and comprehensive sound of their own. Then of course there is Mick Ronson who produced **Amy Winehouse's** "Back In Black," Among all this, let's not forget George Martin, the truly brilliant and charismatic producer of the **Beatles**. Fortunately, after all these years, I was finally able to shake hands with him at the 2006 Hall Of Fame Awards at the Alexandra Palace in London. Unfortunately, experience has taught me that in choosing the wrong producer, you may well pay the supreme penalty of abject failure. Unfortunately, I should know as it has happened to me on more than one occasion.

A good example of having a major record company behind you is **AC/DC**. As a completely unknown band they supported **Back St Crawler** at Surrey University while I was the latter's co-manager. Fortunately for them, the whole of Atlantic Records American hierarchy who were present, saw them, and decided to sign them. Personally, I thought they were nothing special, but it seems they were able to see something which I didn't, and still can't. Within months, after huge full page adverts in the music press, thousands of dollars spent in America on television and radio promotion, a top studio together with a brilliant producer in Mutt Langer, followed by headline spots at major gigs with top class equipment, they quickly became huge. In fact, to me, it was readily apparent that they had achieved success by having a whole marketing machine unleashed on their behalf. In cases like this, in my opinion, initially the general public is being force fed into believing a band are much bigger than they really are. Later, when going to see them live under an array of professional lights, huge PA, and a multitude of adverts in the press, one cannot deny that they must be big, especially if as usual, the gigs are all sold out. However, in real terms its hype, or to give it its full name, hyperbole. Having seen them both in Dortmund and at Donnington Festival, I still haven't changed my opinion. In fairness, Brian Johnson the lead singer is a wonderful down to earth chap who isn't the slightest bit affected by his megastar status. Fortunately, he remains the same person that I knew when he was struggling and despite my critical observations, I am truly and genuinely delighted at his world wide success.

Soon, the possibility of actually being signed after the group's appearance on "The Tube" had everyone on an ever increasing high. Back home a few days later, the telephone rang. "Saw the band on "The Tube," said an executive of Jive Records in London. "I'd like to put them into our studio for a couple of days to hear some more songs. Would that be possible?" he inquired. Once again, my heart began to race as I was confident that the band had an abundance of excellent songs and it was now just a question of choosing one which would impress him. Later, I walked into Louis' coffee bar in the town centre. Here, the sadly deceased Tony Maggiore, one of the three brothers who were the proprietors always kept a dictionary beneath the counter and was never at a loss to explain its meaning when a difficult word cropped up. But today was different. The group had recently appeared on national television and would soon be travelling down to London, with a possible recording contract in the offing. Just then, the keyboard player walked in with a certain swagger. By now, he had become their unofficial spokesman and seemed to hold a certain mystical power over them which the others looked up to. Whether this was healthy or not I was undecided, but with his guidance they had got this far and as yet, there was no real cause for concern. "What song are you going to record?" I asked. "Hungry for Love," he replied. On hearing this, my jaw dropped.

151

I looked at him with a certain disquiet, knowing that while he had undoubted musical talent, he lacked experience of major recording studios as well as the uncompromising and corporate machinations of the music business. It was also (in my opinion) a very poor song and Rob the lead singer always seemed to struggle with it. "You can't possibly do that," I pleaded in desperation. "You have songs which are far superior," I implored. His reaction was cold and impassive, tinged with a touch of arrogance. "That's the song everyone wants to do," he replied dismissively. "Everybody likes it and it always goes down well at live gigs," he countered. "Yes, but whenever you've played it the audiences has had a few drinks and Rob's stage presence succeeds in putting it across. However, in the studio, it will be seen for what it is, a very average song." "You may think so, but we don't," he informed me abruptly. Horror stricken, I slumped into a corner and relived the long drive to Nottingham in order to pick up his new Roland keyboard as well as the £1200 cost of it. All the hard work to get them on "The Tube" and the years of slaving away to acquire this opportunity also came to mind. Just then, I could see failure staring us in the face. But how do you convince someone who has not the slightest respect for your own opinion? Despite this, there was just a chance he was right, although in reality, I failed to see it. However, that's stardom for you. One TV appearance and a possible major record contract in the offing can quickly elevate someone to heady and far reaching heights which most of us can never hope to achieve.

Meanwhile, I secretly harboured hopes that other record companies might also ring. After all, "The Tube" was a national TV show which had made major stars of previously unknown acts. Unfortunately, as each day passed, the much hoped for calls failed to materialise which meant that everything now hinged on the trip to Battery Studios in London. Ironically, this was where **The Cars** had recorded their big hit, "Drive." Meanwhile, just to step into the same studio as them felt really exciting, especially as there remained a distinct possibility of following in their footsteps. Once there, the group pleaded with me to ask for an extra day to "mix" the song,, or in layman's terms, to get the balance right, which would also give them more time to record the song. "We need three days, not two," I suggested to

David Rose their A & R guy. "I'll see what I can do," he replied hopefully. I liked David Rose. Ever since the band's TV appearance he had kept his eye on the group and had been very influential in getting us noticed. "Okay, you've got the extra day," he informed me a few hours later. The following day the band was in the recording studio. "The lead singer is not quite hitting the note," confided the engineer. I nodded in agreement, having already heard him through the speakers in the control room. As the song progressed, my worst fears began to be realised. I was aware the group was now 300 miles away from the crowd who had supposedly cheered the song and the portents were far from good. There appeared to be a hesitancy about Rob's voice and a complete lack of smoothness in his rendition. In places it felt strained and unnatural as well as extremely uninteresting. Inside I felt sad, knowing how hard he was trying to clinch the record contract which meant so much to him and the band. However, sadly, and unknown to any of them, it appeared to be rapidly slipping away. Having completed the recording, four days later I walked into the managing director's office. I glanced at David Rose's face which looked extremely glum, while his boss's looked positively downcast. After the usual exchange of pleasantries, he gave me the news I had always feared. "We have decided to pass," he said. "I wish you all the best in the future and you can have the master tape to play to other record companies," he advised. On hearing his words I slumped dejectedly in my seat. Master tape. The words somehow seemed ludicrous, conjuring up expectations of something wonderful to listen to, but I knew different. "How can you play a seriously mediocre tape to other people?" I wanted to ask. I turned and left with a heavy heart as the girl on reception smiled. Whether it was routine or sincere was irrelevant as I made my way to the exit.

Rejection is a bitter pill to swallow, even if it is half expected, although it definitely fails to soften the blow. Once outside I glanced down at my feet. It was a habit I had acquired in tense situations like this, which in some way seemed to signify I could no longer face the world. In fact, I couldn't face anyone, not even the ticket inspector at the tube station. Suddenly, it began to rain as the droplets rolled off my face and onto my clothes. Inside, the feeling of despair and failure represented a major setback. Why had it happened and could it have been avoided? If only I had dug my heels in and been more insistent. These disturbing and unsettling thoughts raced through my mind in a never ending assault on my shattered senses. By now, I was at bursting point and realised the frustration had to have an outlet. I became angry knowing that opportunities such as this are extremely rare and must be seized with both hands. Unfortunately the prize had slipped away because someone with a one dimensional and arrogant viewpoint had decided he knew best. Of course the same accusation could be levelled at me. However, I was brought up to work as a team. Dad had instilled this highly important ethos into us on any occasion which warranted it. The bill for the hire van, the petrol and telephone costs, all paid for by my two business friends came to mind as well as the long drive and completely wasted effort. However looking back seemed futile and counter productive as I wondered whether they would learn from this experience. I certainly hoped so, but only time would tell. Later, I walked into the flat they were staying at in Roman Rd, Bow, which had also been provided free of charge by my two friends. After informing the group of the record company's decision, one of them sent me into fits of apoplectic laughter. "Well, **The Beatles** got turned down at first didn't they?" he cried. There was no denying he was right, but at least once they were in the studio they could hit the right notes and write a mean tune, I thought to myself.

Back in Sunderland, my enthusiasm was at an all time low. "Saw the band on "The Tube." Did you get a record contract out of it?" asked a friend of mine. "Afraid not," I replied glumly. "Oh! I thought once you appeared on it you were almost guaranteed to get signed," he exclaimed. My heart sank knowing the real tragedy was that he was just about right. But where there's success there's always failure, and of course it had to be us. A few days later, in a rush of blood to the head, (thanks **Coldplay**), I awoke with a renewed sense of purpose, knowing that somehow I had to get the band a record contract, despite my resolve being tested to its absolute limit. I recalled how an unknown **David Bowie** had once pleaded with Wilf Wright at Chrysalis Agency to help him find work. Also, **Rod Stewart** was once sacked from **Shotgun Express** because they thought he wasn't good enough and look what happened to him. However, despite the setbacks, I recognised the importance of keeping the group in the public eye, especially in London. Fortunately, Jack Barrie remained most helpful and loyal as he continued to give them a headlining residency on a monthly basis. During this period, I continued to press unstintingly and wholeheartedly for another chance to appear on "The Tube." "Sorry Geoff, we can't put them on again otherwise it would look as though it was just a regional programme, when in fact it's a national one. Besides, you've had your chance." The producer Malcom Gerrie's words hit me hard. He was right and I knew we'd blown it. If only I could get them on again. Surely this time they wouldn't repeat the same mistake, I thought to myself. I tried, oh how I tried, but it was to no avail. Meanwhile, at the Marquee, they continued to be excellent and began acquiring a professional polish which lifted my heart and spurred me on to greater efforts. Months went by and still there was no breakthrough as the sheer frustration of it all began to creep in. Back in Sunderland, bereft of enthusiasm, while at the same time having had my willpower tested to near breaking point, I again walked aimlessly through the streets and instinctively kicked out at an empty drinks can. Such conduct could be described as loutish or anti social, but in reality it can only be described as a form of escapism. Suddenly, a policeman loomed and I glanced at him, knowing he was a figure of authority, but I didn't seem to care. As uneventful days and weeks went by, time dragged on through inexorable and meaningless days of rehearsals. Once back in London, and after a series of unending and persistent phone calls, it seemed all my efforts were about to pay off. Days earlier, at the invitation of Dave Ambrose, the head of A&R at EMI Records, I'd arranged a meeting with him in his illustrious offices. Might have a better chance there I reasoned as I made my way there. Didn't they have the foresight to sign **The Beatles** when others had turned them down? It was an encouraging thought as I sat in reception amongst a whole myriad of platinum and gold albums hanging on the walls. Eventually, I was called upstairs to meet Dave who wielded power far beyond the dreams of any unsigned group. In doing so, my heart raced as each of my fateful steps took us nearer to possible stardom. At that moment I recalled how I'd followed **The Beatles** to Hamburg, had slept in the same seedy hotel as them, and sat in the same tiny dressing room at The Top Ten Club where they had previously played as unknowns. Now here I was following them into EMI Records. My head began to spin knowing a local jeweller in Sunderland sold gold and platinum rings to the delight of loving couples who proudly displayed them to their friends and relatives. However, gold and platinum albums sounded much better. For a start they were much bigger and if you were lucky enough to "make it," they gave them to you free of charge, not forgetting the accompanying cheque. Looking around, pictures of **The Beatles** were everywhere, not that I needed reminding of what they looked like. Also, the group I represented were much younger than them, surely that had to count for something, especially where girls were concerned. Finally, I was ushered into his office. "What's your name?" he inquired in a rather aimless and disinterested tone. "Geoff. Geoff Docherty," I replied. "Why are you here?" he asked. My morale instantly sank to zero as I realised the 300 mile journey and dozens of phone calls seemed to have been a futile gesture which had failed to register in his memory. "I'm the manager of a band called **Well, Well, Well,**" I replied, while at the same time trying to hide my intense irritation. Seconds later he slipped the highly prized demo tape into his cassette machine while looking totally bored. As he did so, I noticed there was a tired look in his eyes and a sluggish weariness about his movements which seemed to indicate he was in urgent need of a holiday or a good night's sleep. Minutes later, he leant forward and casually handed back the tape as I sensed the portents looked far from good. In fact, nothing looked good, as his face, the weather, and my disquieting thoughts all merged into a raging morass of outright apathy and rejection. "It's not for us," he informed me in a matter of fact and uncaring manner. I swallowed hard. This was the heart of EMI Records and I had been thrilled when I had first stepped through the door. Now, I made my way out with my hopes dashed, accompanied by the sheer disbelief that one man had such overwhelming power. Once outside, my heart was heavy and I couldn't help recalling the Charles Dickens classic, "Great Expectations" knowing mine had just been cruelly shattered. "Have a good day," someone had said earlier. Thinking about it, all I could do was laugh, having experienced the absurdity of what had just occurred. Suddenly, while walking, I realised the tape in my pocket was proving to be unnecessarily bulky, especially as it had failed to make the slightest impact. Now, it was just excess baggage and in many ways, I felt that I was too.

Later that day, I wandered into an alehouse in Soho and quickly began noticing people laughing and joking as if they didn't have a care in the world. A mixture of office workers and attractive girls mingled together, creating an unrehearsed and natural jollity that was most refreshing to witness. The warm and cosy ambience quickly became infectious. Before long, someone laughed heartily and as it reverberated around the room, I began to smile. Why the person was convulsed or besieged with such merriment seemed of little significance. What did matter was that they were human beings too and deserved life's rewards and pleasures just the same as everybody else. After a few sips of beer I began reliving my short visit to the much vaunted EMI Records. I consoled myself with the thought that at least I'd managed to get inside and surely this in itself was some sort of achievement, no matter how brief. A couple of beers later, the immense disappointment began to slowly ebb away and I began wondering if I got down and prayed, would that make any difference? In order to get that elusive record contract it seemed it was the only option I had left, as I'd tried everything else. Later still, I wandered past Raymond's Revue Bar in Soho where lots of pretty girls in near naked poses were displayed on coloured photographs outside. The eagle eyed doorman gave me the once over, but failed to smile as I wandered on. Life seemed aimless as a hostess with far too much make-up on beckoned me inside a club, or should I say "clip joint." "Want business love?" asked an attractive girl as I wandered further along. I smiled before shaking my head in a clear sign that I was declining her offer and continued to walk on. Ironically, earlier that day I certainly had wanted business, but not the sort that she had in mind. However, tomorrow was another day as I wondered what frustrations it would bring? Once back at home, and despite everything that had happened, the group's expectations continued to be exceedingly optimistic. Fortunately, they were young and not yet acquainted with the disquieting and sobering realities of abject failure. Nevertheless, my protective arms were beginning to tire knowing that it was clearly becoming apparent that no one wanted to sign them and it seemed the end was near.

A few days later, the telephone rang. "Is that Geoff Docherty? It's Geoff Wonfor here, the director of "The Tube." Are you still managing that group?" he inquired. "Yes, I certainly am" I replied. "Can you have them at the Marquee in London for nine in the morning? We have a film crew there all ready to film a band, but one of them is ill and they can't make it, can you?" I immediately glanced at my watch. It was 11am, we were 300 miles away and I didn't have a clue where the band members were. "We'll be there," I gushed excitely. "Okay, but don't be late, see you in the morning," he uttered. I put the phone down in stunned silence and took a deep breath. Another appearance on "The Tube." It sounded too good to be true but it was no dream; we really were being giving another chance. Now began an urgent search to find the group and inform them of the fantastic news. Within two hours I'd contacted four of them but there was no sign of Colin the guitarist. Panic stricken, we searched every pub and café he usually frequented, but it was all to no avail. The clock ticked inexorably away and by now it was 5pm and dark. In desperation, I asked the manager of the local ABC cinema if he would flash a massage on the screen during the interval in case he was there, but he refused. "It has to be an emergency before we can do anything like that," he informed me. "This is an emergency. The group has a chance to be on national television which may lead to a major record contract," I urged. Despite my desperation, he looked at me in a cold and dispassionate manner without the slightest semblance of concern or sympathy. However, I reluctantly understood his viewpoint as I walked disconsolately back into the street before quickening my step. I knew it was imperative that we find Colin as everything hinged on it and unknown to him, he was holding everything up. "He may have gone shopping in Newcastle with his girlfriend," suggested someone. On hearing this, I cringed at the very thought. If he had, it would mean we would have to travel overnight and the group would be extremely tired for the actual filming. Just then, an even worse thought occurred to me. What if we were unable to find him? Aside from the missed opportunity, I knew Geoff Wonfor would be absolutely furious after I had assured him we would definitely be there. The search continued as dozens of phone calls were made, numerous messages left, and all possible locations searched. It was 6pm when miraculously, he finally appeared carrying his guitar. "I got your message off my girlfriend's dad," he informed me in a breathless voice as I heaved a huge sigh of relief. "What about our equipment?" he asked. "We only need guitars and keyboard. They have hired everything else including the PA and drums," I hurriedly informed him. Within thirty minutes we were on our way with Mac the roadie, together with six of us and instruments packed like sardines into my estate car. After a long and tortuous journey we finally arrived in London in the early hours at the flat kindly provided for us by the two business partners of mine.

After just a token few hours sleep we finally made it to the Marquee to be warmly greeted by Geoff Wonfor. Here, it must be pointed out that he is a big friendly sort of chap with a great and unbridled sense of humour as well as being an avid Newcastle United supporter. Later, he went on to film **The Beatles Anthology** for which received world wide critical acclaim. Affable and efficient, he quickly set about his task in a true workmanlike manner, while never once having to raise his voice. Inside, I looked at the stage together with the camera crew which seemed all too unreal. In the past, I'd been there so many times and seen so many groups; I'd never imagined anything like this would ever happen. However, this was no dream; it was reality, and an exciting one at that. All kind of mixed emotions crossed my mind knowing that possible stardom beckoned once again and it seemed like the equivalent of landing on the moon. "One giant step for mankind," uttered Neil Armstrong on that never to be forgotten day. Sitting in the empty bar those memorable words came to me, knowing that we too might well be taking a giant step into the hallowed portals of musical fame. Dad had often said "learn all you can son." Years earlier he had passed away and I couldn't help thinking of how thrilled he had been when he first met **John Peel** in my small flat in Sunderland. I also recalled how while sitting in Castletown pit canteen after a hard shift underground he would offer me half his dinner because he was extremely worried about my small stature and wanted me to put on weight. Suddenly, the group were about to appear on national television for the second time and I felt sad that he wouldn't be there to see them. Now, everything hung in the balance as countless immediate concerns about the group began to surface. Would they finally acquire that ever elusive and tempting record contract? How would they come across on national television and would they eventually achieve stardom? Just then, Geoff Wonfor, the man who had gifted us with this last fateful chance after seeing the band playing at a club in London, wandered towards me. "Are the group ready?" he inquired in a highly professional and friendly manner. "Yes." I replied. Now, once again, it was all up to them. An hour later, with all the equipment nicely plugged in and a sound check completed, filming finally began to take place. I looked towards the stage and was elated at realising the lights, the live sound and the song the band had chosen all seemed to merge into a harmonious and pulsating picture of sheer bliss. A few days later, there they were on national television once again as I held my breath in anticipation. For all this to be happening seemed so surreal, while inside I felt an immense amount of personal satisfaction. "Everything comes to those who wait." At that moment this well known proverb suddenly began reverberating around in my head. If it held true, I sensed that finally all the hard work was about to pay off. Seconds later, the opening television sequence came up. "Here is a band that is going to be very big," announced Paula Yates as she stood at the entrance to the Marquee with a poster of the group prominently and proudly displayed alongside her. Her upper class voice sounded genuinely sincere and without her spellbinding introduction, I'm convinced their appearance wouldn't have had the same impact. I continued to stare in disbelief at the screen, still stunned at such a wonderful introduction. I hadn't expected anything quite like it and somehow the sincerity in her voice convinced me that things would almost certainly be different this time. Once on screen, the band broke into a song entitled "Set Me Free," which I thought was excellent while Rob the lead singer came across exceptionally well. Quietly confident, I hit the replay button on the video and proceeded to play it over and over again. "This is more like it" were the first words that came to my mind, but what would the reaction of the record companies be? Once again, their whole career was in the lap of the gods.

Chapter 9

"Hello, is that Geoff Docherty the manager of the group **Well-Well-Well** who appeared on The Tube last week?" asked a voice on the telephone which I failed to recognise. "Yes it is," I replied. "It's Mickey Most here. I saw the group on "The Tube" and thought they had potential. You haven't signed a record deal yet, have you?" he inquired. "No, I haven't," I eagerly informed him. "When will you be in town?" he asked. "Next week," I replied. "When you get here, can you give me a call as I'd like to take you out to lunch and discuss a record contract with you," he continued. After finalising the details I replaced the receiver in stunned silence. After all, it's not every day a group manager gets a call from someone like him, especially as he had produced dozens of hits including **The Animals,** "House Of The Rising Sun" and **Jeff Beck's** "Hi Ho, Silver Lining, as well as being the owner of an up to the minute 24 track recording studio. It seemed like a fairytale come true and I was in a complete state of awe at the news. Suddenly, the show was back on the road, and "The Tube," Paula Yates and Geoff Wonfor had done us proud. Later that day I walked through the town centre with a new sense of purpose while feeling as though I could almost walk on water. Lunch with Micky Most. Thinking about it brought a quiet feeling of optimism and the mere thought of being able to meet him once again gave me a tremendous sense of satisfaction. A few days later after a trouble free journey I alighted from the train at Kings Cross Station in London. Looking back, many years earlier I had done exactly the same thing as a naïve teenager when first making my way to join the Fleet Air Arm at Lee on Solent. On arriving at Kings Cross, a uniformed Petty Officer was waiting to greet the six of us who had made the journey and I felt very nervous when we finally arrived at our destination and had been shown to our quarters. Having done so, he quickly summonsed us to gather round him. As he spoke, his warning words appeared to be extremely harsh, unfriendly and overbearing. "From now on you have lost all privacy and must immediately obey any orders given to you," he warned. "Failure to do so means that you will be taken before your divisional officer and charged. This could even lead to a court martial depending upon the seriousness of the offence. If more than two of you rebel, it will be classed as mutiny and you will be severely dealt with. If convicted, after serving your prison sentence in Colchester Military Prison you will be cashiered out of the service with a dishonourable discharge which means no one will ever want to employ you." As his stark and chilling words reverberated around the room, I felt as if my own life and any attempts at self reasoning had instantly been taken away from me. One fateful signature together with the Queens oath was all it had taken. However, this time was different as I was no longer so naïve. At least, in a moment of irrepressible pride, I liked to think so, despite Micky Most's persuasive charm and captivating friendliness on the telephone.

Days later we met in Cranks health food restaurant just off Carnaby St, which was always a personal favourite of mine. Here, it must be said that meeting Mickey Most for the second time turned out to be a wonderful experience. (I'd met him years earlier in his office when I'd first booked **Led Zeppelin** where he was in a business partnership with Peter Grant, their manager). There wasn't the slightest sign of ego and I found him to be extremely friendly and completely natural. Within minutes he had laid out a lucrative deal before me which to say the least, was very tempting. "I need to speak to the band first," I informed him after a few minutes of deep contemplation. "Why don't you bring them down to London and let them see the studio and the flat in which I will accommodate them while they are recording," he suggested. The more we talked, the more interesting his offer became, which seemed almost too good to be true. A week later, one of his staff took me and the group to visit the studio before going on to view the flat. It proved to be a revelation as, coming from a working class background, it personified sheer luxury. The curtains opened and closed electronically and a wide screen television appeared at the touch of a button. There was also a beautiful bathroom with every facility together with a split level lounge that was richly carpeted throughout. I can't remember how many bedrooms it had, but they were certainly lavish. On viewing its luxurious interior, the band immediately fell in love with it and I can't say I blame them. Nevertheless, as a manager it was incumbent on me to be suspicious. By now, having moved a little further along life's path, it had become a trait of mine and one which any sensible or experienced person develops. Unfortunately, despite his caring and overwhelming kindness, there was one major snag. The record company which he owned was Rak Records who had had a string of hit singles which had all consisted of lightweight pop, **Suzie Quatro** being one I remember. In those days there was a certain stigma to a label like his which meant that any "underground" or discerning music lovers refused to take acts on his label seriously. Being fully aware of this, it was my job to steer the group towards a long selling album career together with one which gave them lasting credibility. A few days later, Dave Dee, (now deceased) who was presently working as A & R for Mickey Most, came to see the band play live. Ironically, I had also previously encountered Dave when he had worked at Warner Bros as head of A&R and often used to go in and visit him. I can honestly say I've never met a nicer person in the whole of my musical career, but unfortunately the relationship was to turn sour and I was completely to blame. To this day, I still haven't been able to forgive myself for not plucking up the courage to speak to him, not that I deserved to. "Yes, we'll sign for your label," I had eagerly told him in answer to a question of his. Having acknowledged my reply he smiled before buying me a drink in the Le Chasse Club in Wardour St, London, so the deal was now all set. A few days later, I bumped into John Wolf, who for many years had been the tour manager for **The Who.** Later, he went on to manage **John Parr** who had previously had a No 1 single in America with "St Elmo's Fire." "Let me contact Chris Cook at Arista Records. He's a friend of mine and I'm sure I can get you a better deal," he informed me enthusiastically with a calm assertiveness that was positively reassuring. "I can't. I've already agreed a deal with Dave Dee to sign for Rak Records," I replied, with words that were tinged with a certain regret. "I can get you a much better deal than he has proposed, but I will want a small percentage," he informed me in an encouraging manner. His words, which were accompanied by an air of complete and unquestioning authority sounded convincing, especially as I had previously promoted **The Who** four times when he was their tour manager. As he spoke, I listened with a fascinated attentiveness while pondering over the possibilities. Finally, and despite my naturally suspicious nature, I decided to wait and see what he came up with. Here it must be pointed out that at this time Arista Records were shifting monumental amount of records with **Whitney** Houston. This, together with their other well established stars was, in my mind, a clear indication that they would almost certainly be able to offer a much better deal

A few days later, Chris Cook, Arista's senior A&R scout, came to see the band who were making another live appearance at the Marquee Club and thought they were excellent. "Unless I'm involved the record company won't sign them," John Wolf quietly informed me. I thought long and hard as I contemplated the lucrative carrot he had thrown into the ring. "I've negotiated a £75,000 advance as well as £75,000 recording costs. What's more, they are guaranteed another £75,000 for the second album and £75,000 to record it regardless of how the first one does. That's a lot better than the £10,000 Rak Records have offered you, isn't it? And don't forget, my artist has already had a No 1 hit in America." His words sounded highly compelling and the deal was undeniably a vast improvement on what was on offer at Rak. £150,000 against £10,000 was very tempting. I tossed and turned, but it seemed it was no contest. Having prided myself on my integrity, I knew that if I did decide to make the change, I'd never be able to face Dave Dee again. However, I had to think about the band's future, together with the potential for economic stability and realised I had an overriding duty to obtain the best possible deal on their behalf. A week later, I met Dave in a London club to find he was in an excellent mood as he immediately started talking positively about his future plans for the group. All the while I shifted uneasily and found I was unable to look him in the eye. Minutes later, with my conscience playing havoc with my emotions, I could stand the deceit no longer. "We're not going to sign for you as we've had a much better offer from Arista," I shamefacedly informed him. On hearing my words he took a step back as if allowing time for the shock to register. "You are joking," he stuttered. "No I'm not. I'm sorry but I've decided to go with Arista and the deal is all agreed," I sheepishly informed him with words which sounded uncaring and cruel. He looked at me with piercing eyes which seemed to go right through me before storming out with a look of sheer disbelief and shock on his face. As I stood there, it was one of my saddest moments in rock, knowing that I'd lost a friend while sensing I had inflicted unnecessary hurt on his professional dignity. Not only that, I had also insulted him which in many ways was hurting me as much as him. Meanwhile, the rest of the evening proved to be a vacant and self chastising blur. Inwardly, my heart was crying as he was such a warm hearted person who had unfailingly made me most welcome whenever I had visited him in his office at Warner Brothers. Thirty pieces of silver. It was part of ancient history but it was as relevant at that particular moment as at anytime I could recall. I had reached out and grasped it with my own eager hands as I consoled myself with the thought that there were five hungry mouths to feed. My own deceitful words, no matter how sincerely intended at the time, had proved to be worthless. Would the trade off be worth it? Somehow, I was already beginning to have grave misgivings.

After intensive negotiations between the lawyers, John Wolf and the record company, everything had eventually come to a successful conclusion. Later, we all met up at Arista's offices just behind Oxford Circus for the official signing ceremony. It was here that I tasted my first glass of Bollinger champagne despite initially refusing it as I normally drink lager or bitter. However, it proved to be a pleasant surprise even though I've never had a glass since. Bottles of it were in abundance and the atmosphere was one of sheer unadulterated exuberance while the band were being photographed and feted as though they were already major stars. Finally, after all the heartache, we were there and thanks to "The Tube," we had signed that long sought after major recording contract. On completion of the signing I breathed a huge sigh of relief. For me, it was a vindication of the personal belief I had always held in the talent and ability of Robert Coyle. Inwardly, I had never waivered in my opinion that he was too good not to make it and despite the setbacks, I'd always felt it was just a question of time before he made it big, especially with such an excellent band behind him. Amidst the euphoria, I took a deep breath and looked around at everyone who was there. Despite holding certain reservations (having been through it all before), it seemed as if the group were now set for a triumphant journey into the higher echelons of the rock world. This was especially so as everyone was in such an optimistic and buoyant mood. To attempt to describe the immense relief I felt is no easy task. Any remaining doubts about the ability of the band together with the setbacks we had suffered were all in the past. Euphoric is a word which instantly signifies an inner and joyous happiness. Ecstatic has more of an outward projection as if wishing to share your immense joy with the whole world, or at least anyone who may be near. At that moment, I was experiencing both and became conscious of a tremendous sense of inner pride together with unbridled optimism. Handshakes, glasses clinking, and Geoff Gilbert the managing director, Chris Cook the A&R chap who had signed them, and a whole retinue of people all seemed to be in a delightful mood. Meanwhile, the next morning my head had cleared and I couldn't wait to get started. "Saving All My Love For You," **Whitney Houston** had sung this song to worldwide acclaim and now we were on the same label. In the record company's foyer her picture was everywhere and she looked positively radiant. Her huge broad smile showing her immaculate white teeth seemed to epitomise everything good about Arista Records while at the same time appearing to give any visitor a warm and welcoming reception. Was I excited at the possibilities, you bet I was?

Nevertheless, I was under no illusions about the task ahead but as I said earlier, life is all about dreams together with its accompanying challenges and endless opportunities. A few weeks later, I instigated a meeting with Rod McSween of International Talent Booking Agency (ITB) in his offices in Wardour St, whereupon he agreed to represent the group. Fortunately, I already knew he handled dozens of major names, including **Neil Young** and **The Who,** having booked many acts off him in the past. Once again, after the opening pleasantries of the day had been affected, we immediately got down to business. "Initially we will start booking them out around the colleges for £75 until we see how the album sells," he informed me. I nodded in agreement as I knew this was the usual procedure for a newly signed band. Unknown to him, sitting in his office felt good as I knew he was a big time operator who was perfectly capable of steering the band into the very highest echelons of the music industry. To have him on board was a major coup and within a few days their first booking came in, which was to be at a college in Oxford. Later that evening, I informed the group and was aghast to find they were far from happy. Unfortunately, I was soon to find out that after signing a major record deal and having had their photographs taken (with accompanying flashbulbs) while drinking Bollinger Champagne, they were now under the mistaken impression that they were major stars and would be going out for a much bigger fee. In other words, they now thought that such a small sum was beneath their dignity. "You haven't sold a record yet," I replied in frustration as I turned away in sheer disbelief. Unfortunately, it had become blatantly apparent that their horizons had prematurely reached unrealistic proportions, while virtually overnight, all the previous bonhomie and hard work appeared to have become meaningless. I can assure you to be involved in such unnecessary histrionics is very stressful. I also realised they desperately needed a steadying hand on the tiller from someone within the group in order to keep their feet on the ground. Unfortunately however, there was no one able or prepared to grasp it. I thought of the sentiments of peace and love which had been such a rallying call in the early days of rock and had imbued everyone with unimaginable hope. I also thought of the majority of kind, gentle and considerate people who had first come to the Bay Hotel and The Fillmore North when I was promoting there. Then I recalled the **Van Morrison & The Caledonian Soul Orchestra** gig at Newcastle City Hall which I'd been fortunate enough to promote. I was privileged to witness one of the nicest crowds I'd ever encountered as they were calm, mannerly, respectful and highly knowledgeable. Just to be present and be able to recall their smiling faces is a never to be forgotten memory. Unfortunately, it was now 1987 and **Well, Well, Well** had blatantly overlooked or chosen to ignore those early ideals. I realised a new and unrealistic set of values had not only overtaken them, but was deeply imbued in their own quest for stardom. However, I remained committed as I desperately hoped that it was just a temporary hiccup and common sense would ultimately prevail.

A few weeks later, the incomparable and ever helpful Jack Barrie came to my rescue once again and kindly agreed to showcase the group at The Reading Festival. Backstage it was sunny and there was an aura of expectation coupled with a nervous confidence that this was their big chance. A major record deal, a big stage, and a huge crowd were the portents for greatness, if I'm allowed to use such a word. Unfortunately, and to my consternation, they proved to be abysmal and failed to ignite the slightest semblance of enthusiasm from the crowd. In an amazing lack of foresight, Rob the lead singer had chosen to wear a pair of tight fitting white trousers that looked ridiculous in the context of a major rock festival. He looked more like a jumped up pop star who was exhorting the audience to look at him, rather than listen to what he was singing. At the end of each song the audience demonstrably booed and to my immense consternation, I realised it was all going horribly wrong. I reminded myself that just a few years earlier **Beckett** had gone down fantastically well and left me bursting with pride. Conversely, while watching **"Well, Well, Well,"** I had become became red faced with embarrassment. In the course of their set, everything seemed to be too smooth and contrived while lacking their usual punch and vigour. Unfortunately, during his tenure, the keyboard player appeared to have orchestrated everything into his own classical ideals. From a promising rock group they had become too formulaic as well as missing the very qualities that had first aroused the record company's, and my own interest. "Alarm and despondency" were three words I'd first heard while serving on The Ark Royal in my earlier days. Among many other things they encompass fear, negativity and an infectious habit of undermining a person's fragile confidence. Now, it seemed that years later, they had come back to haunt me on completion of **Well, Well, Well's** dismal and uninspiring set. Afterwards, I walked backstage in a sad and disillusioned frame of mind. "What did you think?" they asked on seeing me. "Don't ask me, ask the crowd, they were booing," I replied with words which I sorely felt needed to be expressed. "No they weren't, the people at the front were clapping. I didn't hear anyone booing," one of them indignantly replied. "From where I was standing they weren't clapping, they were definitely booing" I answered in an effort to justify what I had just witnessed. In unison, the band glowered at me in disbelief for daring to have the temerity to speak out. Realising there was no point in prolonging the discussion; I turned and retreated towards the beer tent to drown my sorrows. Their first festival was over and unfortunately, the group's impact had been less than minimal as well as an immense disappointment.

A few weeks later, I picked the band up in my car while their faces looked far too serious for my own comfort. "We want a wage rise," demanded the keyboard player. "But you are already getting £100 a week" I reminded him (today's equivalent value, around £300). "We want it doubled. The money that is left from the advance is ours and we can't live on what we are getting," he trumpeted in an overbearing and unfriendly manner. "That would mean paying out wages of £1,000 a week and there is only £37,000 of the advance left, that is, if we ever receive it," I reminded him; (the advance was split into three payments which will be fully explained later). "You all have brand new equipment and there are lots of other expenses to take into consideration. Don't forget there are roadies' wages, petrol, bed and breakfasts, telephone calls, and you need a new van to carry the equipment. Anyway, if the single doesn't chart it would mean you only have a life expectancy of 37 weeks and then you will be back on the dole from where you first started. I'm sorry to point this out but in reality the money is the record company's and they have entrusted it to me to be spent wisely," I pointedly explained. His face immediately dropped as I went on to spell out the harsh reality of what myself and two business friends were doing for the group. They had been living rent free in a flat near Bethnal Green with free electric and heating, a telephone, the cost of advertising posters, hire of the PA and lights, hire vans and petrol all paid for over a period of two years. Also, they had free rehearsal facilities at a company warehouse and they hadn't even released a record yet. More importantly, none of our management percentage or costs had been taken out of their record advance, and now they wanted more. I was positively furious as they began to cold shoulder me, or should I say sulk. It was at this juncture I quickly realised that far from keeping their feet on the ground, their heads were already high in the clouds and it was all going terribly wrong. Meanwhile, I had also negotiated a further deal with Arista for a £15,000 advance (1987 value) in exchange for the song publishing rights of the band. It was an excellent deal considering they were virtually unknown and also meant that the song publishing department would assist in helping them to become established as well as supporting any attempts to acquire future airplay. Back at the flat, on informing the songwriters Rob Coyle and Steven Clifford of the £15,000 song publishing deal, they seemed highly delighted. "Share it between all of you," I advised. "Why should we?" riposted Rob Coyle. "We write the songs so that money is ours," he insisted. "It would be much better if you shared it out equally as there are so many arguments between groups who don't and it will keep everyone happy," I advised. I also pointed out that in the past I'd seen so many groups split up or have endless arguments because of it and was determined the group wouldn't fall into such a mine laden trap. "Don't forget, we are all in this together," I reminded them in an effort to placate their concerns. Here, it must be pointed out that by law, the songwriter or songwriters are wholly entitled to the full song writing royalties, less the management percentage. However, remember, I was sharing my percentage with my two business partners should the group ever reach the heady heights of stardom. Unfortunately, my plea was categorically and blatantly ignored, despite my pointing out that that there were groups who did do this. As I write **"U2"** is one who immediately comes to mind. Meanwhile, the album was being recorded at Livingston Studios in London, (not far from Holland Park and costing £1,200 per day) where I listened to some early cuts. The group did have some excellent songs, but on listening, they appeared to have lost their original bite and naturalness. I couldn't help noticing there was distinct lack of passion, while most of the tracks seemed to have been over produced and lacked "feel" or soul. On completion, at the end of the recording session, I spoke to the group about my concerns but it was to no avail. On the way home I spoke to Rob about my deep reservations. "We've made it," he proudly informed me. I was astonished at such naivety and couldn't believe what I was hearing. "You haven't made it yet, not by a long way," I informed him. However, it was no use. A huge record contract and being advised by someone who was managing an artist with a No 1 in America had undoubtedly turned their heads. Ironically, it was I who had first introduced the group to him. Six weeks later, I received a letter from lawyers the group had been advised to consult. In substance, its words were stark and to the point. "You are advised that you are no longer the group's manager and we must inform you that the contract you have with them is completely unenforceable on a number of counts. Please do not attempt contact them in any way as from now you are advised that we will be dealing with all further matters concerning them." I held it in my hand for a number of minutes and thought of all the times I'd slept in the van with the lead singer. Then there was all the money we had spent on them, notwithstanding the thousands of telephone calls of their behalf. I also thought back to a freezing cold day at a motorway service station. After years of travelling on the motorway I had complained that it always seemed to be me who got out into the cold or wet to refuel the car we were travelling in and to check the tyre pressures. "I can't as I don't know how to do it," the lead singer had said. I looked at him with a mixture of contempt and pity. It was the only thing I could do, but now it had all proved to be academic and would no longer be necessary.

Once again, I thought back to while I was serving on the Ark Royal. On one occasion, I'd attended a burial at sea and watched the poor unfortunate shroud wrapped body plunge into the deep waters of the South China Sea as the ship sailed steadfastly on. It was an immensely sad moment and I counted my blessings it wasn't me. But somehow, by a strange quirk of fate, it equated to the piece of paper I now held in my hand. It was quite apparent that the group in all their majestic pomp were effectively consigning me into the same murky depths of morbid and strangulating anonymity while heading for their own future stardom without me. It was a bitter pill to swallow and totally unexpected, and yet in retrospect, the warning signs had been there all along. My confidence had now sunk to its lowest ebb as I swallowed hard. Once again the elusive prize had been wrenched from my grasp just when it looked realistically attainable. This time, I felt a deep resentment and promised myself I would do absolutely everything in my power to redress the injustice that I felt had been so callously perpetrated against me. A few days later I consulted a top music business lawyer and pointed out that the group had, on three separate occasions, been quite happy to renew management contracts when they were completely unknown and penniless. This was over a period of four years struggle and in the singer's case, eight. Call it bitterness, but an ability to meekly accept a situation where my services were no longer required is not one of my strongest traits. Somehow, I sensed these people had to be taught a salutary lesson and a deep resolve to do so became firmly entrenched within me. I also thought of Dave Dee and my own obsession with negotiating a more lucrative deal. Once again, Dad's words hit home, wounding me even deeper as I thought of them. "God has funny ways of working son. If you try and do what's right, right will come your way," he had often reminded my brother and me. Unfortunately, it seemed bewildering advice as it appeared that despite my trying to do the right thing, no good had come of it. However, no matter which way I looked at it, I realised the dastardly and uncaring actions of the group needed to be challenged in the most forthright and strongest manner possible. At that moment, and unknown to the group, I was going for their jugular and had already set out a course of retaliatory action. Whether it worked or not, only time would tell. I re-read the lawyers letter informing me that I was no longer the manager of the group which left a sad and bitter taste in my mouth. To be abruptly dismissed in such an offhand manner was highly upsetting as well as unbelievable. Having just got back from a two week holiday in the Canary Islands with my friend Gary Pearn, it seemed the plot had been secretly and conveniently sprung in my absence. In many ways it seemed equivalent to a coup d'etat. Ruthless in its execution, I had to grudgingly admit it had certainly been carried out in a heartless and carefully arranged manner. The proverb "familiarity breeds contempt" immediately came to mind, or should I say it now appeared that greed does. Nevertheless, I remained wholly philosophical as well as fiercely determined to fight on. Had they sprung the trap too early? How would I react? These were questions that I knew both parties would now be asking themselves. Meanwhile, the law has to be obeyed. This is fundamental to any free thinking society. However, with any contract, there is a whole labyrinth of complications and interpretations which can totally confuse the issue. How smug they must have felt when they received their advice. Now that I had been so callously and contentiously removed, they were obviously under the mistaken impression that they were free to go on and pursue their own wonderful and exciting avenue of untold riches and dreams. Here, it must be said that where a deeply held feeling of injustice is concerned, a "Cause Celebre" rests more easily on the shoulders. It unceasingly fans the flames of resistance with even greater intensity as it attempts to restore a deep wounded pride to an aggrieved or bitter person. Is it mistaken pride an impartial observer may well ask? Perhaps some people may well think so. However, dad hadn't brought us up to lie down so easily. Deep down, I knew that pride, whatever its interpretation, had to be restored in a somewhat dignified and controlled manner. But who sets the parameters in such a dispute and what would be my riposte? Inwardly I smiled. Only I knew and if they had previously consoled themselves with the thought they had been less than ruthless. If necessary, I was about to introduce them to the true meaning of the word.

Soon, word reached me that John Wolf was hoping to manage them. It would appear that he was a far more attractive proposition than me. However, was this suggestion true? It was a pertinent question and time for me to find out. "Is that John Wolf?" I asked on the telephone. "Yes, it is," he replied. "Are you contemplating managing the group?" I inquired. "Well, they have asked me," he replied in a somewhat confident and self satisfied manner. "Does that mean you are going to?" I questioned. "Well, I'm thinking about it," he answered. There being no reason to continue the conversation, I replaced the receiver. Whichever way I looked at it and for whatever reason, it seemed he was certainly considering the prospect. With a major record contract in the bag and years of hard preparatory work already done, it seemed his opportunism had been well timed. Furthermore, £25,000 of the first advance was still due as it was payable in three stages. £25,000 on signing, a further payment on completion of the album, with the third payment on its release. Then of course there was the second £75,000 due. There was no doubt about it. His timing had been impeccable, especially as I reminded myself it had all happened while I was away on two weeks holiday. Unfortunately for the group, I possessed some knowledge of contracts and was fully aware that it is an offence to induce any person to break one. Here, it must be pointed out that the only way a contract can be legally pronounced invalid is by a court of law or a presiding judge at an appeal court. As far as I was concerned their solicitor's letter was merely the first warning shot fired across the bows and in my eyes, in no way constituted a reason for premature celebrations by the group. If they were labouring under the foolhardy and false premise that the management contract had been annulled, it was about to be tested with my full and unremitting vigour together with an energy that would surpass anything I had previously achieved on the group's behalf.

"If it does go to court, just explain to the judge how much time and money you and your two partners have spent on the group. Remember, they were on the dole when you first met them." My brother Leo's words were very encouraging as well as pertinent, especially at a time when moral support was sorely needed. As youngsters we'd been in homes together, faced adversity together, and come through unscathed. However, unfortunately the law isn't as simple as that. Now it was time to fight, while inside me was a feeling of strength which was culled from that one word, justice. Like an erupting volcano, the energy and unrelenting search for it came from deep within the soul. After a series of meetings with top music business lawyers in London, they pointed out that my 9 year contract was too long, the 25% management fee was too high, and that the group hadn't received independent legal advice before signing the contract. "To make a contract legally enforceable, it should be no longer than three or four years and the management fee should be no more than 20%," they informed me. "Yes, but it can sometimes take years before a group makes it and they were quite happy to renew it on three separate occasions, so I can't have been that bad," I protested. "Also, what about the very large sums of money we have spent on them?" Nevertheless, the lawyer's words were very discouraging even though I pointed out that when a young person enters an army recruitment office, once he signs for nine years or more, it is a legally binding contract. Compounding this is the fact that even though they are never given any independent legal advice, it still remains enforceable in law. I also pointed out that footballers had five years contracts and our management fee had to be split three ways, (I was still in partnership with two business friends and received just over 8% as my share should they ever make it). I reminded them that a record company invariably does five album deals that can take up to ten years to materialise while taking a hefty slice of record royalties, far in excess of 25%. "What is the difference between a management contract and a record contract?" I asked. "They have invested a lot of time and money in the act," came the reply. "But so have we and I've spent eight years with the lead singer as well as four with the rest of the group," I informed him. He shrugged and pointed out that if it went to court we had every possibility of losing. Disheartened, but not discouraged, I walked out of their Soho Chambers determined to fight on. "There is one law for the rich and one for the poor," dad had often said. Now, I knew what he meant.

Somehow, a sixth sense told me that if it did go to court and all the facts were explained to the judge, he might just think differently. Here, it must be pointed out that justice had been an important word in our family and I was determined to seek it. If it meant breaking legal precedent, then that's what I was prepared to do. On explaining this at a later meeting, a resigned look appeared on the lawyer's face. He was a highly educated person with undoubted legal qualifications but I had read the daily papers since I was a small boy and knew that verdicts were often overturned on appeal. In other words, even learned judges sometimes disagree with their fellow advocates. A film adaptation of an absolutely true and amazing story entitled "The Winslow Boy" starring Robert Donat (the brilliant original film and not the remake) which I had once seen came to mind. It had been a famous case in America where the father had sacrificed everything to clear his son's name after he had been found guilty of stealing from a fellow naval cadet's locker, despite vehemently pleading his innocence. His father's belief and determination against seemingly overwhelming odds in his son's blamelessness was a truly heartrending story which brought tears to my eyes. Despite being constantly and forcefully told that he was wasting his time and that the verdict was cast iron, he bravely fought on. Eventually, after years of hardship, struggle, and near bankruptcy his son was finally found to be completely innocent and was pardoned together with compensation and costs. It was an incalculable lesson in never accepting defeat, no matter what the odds. Personally, I think every schoolchild should be encouraged to read it as I feel it is just as important to convey its message as it is to read Charles Dickens or Shakespeare. Soon, a letter from John Wolf's solicitors arrived informing me that he was not the manager of the group and never had any intention of doing so. It was a highly encouraging sign. It meant the group were now in a state of limbo without a manager and would have to handle any future difficulties by themselves. The next step was to send a letter off to Arista Records pointing out that we still had a legitimate management contract on the group and would sue if they forwarded them any money without first ensuring we received our percentage. A reply swiftly followed which, cutting through all the legal jargon, basically read, "No party will be given any further monies until this dispute has been satisfactorily settled." I felt elated on reading it. Now, not only were the group without a manager, they could no longer get their hands on the money, or the lucrative pot of gold which they had been so eager to grasp.

A few weeks later, their album was released to coincide with a London showpiece gig at The Marquee. Unknown to them, a friend of mine, Wilf Wright, had gone to observe what exactly took place. His observations made sobering listening. As the record company executives arrived for what they thought would be another sell out night, the first shock was about to hit them and the group. Inside, the place was only half full as no one had mailed out the complimentary tickets, something which I routinely did. Soon, a review of their debut album appeared in the highly influential Melody Maker which was short and to the point. "This group need a new name and a new song writer," it pointed out. Reading it, I felt sad. I had opposed the name from the very onset but was convinced they did have some good songs. Unfortunately, as I said earlier, the dynamics and sparkle had dissipated into a limp and over-produced orchestration, due to the keyboard player's interpretation of his own ideals. Once again it was time for reflection. In a perverse way I took no satisfaction in watching them self destruct, and yet at the same time, felt vindicated as well as relieved that they were no longer my responsibility.

Meanwhile, I thought of Geoff Gilbert, the managing director of Arista, and how I had asked to see him one last time after being summarily dismissed by the group. All I can say is that I had found him to be a real gentleman from the very first and on any subsequent occasions whenever I met him. Now that I had become the sacrificial lamb, I felt compelled to say goodbye. Kindness, when dispensed with an accompanying and genuine sincerity is a wonderful tonic for someone to experience when they are at their lowest ebb. I'd entered his office as a shadow of my normal self with my self esteem in shreds after being so publicly discarded. Furthermore, it was both humiliating and humbling, especially after attempting to help five unknowns from obscurity to world wide fame. However, this time there was to be no champagne or photographers, just a few farewell words which brought a lump to my throat. "I just want you to know that what has happened isn't my fault, it's the group themselves," I tearfully informed him. "You have always treated me with great respect as has Chris Cook the talent scout who first signed us. All I can say is I'm very sorry." He smiled, accompanied with natural warmth, before informing me that deep down he realised it wasn't my fault. We then shook hands before I turned and calmly left the building for the very last time. Unknown to him, after hearing his reassuring words, I was already beginning to feel like a man again. Once outside, it was time to reflect as in reality there was nothing else I could do. A feeling of complete worthlessness entered my thoughts while each step felt leaden and without purpose on realising the future looked bleak and uninspiring. To dress it up as anything else would be totally false as well as foolhardy. Confusion and mixed emotions whirled around in my head in a never ending search for an answer, but unfortunately there wasn't one. A few yards away, Oxford Circus was as busy as ever while the famous BBC building in Upper Regent Street where I often used to sit in with **John Peel** while he broadcast was only a stone's throw away. On thinking about it, they were happy and enlightening times as well as giving me a deep and inner self belief. **Well Well, Well**. How ironic those words had become, and in some strange way, rather comical. Within weeks, the record company sent me the sales figures for the album which had sold only a few meagre copies. Soon, I envisaged seeing it in the bargain bins and yet the very word appears to be a strange and unworthy misnomer. After all, how can a mediocre album possibly be a bargain? Over the next few weeks, the fight for justice went on as I fired off a series of letters to their lawyer informing them I was quite happy to take the matter further and contest the validity of the contract in a court of law. A few days later, I bought the local paper and there was a prominent photograph of them smiling while outlining their wondrous and far reaching plans for future stardom. How comforting for them, I thought. However, unknown to the group, they were about to find out that life is never quite that simple, not if I could help it anyway. During all this, I met one of the keyboard player's friends in the full knowledge that anything I said would be instantly relayed back to him. "I'm telling you this in strict confidence so you must promise not to tell anyone," I instructed. He nodded in agreement as I spelt out my next move. "I intend to put him in the witness box and keep him there for two whole days," I threatened. "I want to go over everything we have done for the group and I want it to be made public so that everyone can make up their own minds about why this has happened." In doing so I spat my words out with such venom and determination, his face went ashen and I sensed he knew I meant business. As ever, time dragged on. The dispute was now into its sixth month as I dug in and prepared for a long war of attrition. Most days I walked aimlessly through the town centre and tried to appear cheerful, but found it impossible. To pass the time I would sit down in Louis coffee bar and attempt to evaluate where it had all gone wrong, but nothing appeared to make sense. One day, a letter arrived offering me a percentage of their future album sales if I would relent and release them from their contract. "Take it," advised a friend. "If they sell a lot of albums you could become very rich and never have to work again." "I don't want their money. They tried to kick me into the gutter and I won't be happy until they join me," I informed him. "To allow myself to be bought off would cheapen the principles I had been brought up with," I continued. "Besides, I wouldn't enjoy spending the money knowing it was begrudged." My friend looked at me in astonishment and I realised why. But the very thought of them pulling up in a record company limousine outside my local coffee bar while dressed in the latest finery had proved to be too much for me to swallow. Dad had always said that revenge is sweet.

However, if this encompassed wilful stubbornness, lack of foresight, or sheer bloody mindedness, I didn't care. One's own integrity is a priceless commodity and when weighed against monetary values, in my eyes, it was no contest. One thing was for sure, the fight would go on.

Finally, a few months later, a letter arrived with headed notepaper. It was from Arista Records informing me that they had decided to drop the group from their roster of artists forthwith. They had also decided not to go ahead with their proposed song publishing deal. It was a moment to savour as I eagerly digested it. Things had gone full circle and it was now their turn to be humiliated while experiencing what it was like to be cast aside, unwanted, and bereft of the comforting arms of a major record company together with its untold possibilities. But how can a record company suddenly cancel a valid contract you may well ask. Please allow me to explain that there are always individual circumstances which are peculiar to each case. In **Well Well Well's** there were to be no further advances and as the keyboard player had already left them, the group was no longer "as known" on the contract." This was the technicality the record company had used as a "get out" clause and any manager worth his salt would never have accepted it, especially as it wasn't an identifying trait such as a lead singer's voice. "That money is ours." Their words had stayed in my thoughts and for some reason I enjoyed recalling them. Far from the two members refusing to share it, it now transpired that Arista had refused to pay out the rest of the advance and they ended up receiving nothing. I can also reveal that the record company, completely unprompted, sent the two business partners from my management company a cheque for £3.000 as a way of recompense towards all their costs. Poetic justice you may well ask? Or had dad's words been proved correct? "If you try and do what's right, right will come your way."

Unfortunately however, it seemed a pyrrhic victory as in reality nobody had won and this made it all the more difficult to understand. How did I feel? Elated, vindicated and relieved knowing their lack of vision together with their greed had impacted with such indecent haste upon their own heady rush for stardom, they had self destructed.

Shortly afterwards, the group split up, penniless and aimless. Over the next few weeks two of them approached me to say hello, but I was no mood for niceties or forgiveness and continued to ignore them. In Feb-2,003 my friend Alan Hogg was drinking in a local hostelry known as The Rosedene and was talking to the ex bass player of the group. "When you see Geoff, please tell him we are sorry," he had instructed. Inwardly I smiled as it was a very satisfying moment. Once again dad's words had hit home with unerring accuracy. "If you wait long enough son, you see all you want to see." His advice hadn't been specific to this situation, but it was just as poignant. The apology had taken 17 years and a few beers and while I bear him no ill will, I haven't the slightest compunction to resume what was a wasteful and belittling experience. "Would they have said that if they had gone on to make it without you?" questioned my brother Leo. "Take it from me; they wouldn't have given you another thought." His words of brotherly advice confirmed what I was already thinking, but it was all in the past. Was I embittered or carrying a grudge? Any fair minded person reading this might be justified in thinking so, but they would be wrong. Looking at it philosophically, it had been a game of chess played out with human beings together with their emotions. In life, some you win, some you lose. No more, no less. If this sounds harsh or unrealistic, then perhaps it was my fault after all.

Chapter 10

A few years later, with time being a wonderful healer and still possessing an inherent love of music, believe it or not, I decided to try again. First however, I had to find a promising group with some excellent songs and hopefully, the will and determination to succeed. During my low key search I bumped into **John Peel** who was filming a Channel 4 documentary at "The Studio" in Hartlepool, Co Durham. "Haven't you found yourself a group a yet?" he inquired. I paused in order to allow myself time to answer what I thought was an intriguing and far reaching question. "It's not just about talent John, it's also about attitude," I replied with an earnest conviction clearly apparent in my voice. He looked at me in a quiet almost reflective mood while remaining silent as if surprised by my answer. Just then, I thought back to years earlier when he had first started his own record label under the name of "Strange Fruit," but had reluctantly decided to discontinue it. No one ever found out why, but somehow I sensed the machinations of corporate thinking had failed to dovetail into his own independent approach to doing things. A few weeks later I drove through to an excellent little pub in Newcastle known as "The Broken Doll" which showcased new and unknown bands. who were forever sending in their demo tapes. After speaking to the landlord on a number of occasions and becoming friendly with him, I began taking an assortment home with me. After days and hours of listening, I finally heard a tape I really liked. The band's name was **Deadpan Joy** who hailed from Newcastle and I immediately set about locating them. Unfortunately, it was to prove an arduous task as unknown to me they had moved to London and no one knew their whereabouts. After placing an advert in the New Musical Express and the Newcastle Evening Chronicle as well as making dozens of telephone calls, the lead singer finally contacted me. His name turned out to be Ed Hayles and he quickly informed me that the band were living at a cramped flat in Seven Sisters Road near Finsbury Park. Two weeks later, I drove down to meet them and was pleasantly surprised at their friendly and enthusiastic manner. After the obligatory handshakes, Ed told me that they had been together for a couple of years and after building up a following in Newcastle had decided to move to London in order to increase their chances of acquiring that all important record contract. By a stroke of good fortune they also informed me that they were playing a gig in a small pub known as "The George Robey" just opposite Finsbury Park tube station the following day. Intrigued, I went along to observe them and found it to be dark and dingy with very few people present. The four piece group took to the stage to play what proved to be a short set. I thought they were poor while desperately needing more gigs, better equipment, and a huge injection of self confidence. However, despite these initial reservations, they also appeared to possess some excellent attributes in spite of the extremely discouraging circumstances they now found themselves playing under. First, they had some really good songs. Secondly, there appeared to be an underlying talent within the group which, although failing to blossom that night, I felt was ultimately there. Thirdly, any group which has the wherewithal and determination to move 300 miles to London to make it while living in cramped accommodation showed a level of commitment which in itself was something to be admired. After what they even agreed was a lacklustre set, I spoke to the group and took the liberty of making some pretty hard hitting criticisms. Call it psychology or even bad timing, but I wanted to see how they reacted to what I believed to be constructive suggestions, knowing full well they would almost certainly encounter criticism at some time in the future unless they were extremely fortunate. Encouragingly, they listened attentively as if having implicit trust in what I believed to be a useful exchange of ideas. Despite this, I was under no illusions being fully aware that a struggling band are prepared to listen to anyone who may appear to promise them a bigger and brighter future no matter how unbelievable it may sound. As has been fully illustrated earlier, attempting to take a completely unknown band from a sparsely attended gig to major stardom is no easy task. However, there was an earthy quality about this group which led me to believe they had distinct possibilities that were worth pursuing. Also, as I was single, I knew I could devote myself wholeheartedly to their cause knowing that to commit to anything less would greatly diminish their chances of making it. However, having previously learnt a hard, painful lesson, I first had to get them under a valid management contract which would stand up in court should a dispute ever arise in the future. Fortunately, after weeks of negotiations with an independent music lawyer I had advised them to seek, they finally agreed to sign a management contract for three years.

Here, I must point out to any budding managers that the final and most obstinate stumbling block in asking a group to sign a management contract is America. Their lawyer in his wisdom had advised them not to sign for it as it would then allow them to appoint an experienced American manager for that country should things start to take off. Of course at face value this appears to be sound advice. However, I, or any other experienced manager would be hardly likely to go through all the hard work only to see someone on the other side of the Atlantic reap the benefits in the most lucrative market of them all should things start to happen. I also pointed out that a host of major British groups had previously signed to their managers worldwide without the slightest detriment to their long and successful careers. Peter Grant (**Led Zeppelin**.) Steve-O-Rourke (**Pink Floyd**,) Paul McGuiness (**U2**) Ed Bicknell (**Dire Straights**,) Wilf Wright (**Robin Trower**) Terry Ellis (**Jethro Tull**) Chris Wright (**Ten Years After**) and of course, Brian Epstein of **Beatles** fame hadn't exactly held their careers back. With this obstacle finally overcome, I then set about the task of helping them to acquire that elusive record contract. In doing so, I was to be reminded at first hand how heartbreaking and disillusioning it is for an unknown and penniless group to gain recognition. Meanwhile, realising the group needed to improve their stagecraft as well as gaining more experience; I set about slotting them into as many gigs as I possibly could. "If we book them how many punters will they pull in?" soon became the most common, and at times, the most frustrating question I was to be asked. Unfortunately, it seemed to be the only criterion, with no additional questions of how good the music was or any suggestion of giving them a residency to see if they could possibly build a following. In fairness, the Mean Fiddler in Harlesden did ask for a tape and liked it. After having assured them that we would strive to get as many people in as possible, they agreed to book the band. After printing "flyers," (advertising handouts) and giving them out to hundreds of people, around twenty eventually came. Unfortunately, I was soon to find out that such a meagre attendance was to be the ultimate life threatening ligature which saddled them with a "no hopers" tag. By this, I don't mean the music, but their obvious inability to draw people in. Here, it must be pointed out that the numerous venues which this organisation controlled had strict instructions that any group which failed to pull in a minimum of 50 people must not be booked back. Why have this rule, you may well ask? It's simple. Each week in London and its outlying suburbs there are hundreds of struggling bands playing on an almost nightly basis and most give out an endless amount of "flyers." Unfortunately, this makes their advertising impact virtually non existent unless they are well known. It must also be pointed out that most venues usually put on a minimum of three groups a night and more often than not it would be around £3 admittance. If each group succeeds in pulling in their quota of 50 people, this means a minimum gross of £450 at the door. In most cases the groups are given £1 from each admission and that is fair enough. Naturally, this leaves the venue with £300 and the bar take. However, if a group fails to pull in the minimum number required, the venue fails to make any money from that particular group. This in turn can be a very contentious issue because an unknown group has to start somewhere in order to gain playing experience and hopefully acquire that all important following. Nevertheless, here comes the rub. What about the unknown groups who come from outside London and don't have a following? In lots of cases they are paid a bare minimum or nothing and as a fair percentage of them are on benefits, they can barely sustain themselves. Meanwhile, if a group from one of the London Universities or a band whose members reside in or around the capital plays, they usually have lots of friends who come to see them. This then gives them a far greater chance of establishing the required following. Once again, this is fair enough and there are certainly no complaints when this does occur. In fact, jolly good luck to them. In the meantime, the poor unknown groups from other parts of the country cannot possibly hope to pull in the required 50 people except in rare cases where they are able to bring in a busload of their own fans. If this proves impossible, there were three other routes for a hopeful group to pursue. These were a Radio One session from **John Peel**, (sadly now deceased), while Joe Whiley or Steve Lamaque were also hugely influential at the time. Secondly, a good write up or feature in the NME, or thirdly an A&R record company scout who on spotting the group has the courage of his convictions to sign or recommend them. Sounds simple enough doesn't it? But I can assure you it isn't as each record company receives dozens, if not hundreds of demo CDs a week. **John Peel** as was widely recognised, was also deluged with hundreds of them while the NME has to field hundreds of calls from hopeful groups or their managers. Countering this, any venue, if questioned will quite naturally explain that they have their own overheads to consider and need to make a profit in order to exist. This too is an undeniable fact and one that cannot be lightly dismissed. Therefore, it appears that there is a justifiable impasse on a venue's ability to take a chance and book an unknown band. However, some of them are making considerable profits and couldn't care less about the validity of the music or the difficulties for a band who have not yet established that all important following. Fortunately, the internet is beginning to play an important role especially as more sophisticated home recording equipment is available which negates the cost of hiring a demo studio. This is of course an exciting and far reaching development which appears to have unlimited potential. Will it work and is it worth pursuing? Just ask **Lily Allen** or unknown group **"The Conspirators"** from North Yorkshire who at the time had no manager or record contract. Despite this, and against seemingly incalculable odds, they entered a reputable independent chart in America at No 1. Therefore the answer must be an unqualified and resounding yes. Unfortunately however, **Deadpan Joy** were too early to benefit from such a helpful development.

Meanwhile, please allow me to move back to the gig and payment situation. When a group continue to play to just a handful of people, word soon gets around to the other influential venues that the group don't draw and within a short space of time, if there has been no music press on them, London rejects them. Ironically, as a promoter this is perfectly understandable as nobody can afford to keep booking groups who fail to attract an audience. Looking back to my earlier days, when I first booked **Free** for £35, only a handful of people came. On realising how good they were, had I not re-booked them with someone who did draw, thus giving them a chance to impress, there is no telling what might have happened. One clear example of this is the night **Deadpan Joy** were playing a gig at The Kings Head in Fulham. Inside, there was a desperately meagre attendance of only eleven people. However, that same night, Fulham Football Club were playing a mid-week floodlit match whereupon afterwards, thousands of people were making their way home right past its entrance. I recognised it was a golden opportunity to attempt to get more people in and try to build a following, so I quickly approached the promoter with a heartfelt plea. "It's obvious these people have never heard of the group and are unwilling to pay the £3 entrance fee," I pointed out as they hurriedly surged past. "However, some of the younger ones might take a chance and come inside to see them if it is reduced to only 50p," I urged. He immediately shook his head disapprovingly before sternly rebuking me. "No way. If they don't pay the £3 then they are not coming in," he replied dismissively having failed to grasp the significance of my intentions. "But they obviously have no intention of doing so. Please let me go outside and try," I pleaded. My heartfelt words proved to be of no avail and as I looked at his heartless face, I realised his intransigence and lack of vision was matched only by his greed. Even more frustrating was that unknown to him, I was a highly experienced promoter who had promoted many major groups, as well as unknown ones who subsequently went on to attain world-wide fame. I'd also been brought up under the old dictum that you should never look a gift horse in the mouth and this was patently one of those occasions. At the end of the night, he duly paid the group £11 and for that we were grateful, even though it hadn't even covered what the group had drunk, never mind their petrol or operating expenses.

Later, I helped the group to load their equipment back into the van. A very mundane task you may well think, but in reality it certainly isn't. Observing four young people who have devoted most of the day to organise and prepare for an evening's gig and then to witness the eventual outcome is a truly demoralising spectacle. Eventually, tired and weary, they slump into the back of the van and you don't have to be psychic in order to read their innermost thoughts. "That was a complete waste of time and we should never have been booked into there. Our manager an experienced promoter? You must be joking. He couldn't organise a shag in a brothel. He'd better put some petrol in on the way back because we haven't any money otherwise we'll all have to walk home. Another thing, where are all the A&R guys he said might be coming to see us? A supposed friend of **John Peel**. I don't believe him. If that's the case, why can't he give him a ring and get us a session on his radio show?" On the way home I take a quick glance at their faces, which remain impassive apart from what appears to be the occasional scowl as a feeling of intense guilt overwhelms me. Just then a policeman with a torch signals the van to stop. There are three of them and they quickly begin to question the band about why they are out so late. Soon, they peer inside while one quickly notices the back rear light lens is cracked, which is obviously an offence. We all hold our breath knowing the wipers need renewing too. In fact, so does the van. Meanwhile, the exhaust is belching out an unhealthy looking thick black smoke in the manner of a war time destroyer trying to avoid its pursuers. Suddenly, asphyxiation or loss of consciousness becomes a distinct possibility for the officer standing at the rear. Just then the engine coughs, or is it one of the officers lungs which are about to expire? Minutes later, they take a last look at our weary faces and sense we are not on our way to rob a bank, having recognised the four gaunt and underfed figures they have stopped wouldn't even be strong enough to open the safe door. Soon, it transpires that one of their sons is in a band which helps elicit a certain sympathy. Eventually, one of them smiles and waves us on our way without the necessity of having to produce the van's documents at the police station. So it seems the police in London aren't so bad after all. How I wish I could say that about the parking wardens or wheel clampers. If only they could be employed handing out the group's gig flyers half as speedily as they issue parking tickets, all of the venues would almost certainly be full. Later, once back in the house, there's a fight for the toaster as they're hungry and haven't eaten for hours.

Unfortunately, they haven't "pulled" either, which makes it a sad and dispiriting end to the night. Unknown to them; it will be the forerunner of many more to come.

Over the following weeks, I continued to watch and listen as they doggedly rehearsed. A friend, in his wisdom, having realised the paucity of their diet, together with their limited funds, asked me why they didn't look for a job. I then pointed out that part time footballers seem to get so far in the FA Cup before they are eventually knocked out by full time professionals. Ironically, it's the same with a struggling group. In trying to make it, they have to be prepared to give 100% of their time and effort. If however they are afraid to leave hold of a convenient safety rail in case they fail, their faint hearts will inevitably succeed in achieving what they hoped would never happen. However, having decided to give it one hundred per cent, it's hard, it's cruel and it's punishing. In fact, it's palpably inhumane. The human spirit can only take so much, which is where the indomitable will to win comes in. At this stage, everything hinges on their strength of character and fortunately, **Deadpan Joy** had it in abundance. Soon, four attractive and I must say well mannered female London University students moved in next door. Fortuitously, they proved to be very friendly and proceeded to invite the group to sample some of their delicious home made dinners on a number of occasions. Kindness, especially when the person receiving it is facing an uncertain future while at the same time experiencing great adversity, is a human trait which can be most endearing as well as heartening. All the while the girl's smiles remained warm and comforting, which proved to be a timely factor in helping to maintain the group's morale. Soon, friendship turned into romance in the case of Ed the lead singer. On stage, being fully aware of his new girl friends presence, it brought a renewed sense of energy and purpose as he proudly strutted his stuff in order to impress. Once back at the flat, the two of them would disappear, locking themselves away in his bedroom, whereupon in the morning he would smile as a contented look crossed his face. Conversely, Stuart the drummer had a succession of girls continually calling round to see him. Soon, they became his friends, but as ever, one proved to be particularly attractive. In fact gorgeous wouldn't be too strong a word as she devotedly hung on to his every word. Andy, the guitarist, had met a girl at The Marquee Club who was well spoken and very appealing although a little unfriendly towards the rest of us. Then there was the Geoff, the bass player. Quiet, intelligent, and in his own undemonstrative manner, handsome, he had his own girlfriend back in Newcastle who often came to visit him. Giro day was also an important event in their lives. Flush with their fortnightly unemployment cheque, they would stock up at the local supermarket where due to their lack of funds, their choice of food didn't always seem to be particularly nourishing. Andy, however proved to be a little more selective and made every effort to eat well. At the fading light of autumn, and with winter fast approaching, his loving mother sent him a duvet to keep him warm and we all laughed. Not in a nasty or malicious way it must be said, just a little light hearted repartee to while away the time. Then there was his dull and seemingly expressionless beanie hat which I personally hated whenever he wore it on stage as it seemed every other group was wearing one. Andy, who was a law unto himself wasn't having it, so regretfully, I had to accept his wishes as it remained steadfastly perched on his head.

With the group's dedication seemingly limitless in the face of such undue hardship, 1 began to sense they had real possibilities. Through persistent telephone calls coupled with a genuine belief in the band I got them gig after gig in places such as The Dublin Castle. The Marquee, The Water Rats. The Monarch, The Wag Club, The Dublin Castle, The Powerhouse, The Moonlight Club, The Swan, and the Amersham Arms in Deptford, to name but a few. These were all recognised places frequented by the music press and talent scouts as I remorselessly continued to plug away. During times of hardship 1 recalled how **U2** had once played to eight people at The Hope and Anchor in Islington and look what happened to them. In a situation such as this, retaining self belief for both the manager and the group is of paramount importance. However, as time drags on, a certain lethargy begins to creep in. It's an inevitable consequence of being constantly ignored or failing to capture the imagination of the people who matter. This, together with poorly attended gigs and lack of money was proving to be immensely disheartening as well as energy sapping. Still, it's well known in the rock business that with a little luck, everything can dramatically change overnight. Even more disconcerting was when the group picked up the weekly music press and read about a band who they firmly believed to be very ordinary. Of course it's all a matter of opinion but it seemed to be happening far too often for comfort. At one Marquee gig, the sound mixer informed me that he was taping the band onstage so that one of its members could review the gig for one of the music papers he worked for. Naturally, it will be a glowing review and will undoubtedly give them a head start. It does and did happen. Out there, it's a jungle, and where stardom beckons, together with an immeasurable amount of money and glamour, anything goes. In time, the band began to toughen up in order to demonstrate to people that they would no longer allow themselves to be pushed around. It also became quite apparent that they had developed opinions which only experience can bring, while I sensed they were becoming infinitely better. Once on stage, there was aggression when needed, accompanied by a subtlety which allowed a song to be expressed in the manner which the writer had originally intended. At some gigs I was immensely proud, knowing that up there were four NE boys taking on London and appearing to be winning while consistently delivering on stage. In earlier days I'd stressed the importance of avoiding snapped strings by replacing them regularly, together with no sloppy intros or endings. Equipment was to be regularly checked and taped down while weak songs had been dropped from the set and superior ones which they themselves had written were introduced. It had all taken time but the most enjoyable factor was that they were implementing all these suggestions without the slightest need for prompting from me. By now, a distinct sense of professionalism had crept in and they were beginning to play with an assurance which augured well for the future. So what could possibly have been missing now that they possessed all these vital attributes? I'm afraid it was three things. Lady luck, the lack of being able to acquire a London following, and the "killer song" I have earlier described as "three minutes of magic." To constantly make excuses smacks of an inability to accept that other people believe the group to be mediocre which seems to be staring everyone else in the face However, to make such a scathing and injudicious assumption you have to be aware of certain facts and without them, to condemn is to rejoice in someone else's failure. The question is, how long can a group keep coming up for air and smiling amidst a continuing myriad of broken dreams? Success hovers and beguiles until you unwittingly become a compliant slave to its every command or whim. Of course, self belief is vitally important. However, it is absolutely imperative it sits on the right shoulders as humility allied to genuine talent and determination will eventually prove to be a far greater asset. If a group is fortunate enough to possess such attributes it will be others who will soon sense they are witnessing something very special. In doing so, longevity, appreciation, and worldwide success may be just around the corner. For a young inexperienced group it's all there, just waiting to be grasped as the joyous and incomparable mantle of success is finally achieved. But take heart. It can and has been done.

By now, the famous Marquee Club in Wardour Street had been sold to property speculators. Having moved to Tottenham Court Rd under new owners, it became one of the group's favourite gigs. Most nights, I would call in to see other bands and soon became friendly with the new manager. On one occasion I watched a Scottish band which had driven down to London that very day in a decidedly cramped and battered vehicle. After their performance I found them hurriedly loading their equipment back into the van and as I had enjoyed them, I got talking to one of its members. "Where are you going to now?" I inquired. "Back to Glasgow." he replied. "What! you mean you are going to drive all through the night?" I exclaimed. "We have to because some of us have to go straight to work in the morning," he said. I glanced at my watch to find it was well after midnight as they finally squeezed their limp and weary bodies into its dark and uninviting interior for the long journey home. Before departing, they informed me that a record company scout who had promised he would be there to see them perform had failed to materialise. On hearing this I felt extremely sorry for them and after offering my condolences he resignedly shrugged his shoulders before setting off. Meanwhile, as they did so, I couldn't help admiring their truly indomitable spirit. Ironically, unknown to them, I had already asked the Marquee manager if he intended to book them back. "Definitely not. They didn't draw enough punters in," he replied unconcernedly. A few days later the same thing happened to a group from Leeds and it was then I realised how cruel and uncaring the music business had become. In London, eager unknown groups are being constantly booked as support bands at various venues. Unfortunately, it appears that most have little or no chance of ever being booked back or even achieving minor success. But does it really matter you may well ask? Here, it must be pointed out that in any sphere of life, where an injustice is patently being perpetrated upon poor hapless human beings, then of course it matters. Bearing this in mind, please allow me the luxury of going back twenty or so years. In those days, the hub of the music scene was, with very few exceptions, based mostly in Soho. If you were that struggling band, it was possible to survive as everything was more centralised and cheaper. But even more important was the fact that other talented and out of work musicians regularly frequented the Marquee or The Ship; a small licensed premises situated just fifty yards away. On reaching London, hopeful musicians from all over the country invariably headed for either or both of these establishments and providing the person had a reasonable attitude, they soon made new friends. Lo and behold, within days, weeks, or at most months, he was in a band and up and running. If that didn't work out, he was soon invited to audition for another until he had settled into one with a real chance of making it. In those days it should also be said that The Marquee was so popular, it was always at least half full, regardless of who was on. Therefore, if you were the support group, you didn't have the problem of drawing people in. Now comes another important point. As most of the record companies were based in the West End, their talent scouts invariably called in for a social drink and word quickly reached them if a group was any good. Also, in those days, techno, or dance music wasn't fashionable and there were a multitude of clubs throughout the country which enabled groups to play and establish a following which duly progressed on to record sales once they were signed. So, you may well ask what happened to fundamentally destroy such a flourishing set-up. I'm afraid it's that old bugbear, rents. Those in the West End kept on rising to such an extent that record companies and agents began to move to less expensive sites in other parts of London. While this fragmentation was merely the start of the process, there were other corresponding factors which helped to accelerate it. Soon, promoters based in London began emerging who did exclusive deals with a group's agent or manager to promote the bands once they had become a major draw in the city and town halls throughout the country. This meant that the smaller venues which had unfailingly nurtured them and helped to give them vital playing experience in their early days were now unable to book them. This had the stultifying effect of falling attendances, culminating in the gradual closure of many of them. It was undoubtedly a sad and regrettable decline. Unfortunately, accompanying this, the camaraderie, the bonhomie and the togetherness all collectively withered on their once flourishing vine. Coupled with this, in those days, **John Peel,** who had a weekly column in the music press, wrote and enlightened people about how good these venues or bands were after he had appeared there. This had the effect of encouraging readers or listeners to his radio programme to personally visit the clubs in order to experience the same excitement and vibes that he had. Furthermore, on hearing about these bands, music lovers would be inclined to rush out and buy the album of any group he mentioned. These would later be played at parties and word soon spread. At gigs I was fortunate enough to promote, people consistently brought a variety of these albums to be autographed before proudly showing them to friends. To witness the immense joy on their faces after having met the group and secured their highly prized autographs was truly one of the great delights of promoting. Accelerating this decline were London promoters such as Harvey Goldsmith, John and Tony Smith, Peter Bowyer, and others who unwittingly helped the process by negotiating hugely lucrative deals in their London offices, without deference to any of the clubs who subsequently suffered. Fortunately, I not only knew these promoters, I was also fully aware of the economics required to counter such single minded and potentially harmful tactics. Why was it so harmful? Is it not a good thing that people could now see all the major groups in comfort at their City Halls? In principle, it certainly seemed so. However, in practice it meant that that all control had been ceded to London on a mainly financial basis, without due consideration to nurturing new and unknown talent. Usually, every support group they chose was one which already had a major record contract or was forcibly thrust upon them by whoever paid the most money to supplement the main acts costs. During all this, groups who were popular locally found it extremely difficult to get the exposure they desperately needed. Meantime, we haven't even begun to discuss the escalation of admission prices. Happily, during my promoting days I was more than able to compete with them as the two venues I simultaneously promoted in Sunderland and Newcastle each held 3,000. As most City Halls held just over two thousand with most regional gigs or colleges being much smaller, the London promoters were at a huge disadvantage when attempting to thwart me. Another important aspect was that if a major group wanted a quick showcase gig, I could respond almost immediately through having block booked both these venues on a regular weekly basis. Of course, there was one other important factor, which was the friendly and overwhelming response of the crowd. To be up on that stage and look out at 3,000 people who were having the time of their lives was truly an emotional experience for any group. Having tasted such a wonderful and memorable atmosphere for the first time, it was relatively easy to book them back, even though they were at the peak of their careers.

Now we come to the present day. To launch a rock group who may take years to start selling albums or to recoup their advance is far too expensive, time consuming, and extremely risky. However, in exceptional cases a record company may go in for the long haul because of their profound belief in a group who are fortunate enough to possess a friendly and hard working attitude as well as talent. For modern day record companies however, it is much easier to sign and promote a pop group using the media of television in order to obtain a quick return on their investment. Fortunately, as I said earlier, there are exceptions such as the New Musical Express, which carries enormous influence as does Jo Whiley and Steve Lamaque on Radio One. Shareholders, corporate dividends, and managing directors that are conveniently replaced if they fail to sustain and improve company profits all enter into the equation. This inherent fear of failure inevitably spreads to lower levels and if there is no immediate "buzz" about a band, they "pass," culminating in the affected group failing to land that all important record contract. Without one, life becomes increasingly difficult if not impossible. It may take time; it may be that a group possesses tremendous stamina and determination to keep going. However, in the final analysis, it means they will end by either splitting up or returning to their own area and resorting to playing "covers" in order to earn a living. Unfortunately, despite such admirable and untold enthusiasm, it's a sad spectacle to witness and one which gives me no pleasure to relate. What can be done to arrest this decline you may well ask? Firstly, it needs risk takers whose love of music is far greater than their inherent desire to make money. Secondly, it needs a commitment from young groups who are fortunate enough to be signed to act responsibly and spend any advance wisely. Thirdly, it needs patience and perseverance to allow a group to blossom and gain vital playing experience. Am I being too idealistic you may well ask? Perhaps I am. However, hope springs eternal and who knows, stranger things have happened.

By now, Deadpan Joy were living in a flat in Harlesden and still continued to gig relentlessly in an effort to gain a vital foothold. At some gigs, I genuinely became awe struck, knowing that by now they had some excellent songs, a commanding stage presence, and an immense amount of experience under their belt. One night, it would be no exaggeration to say I couldn't help being reminded of The Who and how fantastic they had gone down at The Bay when I had first promoted them. It proved to be a sell out while an eager audience immediately took them to their hearts. Their commitment, their desire, and their talent remain indelibly entrenched in my memory together with hundreds of others who were present that night. Realistically speaking, Deadpan Joy were certainly no Who. However, there were certain characteristics that reminded me of them as they also possessed an unbridled ferocity in their playing which included a genuine subtlety that was immensely memorable to witness.

On another night, sadly, there were only three people present. It was positively heartrending and yet they were still majestically superb. The sheer effort they put in brought tears to my eyes and led me to believe that justice would surely prevail in the end. Conversely, on another night at the Powerhouse in Islington, the place was freezing and only a handful of people turned up. Unfortunately, the group played an uninspiring and lacklustre set on the very night that five record company A& R scouts who I had personally invited turned up to see them. Helpless and in despair, I watched as their weak, futile and inept performance appeared to have consigned them to the eternal abyss of no hopers. Of all the gigs for record companies to come and see them, this was definitely the worst possible one and I was practically reduced to tears. Later that night I lay in bed and reflected on the day's dismal and apathetic events. Ritchie Blackmore of **Deep Purple** had once informed me that you never become a really good group until you have developed the ability to play consistently well at every gig, no matter what the circumstances. As a promoter, I'd had a lot of triumphs together with disappointments. Unfortunately, with **Deadpan Joy** there was one great difference in that their triumphs appeared to be systematically going unnoticed and I'd never felt so frustrated in my whole life. However, five record company A&R men drinking at the bar sharing some light hearted repartee among themselves as they watched an uninspiring band is not a joyous occasion to recall. Meanwhile, unaware that five record companies were present, the group relentlessly played on. It is said that as the Titanic sank, the orchestra did likewise despite the ever growing danger. As the group continued to play on, they appeared to have taken over the mantle from this immensely sad and tragic occasion. Merely going through the motions isn't an exact science. To do it properly you have to be well rehearsed, couldn't care less, or possibly inebriated, while treating the sparse crowd as if they should never have bothered to come. On nights such as this it must be said that managing a band is most definitely a brutal and unfulfilling path to follow. Desolate, weary, and unmistakably depressed, I began to really become aware of the frailties and futility of attempting such a thankless venture. So this was the alleged path to the big time I thought to myself. Move to London, invite record companies to come and see the band, sign a major record deal, enter the charts, tour America and years later, sit back and retire on the royalties. Initially, it had all seemed such a simple and exciting strategy while the outline plan seemed to have little in the way of any visible obstacles. At school in my earlier days, I again recalled how a teacher had once remonstrated with me over a seemingly minor offence. "Stop dreaming Docherty or you will never make anything of yourself" she had happily admonished me in a stern and unyielding voice. On hearing my name, I jerked upright in the full knowledge that it was a harsh and unforgiving indictment to be so forcefully thrust upon the young shoulders of a mere eleven year old. Now, safe in the knowledge of what was presently happening, it appeared she may have possessed a far greater insight than I had at first realised.

Nevertheless, initially, the first part of my supposed grand master plan had worked. After moving to London the record companies had undeniably turned up to see them. Unfortunately however, they had failed to be suitably impressed by what they had witnessed or listened to. Once you have experienced such overwhelming rejection, a vacuous feeling of inadequacy stubbornly lodges inside you. This quickly develops into conflicting ideas as to how to remedy what appears to be a grave and wrongful injustice. Logic, disagreements and heated discussions with the group long into the night all become the norm. Underpinning this is the immense frustration that everyone involved is experiencing. This then is undeniably the danger period as a constant powder keg of tangled emotions threatens to destroy their last vestiges of hope. As a manager, the warning signs are all too apparent as you painfully twist and turn in an effort to right the rapidly sinking ship. Worry quickly turns to distress which in turn soon manifests itself into what appears to be a hopeless or lost cause. The furrowed brow remains ever more deeply lined as the overworked bilge pumps fail to cope with the ever rising frustration levels. Suddenly, everything is spinning out of control. You can feel it as well as sense it while secretly beginning to look forward to the end. All the while, that once inner pride has been replaced with overwhelming apathy and disillusionment which has crept up on you with such stealth, you are not wholly aware of it. However, unfortunately, others are. Their comments soon become more barbed and painfully direct as if they can already foresee a tragedy in the making. Suddenly, a mere morsel of what appears to be misplaced pride forces its way to the surface, breathing new life into your aching limbs while urging you into making one last effort. Can it be done and is it worth it becomes a taxing and overriding question. A subdued but resounding "yes" outweighs your doubts, as the last remnants of common sense are ignominiously and brutally cast aside. Suddenly, the fight to seek that seemingly ever elusive stardom finally pushes its way to the surface and the struggle goes on.

A few days later after making what appeared to be an encouraging telephone call, I was personally invited to Virgin Records to meet one of their A&R ladies. This most welcome and unexpected invitation appeared to be highly promising. I took Geoff the bass player with me to allow him to witness at first hand what actually took place. Fortunately, he had proved to be one of the nicest chaps I've ever managed and was good to have around. As we entered the high-flying portals of the renowned record company, she smiled before shaking hands and offering us a seat. For some strange reason an uncomfortable silence descended over the proceedings which for a few moments made me feel as if we were attending a job interview rather than listening to the group's demo tape. On taking our seats, she calmly eyed Geoff up and down as my heart raced on realising what exciting possibilities might lie ahead. Seconds later, she inserted the tape and leaned back to listen as an air of expectancy entered both mine and Geoff's thoughts. Three songs later, and without any great fuss, she handed it back. "It sounds like the **Smashing Pumpkins** to me," she quietly informed us. By now, her voice had lost its initial heart warming friendliness as danger signals began to flash in front of me. Meanwhile Geoff and I looked at each with a certain discomfort knowing that Virgin Records had both an air of credibility and respectability about it. During these tense moments, the unanswered question was, would she still be interested in signing them despite her critical observation? Unfortunately, as we had feared, it proved to be an emphatic and very disappointing no. When something of this nature occurs the frustration increases ten fold. To be invited into the inner sanctum of a well known and established record company only to be summarily rejected is mind blowing as well as depressing. Once again a mixture of apathy, lethargy, disbelief and heartache all eat into the very fabric of one's precious and long held hopes. In discreetly observing her on the other side of the desk she seemed calm and unruffled, and in some ways, uncaring. In physical terms you are only feet apart. But in idealistic terms, the chasm which her large imposing desk had imposed upon us immediately became huge and insurmountable. I couldn't help thinking of the months of rehearsals, the cost of recording the demo, and the art work to impress. Unfortunately. it had now become a heartrending and meaningless exercise which had only led to shattered hopes and disillusionment. Ironically, a few years previously I'd met Richard Branson at a Leeds TV studio and he proved to be most friendly, polite and self assured. Inwardly, I felt that his young A&R lady was decidedly wrong, but in the manner of corporate thinking, she undeniably held immense power. To say such power embodied life and death would be a gross exaggeration, however at that moment, that's how it felt. Later, I tried hard to think of any mediocre albums the company had allowed to be thrust into the public domain. In truth, I couldn't think of any. On reflection, perhaps it was a childish thought which in many ways lacked an understanding of the pressures under which this A&R lady was compelled to work. Then again, it was her personal opinion to which she was fully entitled, but I can most certainly assure you it failed to soften the blow.

Once outside, Geoff the bass player looked shocked. Having never previously experienced the feeling of outright rejection, I could certainly understand why. Even worse was the knowledge that it seemed they would have to start at the beginning all over again. Back at the flat, he attempted to explain what had occurred to the other three band members as they listened with a mixture of blank and disbelieving expressions on their faces. The unpalatable truth was that their songs, so carefully crafted and rehearsed, had failed to ignite the record company's enthusiasm. Having heard the worst, the group's only comfort was to visit the fridge in order to stem their disappointment, but unfortunately it proved to be empty. On seeing this, a tear came to my eye as an overwhelming sense of failure enveloped me. Once again, apathy, disillusionment and bewilderment all hung heavily in the air. Later, night time finally arrived as I flopped into bed causing the springs to creak. The incessant draught from the bottom of the ill fitted door ensured a plentiful and unwelcome blast of freezing Artic-like air enveloped me. Having awoken, in the morning I rushed downstairs to buy the music papers before quickly perusing them. Unfortunately, despite some excellent gigs, there was no mention of the group which meant another interminable week of obscure and unrelenting nonentity. Meanwhile, in the kitchen, Andy is elated on finding the mousetrap he had so carefully set had finally caught its unsuspecting victim. Victory over such a cunning adversary immediately became infectious as we all happily shared in his joy. Next morning, it was time for a jog, knowing that fresh air has the ability to pump renewed vigour not only to the body, but to the mind as well. On answering the phone, the group eagerly look towards me in the hope of some good news. Is it their girlfriend or parents, or more importantly, has another gig come in? The answer is in the affirmative. It's at the Monarch in Camden for £15 and they are support to a group they've never heard of. Exciting? You must be joking. It's smaller than the toilets at the Mecca ballroom where I used to promote. Also, the sound is abysmal, but no one dare speak out for fear of being classed as difficult, troublesome, or opinionated which could lead to them being permanently frozen out of the London circuit. Being aware of this, a discreet air of diplomacy is the order of the day while remembering the proverb "a wise head keeps a silent tongue." Later, while the group is up on stage, two record company A & R men walk in, making me feel much better and I'm elated. However, up on stage, Ed the lead singer appears to look utterly bored. He doesn't seem to be trying and lacks any spark or vibrancy which gives the impression he thinks he's too good for the venue. In some ways there's certain truth in this but I've taught him different. "Every gig is important, even if there's only one person present," I had always preached. He would nod as though completely uninterested in hearing me saying it, but tonight, all my preaching would be put to the test. Second, third and fourth song in, it quickly became obvious that he was merely going through the motions. Sensing this, I inched forward through the sparse crowd to try and catch his eye, but it was to no avail. Unknown to him, their whole future could be in the balance and he didn't even realise or look in the slightest perturbed. To witness this was highly distressing as I desperately prayed that he would come to life in the remaining part of the set. Meanwhile, the Monarch's resident sound engineer also appeared to be totally disinterested. Later, at a noticeably important juncture in a song, the sound engineer failed to turn up the lead guitar in order to highlight Andy's soloing which is pretty good and deserves to be heard. All the while the headlining group were becoming extremely anxious as they waited to load their equipment on stage, with time becoming critical. Ed's vocals continued to go from bad to worse and soon confirmed my worst fears that not only was he failing to try, he'd all but given up. Inside, I was seething with a mixture of rampant anger and frustration. To think of all the excellent gigs they had done in the past and fate had decided that two record company men had chosen to come to this one. Finally, and excruciatingly, it was over as I quickly discovered the two A&R guys had hurriedly left, and who could blame them. Once back at the flat, I ripped into Ed despite his girlfriend being present. In the mood I was in there was no time for niceties as a torrent of abusive criticism began to flow from my lips. Unfortunately, it soon became apparent it was not having the slightest effect. Moments later he rushed out, heading for his own room as the rest of the group remained fitfully silent. Inside, I was hurting, knowing the chance had slipped right through the group's fingers and everyone knew it. Afterwards, apportioning guilt or blame appears to be the easy part while manfully accepting it is undoubtedly unpleasant and distinctly unpalatable for the recipient. Next day there was tension in the air as Ed and I didn't speak, but somehow I sensed he'd reluctantly accepted what gilt edged opportunity had presented itself and realised he'd blown it. Three days later, in my absence, he admitted to the group that he had never really tried and had failed to realise anyone of importance was there. There was no apology, no histrionics, just his innermost regrets laced with a little of his characteristic stubbornness.

So you want to manage an unknown group and decide to ask me what it's like. The first emotive words that comes to mind are sorrow and abject pity. I don't know why, but they do. So you want to push me further and insist on an answer which possesses some scrap of commonsense or foresight? Oh dear, this makes it even harder but I'll try. It can be fun, hell, exciting and soul destroying all at the same time. It's the challenge which is highly compelling, while an innermost driving force coupled with a deep sense of ambition takes root and becomes difficult to resist. Accompanying this, an overestimation of one's own ability while an unrealistic assessment of a group's potential also come into it. But who would dare admit it? Not me, that's for sure. Here it must be said that where I reside not one group from the hundreds over the years has ever made it in a really big way. In saying this I'm thinking of platinum albums and America. However, we do have two who might just break the mould. These are **The Futureheads** and **Frankie and The Heartbreakers**. However, individuals who have moved to London most certainly have. Dave Stewart (**Eurhythmics**), Mick Grabham (**Procol Harum**), Nigel Olson (**Elton John**) Bryan Ferry, (**Roxy Music**) and Sting (**The Police**) all come to mind. Why is this you may well ask? I can categorically say it certainly isn't through lack of talent as there is an abundance of it out there. Is it ego, an attitude problem, bad luck, lack of finance, or wanting too much too quick. All I can say is that perhaps it's a combination of all five of them.

Having arrived in London, the initial plan for **Deadpan Joy** was to make a resolute and wholehearted effort to "make it". However, in the fullness of time, reality began to weave an uneasy sense of trepidation which soon led to the first signs of apprehension and fear. Nevertheless, the thought that someone out there must eventually listen acted as an unwavering spur to all our long held ambitions. Within just over eighteen months, desperation had slowly begun to creep in. All the while The London Evening Standard and the music press had failed to mention the group in their highly influential columns, despite my constant exhortations in order to alert them of their potential. Nonetheless, despite their recent seatback with Virgin, the group bravely continued to rehearse and write new songs. Even so, I began to sense they were beginning to question their own fundamental and idealistic values. Whenever failure hangs its unwelcome mantle around a group in what appears to be its cruel and debilitating attempt to stifle their enthusiasm, heart searching questions soon begin to linger. Witnessing sad and disillusioned faces desperately attempting to fathom out a new approach which constantly results in stalemate, shreds their puzzled and dejected nerves to breaking point. Having sensed the possibility of apathy clawing its way into their psyche, I decided to speak to Geoff in order to discuss possible future strategy and where he thought we might be going wrong. Fortunately, as well as being a visionary, he was the quiet one who could always be relied upon to think rationally while at the same time possessing a wealth of common sense. "What do you think about that new song entitled "Eskimo Wagon," I inquired? "It's not going down very well at the gigs and when you play it, it invariably seems to be the point at which people begin to retire to the bar or walk out. Personally, I think it's very ordinary," I harshly informed him. He looked at me in his deep pensive manner and remained silent for a few moments before replying. Knowing I had just made a confrontational statement, I was fully aware the criticism was hurting but was keen to see his reaction as well as his honest opinion. "We're still working on it," he replied calmly. Inwardly I smiled. It was a beautifully evasive answer and one to which there appeared to be no suitable reply. Nevertheless, I obstinately pressed the point home. "What's it about?" I inquired. "It's about a journey we had in the van when it was freezing cold so we decided to write a song about it," he replied. "It's terrible, I imagine you must have been up all night to write such banal lyrics," I exclaimed with a barbed hint of sarcasm. His face immediately took on a pained and sorrowful expression, which was reminiscent of someone who had just been stung by a horde of bees, while simultaneously wading through a bed of stinging nettles in order to escape. Even so he remained remarkably calm and composed which was something I always admired about him. But what was he thinking, and more importantly, would he be able to convince the group to act on my critical observation? With failure staring us in the face, I genuinely felt an urgent shake up was necessary and dad had always said "you have to be cruel to be kind." But would it work? Only time would tell.

"Eskimo Wagon" proclaimed Ed the lead singer defiantly to the sparse crowd who were present a few days later at a gig in a Brighton pub known as "The Ship." A surge of immeasurable disappointment immediately raced through my thoughts as the crowd shifted uneasily half way through the song. In observing such apathy, I felt an inner sadness at the futility of the situation in which they now found themselves. In many ways it was a public rebuke of everything I stood for which made it even sadder. During the song, I noticed the band had begun sheepishly looking at each other as if to gain confidence, having finally realised they were losing audience contact. Soon, as I feared, people began drifting remorselessly towards the bar. As a manager, witnessing such a spectacle is heartbreaking, especially as

I'd experienced it on a number of previous occasions. However, as I said earlier, they weren't just members of a band desperately seeking success; they were also human beings who possessed an abundance of fragile and sensitive emotions of their own. Later, in the dressing room, the dark sullen expression on their crestfallen faces portrayed its own sad and telling story. They remained quiet and subdued as if by booking them into such a sparsely attended gig, I had personally committed the most heinous and life threatening crime. However, as a manager you soon learn to accept critical or hurtful innuendoes as well while being constantly given the blame when things go wrong. Amidst such indifference, you can't help imagining what their thoughts are, knowing they have just experienced a sparse attendance and a poor audience response. "It was Geoff's fault for not making sure it was advertised properly. Another thing, we went on far too late and it's not our fault if everyone had prematurely departed for the late buses. You must agree, the first band on were terrible and that's why most people decided to leave early. The on stage monitors and PA were a joke and it's no wonder we didn't go down so well. He should have made sure they had a decent PA before booking us in there. It's not the first time it's happened either. Does he know what he's doing? It's all right for him? He doesn't have to get up there and play and if he did he'd soon learn how hard it is to please an audience who has never heard of the group. Still, we're stuck with him now and when he comes into the dressing room don't say anything because you know what he's like. He'll probably blame us again and I'm getting really fed up with it. Sshh, here he comes now." The actual reality is that on these occasions there is nothing anyone can do as a bad gig is a bad gig. When a band has reached this stage, it is not only soul destroying, it also becomes manifestly evident that it appears a cruel and heartless task has been thrust upon them. In many ways it's a form of self inflicted cruelty which invariably surfaces when a band is at its lowest ebb. The bleakness and despair now stubbornly languishing over them quickly becomes lost amidst a sea of alcohol and girls. Soon, to compound the heartfelt misery at the end of another disappointing night, the promoter sticks £15 in my hands which hardly covers the petrol back to London in a fully loaded van. Later, back at the house an attractive young lady giggles as she sits on Stuart's lap as he giggles too. However, instead of holding drumsticks his hands are now occupied with caressing something far softer and more alluring. "What's wrong Geoff?" he inquires. His concern is very touching but lasts for only a few seconds as their lips meet in an impassioned search to experience even greater pleasures. I can't help noticing she's leggy, intelligent and appears old enough to stay out late, not that she has any choice as all the tube stations are already closed. Ed, who is a private person has already quietly retired to his room, which makes it harder to really get to know him. Meanwhile, Geoff is listening to the **Red Hot Chilli Peppers**. He's been singing their praises for months now but no one seems to have taken him seriously. However, in the fullness of time he has the satisfaction of seeing them become world wide stars but modesty prevents him from reminding us of his foresight. Minutes later, I retire to bed as I seem to be the only one that's not enjoying himself. Where is all this taking us? I wonder. Who knows, but it seems it's certainly isn't stardom.

The next day the group are due to play outside in the open air at the seaward end of Brighton Palace Pier for an annual Surrey University gig. It's a heaven sent opportunity to retrieve the situation as well as the possibility of gaining a following in the area. Knowing this, there's certain exuberance in the group's attitude as they take in its bracing sea air before walking its full length with a renewed sense of purpose. For sixty minutes, it will allow them to lose their own troubled identity crisis and become the centre of attention once on stage. This is more like it. Michael Jackson, Faye Dunaway, Princess Grace of Monaco, and Brighton's own Olympic gold medallist Steve Ovett together with a list of endless luminaries have all trodden its history steeped path. Now it's **Deadpan Joy's** turn to follow in such exalted company as an air of excitement begins permeating through our every thought. At times like this, music proves to be a wonderful and intoxicating tonic. Enthusiasm abounds, lifting spirits to new heights with an invigorating and unstoppable surge of renewed optimism. It resolutely channels its way into every thought while consigning past failures or rejections into the oblivion of futile and highly unwanted setbacks. Soon, the invaluable bracing sea air expands the lungs and quickens their step as they look out at the vast expanse of the ocean. Cheerfulness, camaraderie, joy and optimism are instantly forged into a renewed and unstinting determination to "make it." Later that day, they will be put to the test and can't wait to hit the stage in order to prove their doubters wrong. Regrettably however, after setting up the equipment on the outside stage, torrential rain begins to descend in a never ending deluge. Accompanying it is a gale force wind which relentlessly drives the rain onto the equipment as we frantically try to protect it. Unfortunately, or should I say tragically, the deluge continues unabated for hour after hour until in the end it's hopeless. Having taken a quick check of the weather forecast, it indicates a whole multitude of dark rain filled clouds will stubbornly remain hovering over the area throughout the evening. With the wind and rain continuing to lash the pier, all possibility of playing on the specially prepared outside stage have to be abandoned. Eventually, in desperation, the band is moved inside to the bar where a weekly karaoke night is being held. This turns out to be not only unsuitable, but highly impractical as well. The tiny stage is less than four inches high, while the people present seem decidedly uninterested in listening to anything other than pop chart releases. Later, after completing a wholly uninspiring set, a weary and dejected band troop off, while at the same time throwing me a withering look of disapproval. The fact that I and my clothes are still soaking wet after valiantly trying to protect the equipment from the earlier rain is of little consequence. Some euphemistically call it paying your dues although this seems little recompense for the day's valiant effort. Still, it was fun. At least I think it was now that I'm able to look back on it within the confines of a warm and cosy environment.

Like dozens of other struggling bands, the group continued to live under austere and difficult conditions. Rigid social security questioning, worn out group equipment, broken drum sticks, snapped guitar strings, split cymbals and essential telephone calls are not good bedfellows. As for any of the group meeting and asking a girl out without any cash, this is not only demoralising, but highly embarrassing. Despite encountering such daunting obstacles, in the continuing quest for success, they bravely soldiered on. Fortunately, in a situation of this nature the sturdy roots of youth possess an unwavering resilience and fortitude which can only be truly admired. All the while, I continued to watch and wait. As I said earlier, patience is a hard and unyielding taskmaster, especially when the baton of responsibility rests uncomfortably on one's own shoulders. It's inflexible and uncompromising as it lingers and tortures while revelling in its mastery over your once prized and precious ideals. Meanwhile, new songs together with the deep rooted will to win, indicate that their determination to succeed, far from waning, has been growing ever stronger. Knowing this, I decided to contact Chris Wright. As he had since started his own label known as Echo and personally knowing him from his previous days as the manager of **Ten Years After**, I hoped he might be prompted into signing the group to his fledgling record company. Sure enough, he decided to send one of his men to come and see them at the first available opportunity. After informing the band of this new development their spirits immediately soared, while at the same time taking on a new lease of life. Suddenly, nothing seemed too much trouble, knowing that once again the door had become open to the real and exciting possibility of finally landing that elusive record contract. Following Chris Wright's instructions, a few days later I booked the group into Backstreet Rehearsal Studios in Holloway Rd in London to enable his A & R chap to assess them. By now the band had written some excellent songs one of which appeared to stand out head and shoulders above the rest. Its title was "Holy" and in my opinion, was positively brilliant. Admittedly there was a touch of **U2** about it, but it was undeniably captivating when played live and Ed sang it to perfection. Inwardly, I felt quietly confident of the outcome as the band's stage presence had improved beyond all recognition. Now, it seemed all the hard work was about to pay off. On the appointed day the chap from Echo Records walked in before making himself known. After warmly greeting him he asked the group to play four of their own compositions. Having done so, in all honesty I thought the band were absolutely brilliant. They appeared positive, confident and relaxed while the songs were played with a verve that was supremely heavenly and undeniably inspirational. Afterwards, he quietly beckoned me outside in order to speak to me in strict confidence. "Yes they're certainly very good and could do really well, but I need a few days to consider whether we should go ahead and sign them," he said. On hearing this, inwardly I winced and to say I was extremely disappointed would be a gross understatement. As he left, I turned to face the band with a dispirited air of uncertainty in my voice, knowing they had rehearsed and worked so hard before delivering a pulsating showcase. His seemingly unnecessary procrastination was heartbreaking, especially as our hopes had been so high. On relaying his decision to them, their eager faces looked bemused and quite saddened. However, all was not lost as he had said he would think about it. On ringing him a week later to find out his decision I was informed he had left the company and we never heard from him again. Shortly afterwards, they signed Julian Cope who had previously been in **Teardrop Explodes**. As he was well known to discerning and well informed music lovers, this, together with his previous success seemed a far safer option and I held no qualms about that. In fact, jolly good luck to him I thought at the time. However, just then, I couldn't help thinking of **Free**. When Johnny Glover and Alex Lesley, the two A&R scouts from Island Records had first gone to see them, they were far from impressed and were reluctant to sign them. Fortunately, Chris Blackwell the founder and owner promptly overruled them, ordering them to sign the group. I can assure you it's absolutely true as no less a person than Johnny Glover himself admitted it to me.

When a band learns that a record company has turned them down, the disappointment runs deep, especially when it has occurred on a number of previous occasions. Their family and friends imagine a huge conglomerate of corporate dignitaries sitting around a table discussing their merits before wholeheartedly rejecting them. However, in reality, and in most cases, it is just one A&R guy's personal opinion. He breezes in and quietly watches a band before quickly making up his mind. In some cases he may see up to five bands a night at different venues. To have your whole future decided in such an impersonal manner is not only frustrating, it is also highly undesirable. This is why it is so important to have a deep seated-belief together with the determination and will to keep going. Nevertheless, depending on the group's inner resolve, if rejection continually occurs, quite naturally, a split is almost inevitable. In relating this story, all I am trying to do is to warn young hopeful managers and the hundreds of groups that are out there, trying to reach the top is certainly no cakewalk. I can assure you there are hundreds if not thousands of other bands who could repeat the above scenario and I feel someone had to tell it the way it actually is. If, in attempting to do so, I have discouraged even one group member or band, it would be very sad. My advice is to go out there and prove to any doubters just how good you really are. Aim high, and if you do achieve success, keep your feet firmly on the ground which will ensure you enjoy it all the more. How do I know? I've spoken to lots of major bands who did just that and it's a pleasure to see them reap their true and just rewards. As I have said earlier, another constant basis for dissent is song writing royalties with very few exceptions. Once money or song writing royalties enter the equation, it seems to bring out the worst excesses of greed and selfishness in some band members. In contrast, when they first set out, everything is sweetness and light and is usually the onset of a honeymoon period and it's wonderful to be part of it. The enthusiasm, the will to win and the high ideals are all there in abundance. However, once the record contract comes along things can change dramatically. If a certain band member or members become too full of their own importance, it can prove to be a nightmare. It starts by squabbling over money, while deep seated motives or previously hidden desires suddenly begin to surface. Amidst all this agonising turmoil, the music appears to become secondary. In the event of a dispute, it quickly takes a backseat, while overnight, lawyers become the all important players. This quickly manifests itself in a profusion of letters which begin dropping through the letterbox like confetti at a wedding and seem never ending. Here it must be pointed out that on the actual day of signing; the manager is a splendid and hard working chap who can do no wrong amongst the overwhelming back slapping and joyous celebrations. A few days and a few drinks later, one or more of the band sidles up before reminding you that anyone could have got them a major record deal as it was only a question of time before someone spotted how exceptionally talented they were. Suddenly, gratitude seems to have been mysteriously deleted from their vocabulary and has been replaced by a condescending nod of the head whenever they need their egos massaging. A few weeks later, now they are "stars," your role has been relegated to one of organising petrol and insurance for the van or other mundane tasks. I had one band member complaining that the bed in the hotel felt slightly damp and it was my fault for booking them in. To prove he was being overly fussy, I personally slept in it and it appears I have suffered no ill effects. Meanwhile, one of their girlfriends is stranded at the station which is when a member of the group informs you that she needs picking up. Far from being demeaning, this should be taken as a good sign as it means you have been promoted to chauffer. This is a highly prestigious position which is not to be taken lightly and one which means the band hasn't forgotten that you still have a very important role to play. Feeling wanted or useful now that you are working for "stars" can be a heady feeling. Money, don't dare mention it because it's all theirs and to ask for some is tantamount to committing a heinous sacrilege. Amidst all this euphoria, is there anyone who dares or has the audacity to remind them that they've hardly sold a record yet? What a cheek. What lack of vision. Aren't you aware that their mothers, relatives and friends all bought it on the first day it came out and think it's miles better than anything **The Beatles** or **Rolling Stones** have ever done? "I don't think I'll sign another management contract when this one runs out," remarks one of the band in a drunken and patronising tone as a look of consternation crosses your face. There is no escaping the fact that it is an implied threat coupled with a complete lack of appreciation for all the work you have put in to help them reach the stage they have presently reached. But don't worry. The royalties will soon be pouring in and you will be laughing all the way to the bank. Did I say laugh? Well, it is funny when you think about it. A royalty cheque? I can honestly say I wouldn't know what one looked like. By that, I mean one that was personally meant for me.

Back to **Deadpan Joy** in preparation for yet another Marquee gig. In preparation for this, I rang Island Records and asked if one of their men would come and see the band. "Sorry, they are all going up to Manchester to see a group everyone is raving about," they informed me enthusiastically. "What's their name?" I inquired. **Perussence** came the reply. At the time, the Manchester scene was exploding with Factory Records, **Happy Mondays** and the **Stone Roses** in particular shifting monumental amounts of records. A few weeks later **Perussence** were signed to a major deal and for some unknown reason their name stuck in my mind. Whether it was sour grapes or frustration I wasn't sure. However, I had to admit they must have been pretty good to get almost everyone from Island Records hurrying to see them. Two years later I was at Reading Rock Festival and walked into one of the side marquees where they were playing to find it was packed to capacity and everything was all set for them to impress. Within minutes they were on stage and what I heard was most disappointing. Watching them, I thought they were very ordinary and lacked even the slightest semblance of stage presence. In between numbers they seemed like really nice chaps who were all well mannered and able to play their instruments with an assured confidence. However, it takes more than this to make a band stand out. Excitement comes in all forms whether it is the sheer intensity and passion of a folk singer's lyrics, or a full-blooded assault like **Led Zeppelin, The Who** or **Deep Purple**. In my option **Deadpan Joy** were a different class to **Perussence** and I thought of the night they had played at the Marquee and Island Records weren't there. There was no bitterness, just regrets that they had missed an excellent gig, and yes, **Perussence** are still playing as I write.

Three weeks later, the band were rehearsing a new song they had written, causing me to instinctively tap my feet while my whole body began moving in an agreeable and uplifting show of approval. There was a spark and vibrancy about it which refused to leave me as they went through it again and again. Suddenly, it was filling the house with a mixture of hope and anticipation. On entering their makeshift rehearsal room the broad smile on my face clearly showed my enjoyment. "What is the song called?" I inquired. "Girl in a Bun," answered Ed. "I like it. It's got hit single written all over it if it is ever fortunate enough to get played on the radio," I enthused. On hearing this, the band members immediately smiled, knowing they hadn't had much to enthuse about recently and seemed relieved at my reaction. "Do you think so?" they asked as if surprised at the possibility. "Yes I do," I assured them. Stu, the effervescent drummer immediately went round his drums as if to endorse his approval. "Girl in a Bun," I repeated as if in a trance. Admittedly it sounded a little bit "poppy, but it was certainly catchy in every sense of the word and I immediately realised the time had come to act. Within days, I had booked them into a studio advertised in the New Musical Express as I began envisaging possible success at last accompanied by an air of intense optimism. Finally, it seemed that the much and long awaited "Three Minutes of Magic" was just a demo away, as I began to dream of acquiring that elusive record contract. I spoke earlier of heady dreams which for any group is a tantalising prospect that allows a whole new vista of exciting possibilities to emerge. Was it to be success at last? I wondered. I certainly hoped so.

Having booked them in to a studio for three days, time dragged inexorably on in the empty house where I now found myself patiently waiting for them to finish recording. Now for a foray into the charts possibly culminating in a No 1, I thought. It was so exciting I was beside myself with joy at the very idea. "Here's the cheque for the royalties Geoff. Great news, it's stayed at No 1 for a second week." I smile with false modesty, knowing that it just had to happen. After all, they were too good for it not to. "Have you formulated any plans yet?" asks a record company executive. "I'm just discussing a major tour of America with **The Who**. It should be really good as I already know them. While I'm there, please keep me informed of the sales as I've got a chart clause in and if it stays at No 1 for a third week we get a higher percentage on our royalties. Incidentally, the group are really looking forward to flying on Concorde and so am I. It should be a great experience. Have to go as I have another meeting with Michael Eavis who wants the group to headline at Glastonbury. I hope you don't think this all this success has gone to our heads but I really must go. I'll send you a card from LA. Bye. Oh! has my limo arrived yet? Good, I hate driving in London especially as I'm not very sure of my way around. That new secretary of yours looks quite dishy. I like her smile and a lot of other things about her as well. Still, I've already arranged to take out one of the leading dancers from the Royal Ballet tonight. Very upper class you know. She's going to teach me croquet at the country mansion where her parents live. Don't know if I'll enjoy it but you can't have everything can you?"

Suddenly, it was back to reality. "How's the recording going?" I asked the group at the end of day two. "Really well," replied Stu the drummer. "We're very pleased at the way its sounding," he gleefully informed me. On hearing his enthusiastic and positive response my heart raced in anticipation. £300 to demo a hit single, surely it doesn't get any better than that, I thought? The following day they played me the finished tape whereupon my jaw dropped as I listened. The song appeared to have lost its spontaneity and failed to swing like it did at rehearsals while its natural rhythm had dissipated into a wooden and lifeless interpretation of the vibrant original. Unfortunately, the studio owner with whom I had done the deal had put a young tape apprentice in charge of the recording and it showed. The £300 it had cost appeared to have been wasted and I was distraught. I knew how a good producer can capture the "feel" and passion of a song, and this had neither. The band's heads dropped as I expressed my thoughts to them and pointed out that in my opinion, no record company would sign them on the strength of it. My words sounded cruel and uncompromising and I hated the fact that it was my job to relay this to them knowing that disappointment in any form is a bitter pill to swallow. However, to witness five crestfallen faces seemed more than any human being should be asked to bear. Disconsolate and sad, they looked at me in complete and abject bewilderment. Broken dreams which have been unceremoniously consigned into the darkened abyss of rejection leave no room for sympathy or understanding of why it may have occurred. Unfortunately, impending failure thrust upon young shoulders is brutal, uncompromising and demoralising. To experience it amidst the turmoil of emotional devastation is not only a setback; it is soul destroying as well. Needless to say, and as I had feared, despite my undying efforts, almost every major record company went on to reject the single after I had played it to them.

Finally, two years of utter frustration were beginning to take its toll. Defeat was staring the group in the face while disillusionment and apathy were the prevalent signs. Witnessing the spectacle of a group who's once bright and burning embers are in the throes of dying is a sad and depressing sight. To enter the house under such circumstances is to enter a morgue where lifeless decomposing bodies appear to be undergoing the last rites before rigor mortis finally sets in. Instruments begin to gather dust, bills remain unopened, while the stench of failure reaches such dismal and asphyxiating proportions, it becomes a gargantuan effort to retain any form of self respect. As each day passes, aimlessness and terminal morbidity begin to creep in with ever increasing intensity. In observing such malaise, it is a clear signal which can only be interpreted as one that all hope has been lost, while to attempt resuscitation would appear to be futile as well as pointless. Soon, the lingering and ever spreading apathy of a once proud group begins to spread. The friendly shopkeeper next door also appears to have sensed it and wisely omits to ask about the group. Suddenly, the mortal decline which has insidiously enveloped them begins to accelerate knowing that the last hoped for call from a record company has failed to materialise. No one needs to speak. The way ahead is just a darkened abyss of shattered dreams and they no longer seem to care. That first heady day when they enthusiastically rushed into the house to claim the best bedroom is now just a distant memory. Their failure is not only theirs, it is mine too. It weighs heavily on the shoulders which are aching from the relentless burden of false hopes. Meanwhile, I detect a decided sadness in the group's thoughts and eyes which unerringly transmits itself to anyone coming into contact with them. Surrounded by such lethargy, I swallow hard knowing they had left their loving homes and risked everything to "make it" as sadly, I recalled Geoff the bass player's words. "We left Newcastle because we knew we were good and felt if we came to London they couldn't ignore us." This alone summed up the damning and unpalatable reality of a failed venture. It seemed London had not only ignored them, but had positively rejected them while crushing their hopes into a wasted and despairing heap of human frailty. Looking and listening to them was heartbreaking, but inside, I was hurting too. Over the following days, I lay on my bed and began thinking things over. I had undoubtedly learnt a lot and felt the group had done some fantastic gigs bordering on as good as anything I'd ever promoted. But I too was weary. The motivation to telephone record companies and gigs had all but deserted me. All five of us had striven manfully to grasp the bottom rung of the ladder before attempting to climb it, but it wasn't to be. Were these hopes born out of an inherent and unstoppable desire to become famous, or an over enthusiastic assessment of their talent? Self doubt is an inevitable corollary of such thoughts and dwells on what might have been. Inevitably, you can't help thinking of the good times, the camaraderie, and the uplifting music you really enjoyed. These things eventually override all other considerations because in the final analysis, it's all that matters. Inside the flat, the group was watching television. In the past, I would occasionally berate them and instil into them the importance of rehearsing and being ready to play at any gig which may suddenly be thrust upon them. Now, it no longer mattered. Apathy and disillusionment, just like woodworm in the rafters of an old church or historic building had eaten into the very fabric of their existence. Just then, one of the group nodded towards me in half hearted acknowledgement. In doing so, the effort seemed all too much for him and suddenly, I felt surplus to requirements. The bond that had kept us together was not only frayed, but had irrevocably parted and it was time to go. "I'm leaving," I stammered to the assembled group. A resigned look crossed their faces and I felt a certain disappointment. The impact of my words had proved minimal and it seemed they didn't care. However, I understood knowing that London had proved to be a harsh and uncompromising city where success is all that matters. Having made my decision, they were now free to pursue their own ideals and I was finally divested of a huge responsibility. As a promoter, I'd reached the very top, tasted success, and had some great times. Sadly, for the band it was totally different. Success had stubbornly eluded them and I felt for them knowing they had given music and London everything they possessed and a whole lot more.

Before leaving, I attended their final gig at a bar in Convent Garden. It was packed with young Japanese tourists and the band proved to be excellent. Afterwards, the manager spoke to me in a highly enthusiastic and appreciative manner. "This group are really good. I'd like to book them back straight away," he informed me. "Once again I swallowed hard before speaking. "They are splitting up after tonight. That was their last gig," I regretfully informed him. "You're joking," he replied. "There aren't many groups who can come here and get three encores," he riposted. Inside I was hurting as I tried not to cry on realising his statement had penetrated my supposedly tough exterior. Nevertheless, I felt very proud knowing the boys had delivered one last time. No record company, no Dave Ambrose, no music press, just the five of us and our memories. **The Animals** together with **Lindisfarne** had come to London and conquered. In reality so had **Deadpan Joy**. It was just that everyone has their own opinion and the fact that it differed greatly from ours was ultimately the deciding factor. In many ways it could be said that I hadn't proved as adept at managing as I had thought I would. However, critical analysis of one's own failures isn't to be recommended. It can be soul destroying and to relive them without allowing time to heal the hurt and disappointment can be highly depressing. In reality, it's called experience and it had most certainly been that. However, in order to obtain it a high price had been exacted. "The devil is in the detail" so they say. However, in our case he appeared to be everywhere. In many ways failure can have a twisted sense of humour as if finally rewarding you for all your efforts. Why, I will never know. Fortunately, in **Deadpan Joy's** case, I have managed to remain friends with all four. This in itself is very gratifying and made all the effort worthwhile. A few months later, backstage at Reading Festival I spoke to **John Peel.** "What happened to that group of yours?" he enquired. "They've split up," I replied. "I listened to their tape and thought they were quite good. It's not the type of stuff I play on my programme but I was going to pass it on to Steve Lamaque for his radio show. What happened anyway?" "We were just bounced around in London and everyone became disillusioned," I explained. It was a bittersweet and in many ways a proud moment. Someone whose ears I respected had finally picked up on the band, but unfortunately it was too late. I walked away and sat down at a nearby table to absorb the sun's warm and invigorating rays before reflecting on what he had just said. So I didn't have cloth ears after all. It was an invaluable endorsement as well as a vindication of everything I had felt about the group. Such are the vagaries of managing an unknown band. Obtaining three major record contracts for groups I have managed certainly can't be regarded as total failure. However, in the final assessment, it seems that it is. I am under no illusions that what I have described in this book has happened in some form or other to dozens of hopeful managers and their groups. I also recall how John Sherry who managed **Wishbone Ash** was once offered **Dire Straights** but turned them down as he said he was too busy managing the **Flying Pickets** who had just entered the

British charts. At the time, it was a mistake he lived to regret but is indicative that no one can foretell how a group will fare. Just ask the record companies themselves whose success rate is just three out of every ten groups they sign. What happens to the other seven you may well ask? I honestly don't know as in most cases they disappear into the unwelcoming quicksand of obscurity. One question I often ask myself is what drives man to attempt things where failure and extreme danger lurk. In saying this I'm thinking of people like Irvine and Mallory who courageously struck out for the summit of Mount Everest and were never seen again. The indomitable Scott of the Antarctic who sadly perished when only a short distance from safety also comes to mind. Then there is Donald Campbell who attempted to break his own world water speed record only to crash and perish in the waters of Lake Coniston. You may well ask what drives these men on and people like them. Surely it's the challenge of the unknown which most humans possess in some form or other. Ironically, it's the same when you are managing an unknown group. Of course to dare align oneself with such heroes as those mentioned above would not only be farcical, but highly inappropriate. Nevertheless, it's the challenge which is irresistible, whatever its form. I mention this in passing because observing sceptics may not be able to comprehend why someone such as myself allows their whole life to be drawn into a quagmire of broken and unrealised dreams while recklessly gambling with ones own future.. However, ambition and the lure of the bright lights are enticingly hypnotic, or alternatively, perhaps it's a personality failure where you feel you have to prove yourself. However, I like to think of it as an honest attempt to create some excitement as opposed to an otherwise mundane or risk free life. There I will leave it.

As a footnote however, having previously had a book published about my exploits as a promoter of major bands, I received a telephone call from Dot Fisher, better known as Dory. She had heard me being interviewed by Johnny Walker on his BBC Radio 2 show. As I had written about her in my first book and having never heard from her for many years, she invited me to visit her at her house in Tiverton, Devon. While there, I spotted an inconspicuous looking CD lying on a table. "Who is it?" I inquired. "Oh! it's just a group that my daughter in law plays in," she informed me. "Let me hear it," I requested. "You can if you want to. The CD player is in the kitchen," she replied. To my surprise, what I heard was wonderful. The name of the group was **"The Fondues,"** and her daughter-in-law "Jules" was the lead singer. Two days later, I enthusiastically attended rehearsals in order to see them play. All I can say it was a wonderful feeling to hear them live. A few weeks later, I arranged for them to play at London University, (ULU). Excitement, together with a gut feeling that something special is happening is a rare commodity. Yet, here I was experiencing it again. The stage was tiny and there weren't many people there, yet this six piece playing jazz funk with two female singers proved to be exceptional. Two months later, they played at The South Pacific Club in London. What can I say? They were brilliant and the packed crowd demanded encore after encore. Hope springs eternal they say. For any A&R chaps out there don't dare miss them. All in their mind thirties and brilliant musicians, I can't wait to hear more. Recently, no less a person than the manager of **Coldplay** arranged to see them play in Devon where they and **Muse** are from. Having been recommended by a friend as to how good they were, he arrived too late. Recently, they have changed their name to **SKA TREK** playing Ska Dub & Reggae with an added three piece brass section. Are they exciting, can they play, are they intelligent? The answer is undoubtedly in the affirmative and I suggest you go and see them. Will they get signed? I certainly hope so as I just love happy endings. Don't you?

Footnote, if any of the band read this, please ring or e-mail me as your phone number must have changed.
fillmoremusic73@hotmail.co.uk

Chronology of Gigs Promoted By The Fillmore North (Geoff Docherty)

Fees paid to artists are correct to the best of the author's recollections. Where none is mentioned, the author cannot recall the fee paid.

1969

Date	Act	Admission	Venue
6 Jan	**Family**	6/-	**Bay Hotel, S'land**
13 Jan	**Free**	4/-	**Bay Hotel, S'land**
20 Jan	Harmony Grass		Bay Hotel, S'land
27 Jan	Keef Hartley	5/-	Bay Hotel, S'land
3 Feb	**Pretty Things**	7/6d	Bay Hotel, S'land
7 Feb	The Web	5/-	Bay Hotel, S'land
10 Feb	Dr.K's Blues Band		Bay Hotel, S'land
17 Feb	**Pink Floyd**	7/6d	**Bay Hotel, S'land**
21 Feb	Ferris Wheel		Bay Hotel, S'land
22 Feb	Circus	5/6d	Bay Hotel, S'land
24 Feb	Aynsley Dunbar	6/-	Bay Hotel, S'land
28 Feb	Writing On the Wall	5/-	Bay Hotel, S'land
1 Mar	Episode Six **(Ian Gillan & Roger Glover)** (Pre Deep Purple Days)		Bay Hotel, S'land
3 Mar	**John Peel, Van Der Graaf Generator & Black Sabbath**	6/6d	**Bay Hotel, S'land**
8 Mar	**McKenna Mendelson Mainline** (from Canada)	5/-	Bay Hotel, S'land
10 Mar	**John Peel**, Spirit of John Morgan & The Music of Jan Dukes De Grey		Bay Hotel, S'land
17 Mar	**Spooky Tooth**	7/-	Bay Hotel, S'land
22 Mar	Leviathan		Bay Hotel, S'land
24 Mar	**Country Joe & The Fish**	10/6d	**Bay Hotel, S'land**
28 Mar	Cliff Bennet & The Rebel Rousers		Bay Hotel, S'land
31 Mar	Idle Race	5/-	Bay Hotel, S'land
3 Apr	Bakerloo Blues Line (Playing Upstairs)	2/6d	Bay Hotel, S'land

219

Date	Act	Admission	Venue
7 Apr	Bakerloo Blues Line (Downstairs Ballroom)	6/-	Bay Hotel, S'land
11 Apr	Plastic Penny	5/-	Bay Hotel, S'land
14 Apr	Terry Reid' Fantasia	5/-	Bay Hotel, S'land
19 Apr	Hard Meat		Bay Hotel, S'land
26 Apr	Eyes Of Blue		Bay Hotel, S'land
12 May	Chicken Shack	7/6d	Bay Hotel, S'land
19 May	**Steppenwolf** (Non Arrival) **Breakthru played**	**5/-**	**Bay Hotel, S'land**
26 May	**Savoy Brown** & This Year's Girl	6/-	Bay Hotel, S'land
6 June	Spirit of John Morgan	6/-	Bay Hotel, S'land
9 June	**Three Dog Night**	**7/6d**	**Bay Hotel, S'land**
13 June	**Jethro Tull**	**12/6d**	**Bay Hotel, S'land**
16 June	**The Nice**	**10/-**	**Bay Hotel, S'land**
23 June	Aynsley Dunbar	6/-	Bay Hotel, S'land
27 June	**Tyrannosaurus Rex, Free** **& This Year's Girl**	**12/6d**	**Bay Hotel, S'land**
30 June	**Yes**	**6/-**	**Bay Hotel, S'land**
7 Jul	**Chicken Shack** (I'd Rather Go Blind No. 4)	7/6d	Bay Hotel, S'land
11 Jul	Writing on the Wall		Bay Hotel, S'land
18 Jul	Marsha Hunt with White Trash		Bay Hotel, S'land
21 Jul	**Family**	**10/6d**	**Bay Hotel, S'land**
25 Jul	Third Ear Band		Bay Hotel, S'land
28 Jul	**The Who**	**12/6d**	**Locarno, S'land**
13 Aug	**Bonzo Dog Band, Eclection, King Crimson** **& This Year's Girl**	**12/-**	**Locarno, S'land**
22 Aug	**Family**, Grail & Bridget St John	**12/6d**	**Locarno, S'land**
29 Aug	Liverpool Scene, Mooche & Junco Partners		Locarno, S'land
5 Sept	**Soft Machine**		**Locarno, S'land**
12 Sept	**Free, Mott The Hoople**	**7/6d**	**Locarno, S'land**
19 Sept	Atomic Rooster, Poet & The One Man Band		Locarno, S'land
26 Sept	**Chicken Shack** (Tears In The Wind-No. 28) & Principal Edwards Magic Theatre		Locarno, S'land
3 Oct	Keith Relf's Renaissance & Blossom Toes	7/6d	Locarno, S'land
6 Oct	**Pretty Things**		**Locarno, S'land**
10 Oct	Noel Reddings Fat Mattress (ex Jimi Hendrix Experience) & Big Fingers	7/6d	Locarno, S'land

Date	Act	Admission	Venue
13 Oct	Pete Brown's Piblokto	3/-	Locarno, S'land
17 Oct	**Family & Man**	**10/-**	**Locarno, S'land**
20 Oct	Writing On the Wall		Locarno, S'land
24 Oct	**Pink Floyd**, Stone The Crows & John Peel	**12/6d**	**Locarno, S'land**
27 Oct	**Roy Harper**		Locarno, S'land
31 Oct	**Savoy Brown** & Barclay James Harvest	7/6d	Locarno, S'land
3 Nov	Principal Edwards Magic Theatre	3/-	Locarno, S'land
7 Nov	Edgar Broughton & Zoot Money		Locarno, S'land
14 Nov	**Christine Perfect Band** **& Mighty Baby (Ex Chicken Shack)**	**10/-**	**Locarno, S'land**
21 Nov	**Free & Qunitessence**	**10/-**	Locarno, S'land
28 Nov	**Tyrannosaurus Rex, John Peel** **& Spirit of John Morgan**		**Locarno, S'land**
1 Dec	Hard Meat		Locarno, S'land
8 Dec	Gypsy	3/-	Locarno, S'land
15 Dec	Rare Bird	2/-	Locarno, S'land
22 Dec	Gypsy		Locarno, S'land

1970

Date	Act	Admission	Venue
1 Jan	Edgar Broughton, Principal Edwards Magic Theatre & This Year's Girl		Locarno, S'land
9 Jan	**Manfred Mann Chapter Three**, Principal Edwards Magic Theatre & This Years Girl	12/6d	Locarno, S'land
12 Jan	Jo-Anne Kelly with The John Dummer's Blues Band	3/-	Locarno, S'land
16 Jan	**Kinks, Quintessence** (Kinks didn't play)	10/-	Locarno, S'land
19 Jan	Stone The Crows	3/-	Locarno, S'land
23 Jan	**Family** + Emily & Muff	**10/-**	**Locarno, S'land**
30 Jan	**Ten Years After** & Junco Partners	**10/-**	**Locarno, S'land**
6 Feb	**Free** & Griffin (recording live album)	**10/-**	**Locarno, S'land**
9 Feb	The Music Of Jan Dukes De Grey	3/-	Locarno, S'land
13 Feb	**Blodwyn Pig**, Audience & **John Peel**	10/-	Locarno, S'land
20 Feb	**John Hiseman's Colosseum** & Jess Roden's Bronco	10/-	Locarno, S'land
23 Feb	Siren	3/-	Locarno, S'land
27 Feb	**Chicken Shack & Quintessence**	10/-	Locarno, S'land
6 Mar	**Edgar Broughton** & Juice	10/-	Locarno, S'land

Date	Act	Admission	Venue
9 Mar	Third Ear Band & **Genesis**	3/6d	Locarno, S'land
13 Mar	**David Bowie** & The Hype Principal Edwards, Circus & Man	10/-	Locarno, S'land
16 Mar	**Chicken Shack**	4/-	Locarno, S'land
20 Mar	**Blodwyn Pig** & Writing On The Wall	10/-	Locarno, S'land
26 Mar	**Ginger Baker's Airforce**	15/-	Locarno, S'land
3 Apr	**Rory Gallagher's Taste & Black Sabbath**	12/6d	Mayfair, Newcastle
10 Apr	**Edgar Broughton** & Juice	10/-	Locarno, S'land
17 Apr	**Groundhogs** + Grisby & Dyke	6/-	Locarno, S'land
24 Apr	**Roy Harper & Humble Pie**	10/-	Locarno, S'land
27 Apr	**Status Quo**, Good Habit & John Peel		Locarno, S'land
1 May	**Keef Hartley** & Black Widow	10/-	Locarno, S'land
7 May	**Colosseum**, Man & Raw Spirit	12/6d	Mayfair, Newcastle
8 May	**Traffic** & If	10/-	Locarno, S'land
13 May	**Ten Years After**		City Hall, N'castle
15 May	**Procol Harum**		Bay Hotel, S'land
22 May	**Radha Krishna Temple** + Local Support	10/-	Barnes Hotel, S'land (Limited Capacity)
25 May	Gypsy	5/-	Bay Hotel, S'land
29 May	**Tyrannosaurus Rex** & Man	10/-	Bay Hotel, S'land
5 June	**Groundhogs**	6/-	Bay Hotel, S'land
12 June	**Family**	10/6d	Bay Hotel, S'land
12 June	**Edgar Broughton, Quintessence** & Dogg (Gigs now running simultaneously)	12/-	Mayfair, Newcastle
15 June	Quatermass	3/-	Bay Hotel, S'land
19 June	**Savoy Brown** & Yellow	10/-	Bay Hotel, S'land
22 June	Principal Edwards Magic Theatre	2/-	Bay Hotel, S'land
26 June	**Free, Kevin Ayres & The Whole World** Yellow & Juice	12/6d	Top Rank, S'land
26 June	Rare Bird & Hard Meat	12/6d	Mayfair, Newcastle
10 Jul	**Chicken Shack** Matthews Southern Comfort & Man	12/6d	Mayfair, Newcastle
23 Jul	Atomic Rooster, Van Der Graaf Generator & Yellow	12/6d	Mayfair, Newcastle

Date	Act	Admission	Venue
31 Jul	**Deep Purple** & Daddy Longlegs	12/6d	Mayfair, Newcastle
7 Aug	**Derek & The Dominoes** &Writing On The Wall	15/-	Mayfair, Newcastle
21 Aug	**Quintessence, Mott The Hoople & Supertramp**	12/6d	Mayfair, Newcastle
28 Aug	**Tyrannosaurus Rex** & Principal Edwards Magic Theatre	12/6d	Mayfair, Newcastle
11 Sept	**Blodwyn Pig**	15/-	Mayfair, Newcastle
27 Sept	**Jethro Tull**		**City Hall, N'castle**
16 Oct	**Free, Deep Purple** Principal Edwards, Cochise & Yellow	£1	**Top Rank, S'land** (Indoor Festival of Music)
22 Oct	Keef Hartley, Strawbs & Pink Fairies	14/-	Mayfair, Newcastle
19 Nov	**Chicken Shack**, Yellow & Traction	14/-	Mayfair, Newcastle
26 Nov	**The Who & Curved Air** (The Who failed to play)	17/6d	Mayfair, Newcastle
14 Dec	**The Who** (Rescheduled Date) Previous Ticketholders		Mayfair, Newcastle

1971

Date	Act	Admission	Venue
1 Jan	**Groundhogs, Quintessence** & Medicine Head		Mayfair, Newcastle
15 Jan	**Chicken Shack**,Third Ear Band & If	12/6d	Mayfair, Newcastle
18 Jan	**Black Sabbath, Curved Air** & Freedom		**City Hall, N'castle**
14 Feb	**Free & Amazing Blondel**		**Empire, S'land**
18 Feb	**Tyrannosaurus Rex & If**	15/-	Mayfair, Newcastle
5 Mar	**Fairport Convention** & Stud		**Top Rank, S'land**
18 Mar	**Led Zeppelin**	12/-	Mayfair,Newcastle
26 Mar	**Mott The Hoople,** Medicine Head & John Peel		Mayfair,Newcastle
2 Apr	**Quintessence** & Stray	75p	Top Rank, S'land
8 Apr	Skid Row, Hardin & York + Stray	85p	Mayfair, Newcastle
15 Apr	**Groundhogs, Chicken Shack** & Michael Chapman	All seats 50p	City Hall, Newcastle
30 Apr	**Quintessence** & Stone The Crows	80p	Mayfair, Newcastle
7 May	**The Who**	50p	Top Rank, S'land

Date	Act	Admission	Venue
14 May	**Buddy Miles Express** (From America) & Kevin Ayres & The Whole World	50p	Mayfair, S'land
21 May	Stud, Hardin & Yorke + Gin House	75p	Mayfair, S'land
28 May	**Rod Stewart & The Faces** + **Reuben James**	75p	Mayfair, S'land
18 June	**Curved Air**, Mick Abrahams Band & Mark Ellington Group	75p	Mayfair, S'land
24 June	**Deep Purple**		Mecca, Bir'ham
25 June	**Deep Purple & Quiver**	85p	Mayfair, S'land
9 Jul	**Groundhogs**, Heads, Hands & Feet	75p	Mayfair, S'land
23 Jul	Colosseum & Osibisa	75p	Mayfair, S'land
30 Jul	**Rory Gallagher & The James Gang**	75p	Mayfair, S'land
6 Aug	**Curved Air** & Medicine Head	80p	Mayfair, S'land
13 Aug	**Mott the Hoople** & Gin House	75p	Mayfair, S'land
27 Aug	**Rod Stewart & The Faces** + **Bell & Ark**	85p	Mayfair, S'land
10 Sept	**Cat Stevens**, Mimi Farina & Tom Jans		City Hall, N'castle
16 Sept	**Ten Years After, Supertramp** & **Keith Christmas**		City Hall, N'castle
17 Sept	**Curved Air**	80p	Mayfair, N'castle
16 Oct	**Yes** & Jonathan Swift		City Hall, N'castle
21 Oct	**Steeleye Span** & Andy Roberts		City Hall, N'castle
22 Oct	**Quintessence** & East of Eden	80p	Mayfair, Newcastle
11 Nov	**Led Zeppelin** (4th Zep Album Released)		City Hall, N'castle
12 Nov	**Led Zeppelin**	75p	Locarno
18 Nov	Edgar Broughton & Stray	75p	Mayfair, Newcastle
1 Dec	**Groundhogs**, Egg & Quicksand		City Hall, N'castle

1972

Date	Act	Admission	Venue
7 Jan	**Rory Gallagher & Nazareth**		Mayfair, Newcastle
21 Jan	**Procol Harum** & Amazing Blondell	60p	City Hall, N'castle
1 Feb	**Free** & Junkyard Angel		City Hall, N'castle

Date	Act	Admission	Venue
5 Feb	**Black Sabbath** & Wild Turkey		City Hall, N'castle
13 Feb	**Free**, Vinegar Joe & Junkyard Angels		Top Rank, S'land
20 Feb	**Argent**, Beggars Opera, Beckett & Brass Alley		Top Rank, S'land
21 Feb	**Free**		City Hall, N'castle
21 Feb	**Jethro Tull** & Tir Na Nog		Top Rank, S'land
5 Mar	**Rod Stewart & The Faces** + Byzantiun		Top Rank, S'land
7 Mar	**Jethro Tull** & Tir Na Nog		City Hall, N'castle
12 May	Heads Hands & Feet + Vinegar Joe		Mayfair, N'castle
8 June	**Lindisfarne, Capability Brown** & Beckett	75p	Top Rank, S'land
22 June	**Family** & Audience		Mayfair, Newcastle
7 July	Stray & Third Ear Band		Mayfair, Newcastle
15 Sept	**Free**, Smith, Perkins & Smith	90p	Mayfair, Newcastle
25 Sept	UFO, Beckett & (Melody Maker Winner) Loyd Watson	Free Concert	City Hall, N'castle
11 Oct	**Free** & Beckett	65p Last ever Free Gig in S'land Locarno	
20 Oct	**Free** & Beckett	£1 Last ever Free Gig Before Splitting Mayfair	
26 Oct	Steeleye Span		City Hall, N'castle
27 Oct	Beggars Opera		Top Rank, S'land
10 Nov	**Fairport Convention**		Top Rank, S'land
11 Nov	**Roxy Music** & East Of Eden (1st Ever Concert Worldwide)		City Hall, N'castle
22 Nov	**Santana** (2 Concerts in Same Evening)		City Hall, N'castle

1973

Date	Act	Admission	Venue
16 Mar	**Procol Harum**		City Hall, N'castle
13 Apr	**Rod Stewart & The Faces,** John Peel & Beckett (Rescheduled gig from non appearance on 24th March 1971)	75p	Locarno S'land
20 Apr	Geordie, Pams People & Medicine Head		Locarno, S'land
27 Apr	**Status Quo,** Good Habit & John Peel		Locarno S'land

28 Apr	**Captain Beefheart** & His Magic Band		City Hall, N'castle
1 June	Nazareth & Robin Trower	65p	Locarno, S'land
19 June	**John McLaughlin's** **Mahavishnu Orchestra**		City Hall, N'castle
20 July	**Lindisfarne** & UFO		Locarno
27 July	**Van Morrison** & The Caledonian Soul Orchestra		City Hall, N'castle

1974

9 Mar	**Bad Company**	City Hall, N'castle
10 Mar	**Bad Company**	City Hall, N'castle
11 Mar	**Bad Company**	City Hall, N'castle
21 Apr	**Ten Years After**	City Hall, N'castle

1977

17 June	**The Jam**	£1	Seaburn Hall S'land
1 Jul	The Vibrators & Penetration	£1	Seaburn Hall S'land
8 Jul	The Saints & Straw Dogs	£1	Seaburn Hall S'land

1988

1988	**Wishbone Ash**	Mayfair, Newcastle
1988	**Wishbone Ash**	Roxy, Sheffield
1988	**Wishbone Ash**	**MGM Nightclub** **Nottingham**

1991

7 May	Still Got The Blues Fat Jeff, also ~The Pencil Sharpeners	7DM University Freshers Ball, Valentino's Nightclub, Dortmund, Germany